LIFTING
THE
WHITE VEIL

LIFTING THE WHITE VEIL

An Exploration of White American Culture in a Multiracial Context

JEFF HITCHCOCK

Crandall, Dostie & Douglass Books, Inc.
ROSELLE, NEW JERSEY

First printing 2002

ISBN 0-9719017-0-8

LCCN 2002104021

ATTENTION CORPORATIONS, UNIVERSITIES, COLLEGES, AND PROFES-SIONAL ORGANIZATIONS: Quantity discounts are available on bulk purchases of this book for educational, gift purposes, or as premiums for increasing magazine subscrip-tions or renewals. Special books or book excerpts can also be created to fit specific needs. For information, please contact Crandall, Dostie & Douglass Books, Inc., 245 West 4ᵗʰ Avenue, Roselle, NJ 07203; phone 908-245-4963.

To my family,

Nathaniel, all brightness and bounce,

Matthew, both irrepressible and reserved,

and Charley, teacher, friend and partner,

who together are the reason

I wrote this book.

Table of Contents

Preface

I had thought to subtitle this book *A Guide to Self-Discovery and Understanding for White Americans Who Live and Work in Multiracial Settings,* but that was much too long and so I mention it here. This book is a labor of love and concern about a topic many hardly know exists. Therein lies the concern. White people form part of the equation of our multiracial nation, yet we've given little serious thought to our role as simply that—white people. Furthermore, it seems everybody but white people has been telling us we need to do some of that thinking. Taking a critical and concerned look at white people, our culture, our history, our ways of perceiving the world, is a timely and important task as we enter the 21st century.

Yet many white people already feel battered and bruised, suffering from compassion fatigue brought on by the constant moral, psychological, and less often, economic wear and tear that race places upon us. We've been told untold times of our sins, alleged or true. Most of us wish only that it would go away, yet deep down we realize we have a lot of hard work to do to make our community, our nation, our world a better place for people of all colors.

It is knowing the goodwill of white people that makes my task a loving one. To me, as a white American, this knowledge comes from within. I could document the failure of that goodwill to produce change on a thousand different occasions, and admit the external evidence of its existence is sometimes poor, yet I know it's there.

Nearly 100 years ago, sociologist W. E. B. DuBois spoke of the veil separating white and black Americans. He spoke of the double-consciousness of African-Americans, who witness both their internal experiences, and the imagery of the dominant white culture that thrusts its own images of blackness back at them. Many sociologists today believe this dual consciousness has become more widespread in our society. White Americans, as always, witness images of ourselves of our own making. But increasingly, images of ourselves produced by other racial and cultural groups penetrate our social world and impose themselves on our awareness. As our nation and our world continue shrinking, white Americans can no longer ignore the larger racial and cultural context in which we live.

Though I have had acquaintances and friends from every racial group, my richest experiences of intimacy and mutual trust with people outside my racial group have most commonly been with African-Americans. Hence, though I touch on the experiences of many groups in the book, there is a decided "black/white" flavor as well. This is not intended to simplify the growing complexity of race relations in our country. I simply draw upon what I have lived.

Chapters 1 through 4 explore reasons why white Americans who care about creating a multiracial society should look to understanding our own culture as part of that process. Chapters 5 through 7 provide details of the history, cultural components, and psychology of white American culture. Chapters 8 and 9 review various perspectives in academic and nonacademic settings that examine and act upon white American culture in an intentional way. Finally, Chapter 10 offers a model for decentering white American culture in our society and centering multiracial values in its place.

Throughout the book, within each chapter are several sidebars. Each may be read and understood independently of the surrounding chapter narrative. In order to not disrupt the flow of the main narrative some readers may wish to read the sidebars either before or after the narrative. This is a matter of personal choice, and I do not recommend one approach above another.

The book, I hope, is readable, personal and autobiographical, opinioned, and informative. Those are my goals, each equally important. It is not a scholarly work per se. That would conflict too readily with the other goals I set. Yet I have taken pains to identify my sources with detailed notes. I do this so that the reader who wants to delve into the topic at depth will have the means to do so. But to those less inclined, the book reads perfectly well on its own and you can simply ignore all those little numbers at the end of various sentences and paragraphs if you like. Just go with the flow.

1

White People—What Do We Want?

A Strange Logic

There's a strange sort of logic at play in the United States, all the stranger because we are a rational people who take pride in being logical. In strictly symbolic terms, if A is different from B, then we expect B to be different from A. When we look at race, this sort of logic seems to go away. We find that black people are different from white people, but white people are, um…, well, we just *are*. We really aren't different from anyone. That is to say, we're really not different at all. We're normal and natural Americans who just are. Hispanic-American people are different. Asian-American people are different. American Indian people are different. African-American people are different. White people, we're just people. B is different from A, but as for A itself, it's not different from anything.

This strange sort of logic permeates our entire society. It's so pervasive and so thoroughly ingrained in our thought and our experience that few people realize it's totally illogical. White Americans are a racial/cultural group with customs, habits, and practices that differ from other broadly defined racial/cultural groups like Latinos and black Americans. This is hard for many of us to see, and this difficulty in "seeing" is an interesting social phenomenon in itself. How can A not be different from anything, and what is A?

Many books on race focus on how racial/cultural groups other than white people are "different." Often they suggest we should do away with those differences. Everyone should become A and there should be no more B, or C or D or E. Unlike many books on race, this book takes white people as its central focus. People of color can rest assured that I am not going to spend countless pages wondering about, probing, or analyzing the condition of African-American, Hispanic-American, Asian-American, and

American Indian peoples and neglecting to discuss white Americans, my own people.

Many white Americans may find this uncomfortable. To them I offer my assurances that I do not intend to point fingers, try to make them feel guilty, or pretend when I talk about "white Americans" that I am not one of you. I know I can't speak for all white people. I won't even claim to try. But I can and will speak from my own experience as a white person, and that experience is, in many ways, typical of a large number of people who are described as white.

What's in a Name?

White is only one of many terms used to describe the people descended from Europeans who have settled in the United States. Other terms are Caucasian, European-American, Anglo, and Euro-American, plus many local, often disparaging terms such as *honky, ofay, haole, cracker,* and *gringo*. In government statistics, this group is sometimes called "non-Hispanic white" to distinguish from light-skinned people of largely European descent who have migrated to the United States from Central and South America.

Each name differs subtly from others. Caucasian, for instance, includes people from the Indian subcontinent of Asia. The term European-American does not. The term white, as defined by the United States government's Directive 15, includes people from Egypt and the Middle East. The term white has also expanded over time to include many groups not previously considered by popular society to be white.

In this book, I am using the term white, as it is commonly used in the United States at present, to designate those people of European descent who do not claim a racially mixed heritage or an Hispanic heritage. This is roughly equivalent to the term European-American, which I find acceptable as a descriptor as well. The former term, white, places greater emphasis on race, the topic of this book. The latter term, European-American, mirrors the term African-American and emphasizes ethnicity and culture.

It's not possible to talk about race without reference to various racial groups in at least some passing way. Nor is it possible to overlook something like racism. So I will talk about people of color at various points. And I will talk about some things that many white people would rather keep silent. If you are particularly sensitive to either of these issues, you may find some things I have to say unpleasant. I'll take pains not to be disrespectful, but I will describe what I feel is true.

What Do We Want?

We often hear white people asking of black people, "What do they want?" Not being a black person, I'm not in a position to answer that. But I think it's only fair to ask the same question of ourselves. Indeed, we might learn something from it. And since I happen to be a white person, I'm on safer ground in forming an answer.

When I listen to other white people I hear many questions and statements repeated over and over. "Why can't we just be Americans?" we ask. "Talking about race is the problem," we say. "My family never owned slaves." "Why keep bringing up the past?" "We're all so different; how can you talk about 'white people?'" "We should get over race." "I just wish it would go away." "We're all individuals." "How can you blame a whole race for a few individuals?"

I believe we want to have a unified American society. I say this with some hesitation, because I don't think our record is all that good. Sure we've made progress, and yes, we don't own slaves and we have removed Jim Crow legislation from the books. Personally, though, I think we have a long ways to go. So I'm not individually ready to grant, as some people do, that we as white Americans have done all we can do and need to do to create a society that lives up to our basic democratic principles.

Still, I really do think most white Americans want to achieve a multiracial society. This goes beyond liberals and conservatives, a distinction that has meaning for many other political issues. When it comes to race, our feelings run deeper. Liberal and conservative approaches to the topic simply represent two ways of going about the same thing: trying to achieve a unified American society in which race does not determine a person's standing.

It touches on the deeper values that we claim as Americans. These are the old standards: liberty, freedom, equality, respect for the common person, progress toward a humane society. Together with my wife of twenty years, an African-American woman, I sometimes find strangers staring at us in a friendly way in public. It seems to me they find something in our relationship that affirms what they hope for in the future of our society and our country.[1] Whether our relationship truly exemplifies the values they project upon us is not the point. Rather, it's the fact that people hold these aspirations in the first place. Indeed, I find these friendly stares more common than hostile ones. My experience is confirmed by other people in mixed-race relationships with whom I have spoken.

In sermons, political speeches, and even movements for "new civil rights initiatives," I hear a longing for the creation of a coherent American character and identity. This longing runs deep within our nation. Our story, as we tell it, has been the creation of a new people. In 1782, in *Letters from an American Farmer,* Michel Guillaume Jean de Crèvecoeur said:

> What is an American? He is either a European, or the descendant of a European; hence that strange mixture of blood which you will find in no other country. I could point out to you a man whose grandfather was an Englishman, whose wife was Dutch, whose son

> married a French woman, and whose present four sons have now
> four wives of different nations....Here individuals of all nations
> are melted into a new race of men, whose labors and posterity will
> one day cause great changes in the world.[2]

It's not hard to find some problems with this passage. The equation of "American" with "European," for instance, excludes people of color. Some scholars question whether even Europeans were melting at the rate de Crèvecoeur implied in the 1700s.[3] The point here is that the ideal of the melting pot, the combining of disparate peoples and nations into a single American character freed of traditional obligations to the cultures from whence these peoples came, is an ideal that has run through American history. Today it continues to be felt very strongly by many Americans, and possibly by most Americans depending on how we express the details. Indeed, the fact that this very passage by de Crèvecoeur is frequently quoted, regardless of its historical veracity, attests to the strength of longing Americans have for this unfulfilled dream.

Among white Americans there are few experiences more painful in a cross-racial encounter than to be called a racist. Why this is so (I'll look at why in detail in Chapter 7) is sometimes puzzling to people of color, and not even clear to the white person who experiences the anguish and anger this accusation provokes. It has to do at least in part with the implication that the white American so accused is working against this dream of a coherent and unified American identity.

White Americans, who form the core of mainstream society in the United States, continue to hold to this dream with a quiet passion. True, in the past and even today there are white supremacist groups. The Ku Klux Klan has not died out. In some places it's even seen a revival. Klan members obviously are white people. So just as obviously it can be said that not all white people are ready to be a "people of many peoples." But it's also not uncommon to see a Klan rally of a dozen participants surrounded by a counter demonstration of several hundred people, most of whom are also white Americans. My heart goes to the counter demonstrators. I believe yours does, too.

Reality and Myth

College professors, particularly those teaching popular courses, sometimes engage in a little exercise at the opening session of a class. They purposefully act in an arrogant and demanding way, emphasizing the dif-

4

ficulty of the course requirements, the necessity of having already taken prerequisite classes on their topic, and the near impossibility of getting a high mark under their draconian grading system. If you have the audacity to return for the second session, you often find two things: (1) fewer students have come back, and (2) the professor actually turns out to be personable and engaging.

The hidden agenda, of course, is to scare away those who weren't so committed to exploring the material offered in the course. Large class sizes and loosely committed students create mediocre dialogue. I've tried to be inviting to this point, but now I wish to play the part of the first-day-of-class professor. There are things I need to say, and I can't spend the time needed to sugarcoat my thoughts, or pander to people who will swallow every positive comment uncritically and then blanch and turn away when one or two negative points are raised.

White Americans are sometimes like this when it comes to discussions about race. We love to talk about our good intentions, the progress we've made, and how we aspire to equality. But if the conversation suggests we may have some more work to do on these issues, some people head for the door.

In fact, I can hear some people leaving right now.

In our aspirations to heal our racial divisions and create a racially harmonious society we are sometimes like overweight people talking about going on a diet. We talk, and we talk. We spend a day, maybe even a week or a month, trying one thing or another, but in the end we really don't change our lifestyle. The weight stays on and the talk, for what it's worth, continues.

With so much talk, we often become confused about how things really are. If you watch or read entertainment media, such as television or the movies, or magazine and newspaper advertisements, you would think most Americans are trim and fit. Of course the reality is quite different, or so our medical professionals tell us. As a people we're overweight, and not showing signs of getting any thinner. The media reflect what we want to be, not who we are.

In racial terms, the same media show a vision of multiracial togetherness. In a September 1995 cover story for *Harper's Magazine,* author Benjamin DeMott thoroughly dissected the entertainment and advertising media's preoccupation with demonstrating that black and white people now exist in a state of individual friendship and harmony with one another.[4] This glut of imagery—DeMott lists 35 recent mainstream movies alone, like *Sister Act, Die Hard, Driving Miss Daisy,* and so on—hides us from the hard facts of race and racism. It obscures our history and suggests "friendship" alone can solve structural problems that run to the core of our society.

Did I just hear some more white people leaving? Maybe they had to catch the latest "feel good" movie.

DeMott clearly supports a liberal agenda and views the popular imagery of interracial friendship as a major component in dismantling liberal efforts to promote racial justice. "The good news at the movies obscures the bad news in the streets and confirms the Supreme Court's recent decisions on busing, affirmative action, and redistricting." Even for a committed liberal, DeMott notes the siren song is hard to resist, saying "the faith has its benign aspect. Even as they nudge me and others toward belief in magic…, the images and messages of devoted relationships between blacks and whites do exert a humanizing influence."

DeMott's debunking of the interracial friendship fantasy machine has implications for us all. Support or contest affirmative action if you will, but don't delude yourself into thinking that's all there is to creating a racially just and harmonious world. Whether you believe governmental intervention and social engineering are the solution, or you feel a search for honesty within your own heart is the answer, the couch potato approach of viewing a "color free" dreamworld only confuses the issue. DeMott speaks of an earlier, more genuine time when "In the civil rights era, the experience for many millions of Americans was one of discovery. A hitherto unimagined continent of human reality and history came into view, inducing genuine concern and at least a temporary setting aside of self-importance." Today, we've grown soft and fat, letting dream makers woo us into self-satisfied somnolence. It's time to get off the couch and take a walk outside.

Are you still here? Well, I'm not through. It's time for a pop quiz.

Pop Quiz

When you want work done on your car, you contact someone who has experience as a mechanic. When you need repairs done to your house, you call someone who has experience with carpentry, plumbing, or whatever skill is called upon. When you suffer from a serious illness, you go to see a doctor. Friends and neighbors are always around to offer advice, and often do. But for the important things in our lives, we look for people who have experience. Maybe we can't afford the best, but if money were no consideration we would try to find the person with the most "hands on" experience we could find. If we suffered a serious accident, we'd probably be reluctant to put ourselves under the care of a neighbor who was a sales clerk, even if he had watched every episode the most current, popular, and critically aclaimed medical television drama.

Experience counts. This book is about some things white people can do to create a multiracial society. Our media tells us we already have this. But how real is that image? What is your measure of experience? For starters, take a look at the list on the next page. It's not really a test. It's what I call a racial interaction inventory, meaning it simply helps people assess how much actual experience they have living in a multiracial world. Give it a try. No one's looking, so how you "score" is a private matter.

I know this checklist is not perfect. How many are? If you are a person of mixed race, the questions won't make much sense. But for white people who are not of mixed race it does get to the heart of the matter. The inventory looks at six areas of experience (household/neighborhood, school, family, work, romance/marriage, and friendship). It asks questions pretty close to home, so to speak, but that's because we all like to fudge when we can. If I asked about your close friends rather than "closest" friend, then you might be tempted to run down your list of friends until you found someone of a different race. That person might even become elevated in the degree of their friendship status for the moment. I'm simply recognizing that's human nature. I do that sort of thing, too.

Racial Interaction Inventory

DIRECTIONS: Please place a check by each statement that applies to your experience. Add up the number of checks and record the total below.

_____ I share a household with someone of a different race.
_____ My closest neighboring household has someone of a different race.
_____ I attended a school where no single race was more than 75% of the student body.
_____ I have been in a classroom/training setting where, numerically, I was a racial minority.
_____ My family has living members of more than one race.
_____ My family has past members of more than one race.
_____ I work with people of a different race.
_____ I have had a boss who is/was of a different race.
_____ I have dated or been romantically involved with a person of a different race.
_____ I am married (however defined) to a person of a different race.
_____ As a child, my closest friend was of a different race.
_____ As an adult, my closest friend is of a different race.
_____ TOTAL

The list makes another point. If we really did have a multiracial society and if we really did live in a world where color did not matter, and if we really did have many harmonious friendships across racial lines, then we should expect to see this reflected in our closest and most personal experiences.

Most white people will be able to check fewer than half the items. Even white people who have been active in support of bettering race relations might find they can only check two or three items. One such person, an elderly white woman, voiced her distress to me after completing the inventory. It made her look "like a racist," she complained. If you believe in the friendship model, then you might react this way. The friendship model is the one critiqued by DeMott. He describes the model, "Whites are part of the solution, says this orthodoxy, if we break out of the prison of our skin color, say hello, as equals, one-on-one, to a black stranger, and make a black friend. We're part of the problem if we have an aversion to black people or are frightened of them, or if we feel that the more distance we put between them and us the better...."

There may be some truth to the friendship model. But the larger and hidden truth—hidden at least for most white people—is that our society and thus our experience, even and especially our personal experience, is racially structured. All the best personal intentions you can muster are not enough to break through the social forces that move white people in one sector of our society and people of color in another. Changing ourselves from within is important. Ultimately no change can come from anywhere else. But gaining the experience we need to guide us toward a real and meaningful inward change means we have to get up off the couch, go outside, and look at the big white house in which we live. Or maybe you still think you can do it by watching TV.

Walking the Tightrope

You can't look at race in any socially significant way without looking at racism. Our society is still racist. White culture is still racist. It is still harder to be a person of color in America than it is to be white, and white privilege still conveys benefits to white people. For anyone who takes time to look into the matter, these become inescapable conclusions. It wouldn't be hard to make a long list of facts to support this contention, though it is often difficult to break through the power of denial many otherwise rational white people exhibit when the finger points at them.

Did I hear some chairs scraping? It seems I've lost a few more white people on this point.

Now, I know I said I wasn't going to point fingers or try to make people feel guilty. And here I am using the R-word. By now you might think I'm an incorrigible, misanthropic curmudgeon bent on finding the worst in white people. Unfortunately, when talking about race to a large and racially diverse audience, it doesn't feel like the usual process of standing before a large group and addressing them from a podium. Rather it feels like walking a tightrope with people arrayed on either side ready to pull you toward them or push you away.

On one side of the tightrope are those who want to hear about the good side of white people. This involves things like acknowledging that white people want to improve race relations and live up to our better values—such as advancing by merit, not letting color invoke stereotypes, and wanting to live in a multiracial society. We've made a lot of progress over time and will continue to do so.

On the other side are people who say there is still a lot of racism in our society and white people have come to assume our central position through cruel and extreme methods, such as slavery and genocide, which are amply documented but seldom spoken about in the mainstream. If we don't look at differences in power, then we are doing nothing worthwhile in regard to race relations.

I've voiced these views in a moderate way, though there are more extreme expressions. Some white people take any reference to race as a suggestion that the speaker is trying to make them feel guilty. One drop of criticism among a bucket of praise is enough to bring charges from this group that the speaker is "racist against white people." Usually they are adamantly against using the concept of race in any fashion, even in a discussion aimed at bettering race relations. Unable to see race, they are blind to racism as well.

Some people of color feel white people are beyond redemption. The crimes of our white ancestors were so unspeakably foul that no white person can escape from their corrupting influence. White culture consists of a consciously shared conspiracy among a racial elite whose only concern for people of color is understanding how better to exploit them.

Actually it's not all black and white between these two sides. Some people of color take the "can't see race, can't see racism" point of view and some white people take the "white equals racist beyond redemption" perspective. My own point of view falls in the middle. I believe our society is still racist, and I believe white people have redeeming qualities and are honestly working to live up to our better values. Since this is true, or so I believe, either side of the tightrope can find evidence to support its view. There are times when I will have to agree with both. Being in the middle on a tightrope is not a comfortable place to be. Like either side, it is also a multiracial location, probably more so. I have found both white people and people of color share this perspective and it can feel like a pretty vulnerable stance. You can count on being attacked from both sides.

There are many books written about race. Few take white people as their main focus. Of this smaller number of books, most are written by scholars. Though extremely important as reference works, they are also narrowly focused and fail to reach, capture, discuss and convey the everyday racial experience of white Americans in everyday terms. An even smaller number of books about white Americans are written for the public. These books take the stance that white people need to learn about racism and do something about it. I quite agree with the importance of these books as well. Since other people have already done it, and done it well, I don't think another book like that is needed.

This book is about white Americans as racial beings. It is a personal work. It's about my people. I am writing it as both an act of love and an act of concern. The love helps me see what we might become, and the concern helps me see some of the hazards that stand in our way. I plan to draw on work from scholars and activists. Much of this work has been tucked away from the limelight, hidden beyond taboos in our culture that say talking about white people should not be done. This is important work, some of it decades old. It should come to light before the public. Most of all, I simply want to talk freely about what it means to be white, in terms everyday people can understand.

Racism Education for White Folk

Although this book does not focus on racism, it is nonetheless an important topic for white people living in a multiracial world. Racism is something people can study and learn about. Many excellent books are available as resources for white people wishing to learn how to identify and work to undo racist elements in our society. Some suggestions:

- Barndt, Joseph. *Dismantling Racism: The Continuing Challenge to White America.* Minneapolis: Augsburg Fortress, 1991.

- Katz, Judith H. *White Awareness: Handbook for Anti-Racism Training.* Norman, Oklahoma: University of Oklahoma Press, 1978.

- Kivel, Paul. *Uprooting Racism: How White People Can Work for Racial Justice.* Philadelphia: New Society Publishers, 1996.

- Shearer, Jody Miller. *Enter the River: Healing Steps from White Privilege toward Racial Reconciliation.* Scottdale, Pennsylvania: Herald Press, 1994.

- Terry, Robert. *For Whites Only.* Grand Rapids, Michigan: William B. Eerdmans, 1975.

Not All White People Are the Same

No, I don't mean we're English, French, Italian, Irish, or Dutch or that we're from the South, New England, the Midwest or the West Coast as white people often mean to say when we use this phrase. I'm using it in a tongue-in-cheek way to make another point. Like any sizable racial/cultural group, white people differ from one another in many ways.

One way in which we differ is in regard to how committed we are to working for a multiracial society. I've suggested that most white people want this to happen. Indeed, I've said it's a deeply held value, though one that has been poorly realized in action. But not all white people feel the same way about this. Many are adamantly opposed. Some say OK, so long as white people continue to be in the center. Some say it's important, but not as important as other issues.

Others devote their professional lives and, less often, their personal lives to doing what they think needs doing toward improving race relations. These people come from many backgrounds and take many approaches in their work. Some are antiracist activists working with social change agendas. Some are members of multiracial families. Some are religious and spiritual leaders. Some are youth who, having inherited a race-conflicted world, want to change what they know is wrong. Many are simply people in the street who for any number of reasons want a multiracial society.

Some of us want a multiracial society and if you are one of them, this book is for you. What we've been doing may have worked in the past, but it's no longer moving us to the future. We need to consider new options, explore new directions. I have some ideas about how to do that—ideas which you may find a little controversial—and I'll lay them out in the following chapters. In the end we may agree or disagree. I won't pretend to have the final answer to an exceedingly complex situation. But whether you find the direction in which I am pointing to be fruitful or lacking in merit, I hope we can remain in harmony on the goal. America must become a multiracial country.

I am a child of the 1960s. Back in those tumultuous times white people went through a lot of changes. The awakening to racial concerns of that era forced us to examine new thoughts, feel new feelings, and take on perspectives we had never been shown before. It was hard work. It was exciting. Even more than that, it was scary. But we felt it was only a matter of time before we learned how to be better and the whole race thing would go away.

Now here I am, a man in my early fifties. My generation is in charge. Where once we made great strides as a people, we've become mired once again. Race is still with us. Even the progress we made back then is now eroding on many fronts. It's not time to be complacent or smug, or to think we've arrived at any final answers, no matter how thoroughly it was taught to us as children or how obvious it seems.

Good. I think I just saw the last complacent person go out the door. Now that we have a smaller but more committed group, it's time to get this conversation going.

We have a lot of work to do.

2

What Will It Take to Create a Multiracial Society?

What Is a Multiracial Society?

Some people say America is already a multiracial society. We have citizens of every color, from every part of the world. In most parts of the country white people and people of color typically encounter one another during the course of our daily affairs. The media shows people of different racial backgrounds mixing with one another.

Today several million people belong to multiracial families, live in multiracial neighborhoods, and work in multiracial settings, but that doesn't mean we're living in a multiracial society. Tens of millions still live and work in fairly segregated settings. To me, and probably to many people, a multiracial society is one in which multiracial relationships are commonplace, where racial tension is not a factor, where justice is not influenced by a person's racial status, and where each person has equal opportunities. In a multiracial society, we would all achieve a high number of check marks on the Racial Interaction Inventory in Chapter 1. Although American society has slowly been moving toward this ideal, it still has a long way to go.

We can't really describe what a multiracial society would be like since we do not have the experience of living in one. We do know what living in a racialized society is like, and many of us are working to remove the unpleasant and sometimes lethal consequences of that condition. But I have to admit I can't describe the utopian future in which racial justice, harmony, and equality are finally achieved.

Still, I can speculate. We may not be able to say exactly how things will turn out, but it's important to develop some notion of direction. For starters, we probably will not have the nearly all-white organizations and settings that still pass for the norm in our society. Examples are the federal and most state legislatures, board membership and executive leadership at our major corporations, and the middle and upper class suburbs of our metropolitan areas. In a multiracial world, we would expect that these locations, in which power and control of resources are most concentrated, would in fact include people from all racial backgrounds.

We might also expect that people in authority over us would just as likely be of another race as of our own. This does not mean that everyone will be equally distributed by racial status. Some neighborhoods might remain predominantly white, or black, or of another single-race composition. Some organizations may reflect a similar predominant trend to one race or another. This would be expected even if race were a randomly distributed factor throughout the population. Sometimes chance alone forms clusters of similar traits. But on average, and as a general rule, we would expect to see a thorough mix of racial statuses throughout our institutions, and especially in the places where power is held, decisions are made, and resources are controlled. We would expect most communities to have a multiracial composition, with people of different racial backgrounds living side by side. We would expect that typical families will themselves be multiracial.

Looking at this vision a little more closely, we might expect the following to be true of a multiracial society:

Color doesn't matter. That is, race does not determine how people act toward one another, and how a person will fit into the overall structure of the society. Skin color will be like hair color, a matter of personal difference, and perhaps stylistic preference, but not a determinant of social position. More to the point, skin color does not determine access to resources and power in society. To say color does not matter is another way of saying race is not a structural feature of the society. Race becomes a structural feature of a society when that society assigns people roles according to their racial background. In a racially structured society, your race has a lot to do with whom you live with, the racial composition of your neighborhood, whom you work with, and who has access to resources and power.

Multiracial settings are the norm. It might theoretically be possible to have a society in which people of various racial backgrounds had equal access to resources and power, but where same-race groupings (families, communities, work settings) were still the normal and accepted way of life. In a truly multiracial society, this would not be the case. The normal and expected way of life would be one in which people of different racial backgrounds intermingle in families, workplaces, churches, neighborhoods, legislative bodies, governing boards, leadership cohorts, and other settings throughout the society. Same-race groupings, while not precluded, would be seen as unusual and marginal, not central to basic and preferred values of the society.

A multiracial society is not a panacea for all our social problems. There is nothing in the notion of a multiracial society per se that will prevent other social concerns such as economic inequality and exploitation, environmental degradation, regional conflict, domestic violence, or any number of other social ills. But a racially structured society, particularly one in which one racial group is privileged and others are oppressed, is an evil in itself. A multiracial society will not lead to utopia, but it is nonetheless a significant goal worthy of our efforts.

What Do We Have Now?

Where do we stand today against this somewhat cloudy but hopeful vision of the future? Our society is racially structured. This is not the same as saying people are individually racist, though some are. This is also not saying race is an absolute, biological construct. Some racial differences are biological, but the important elements of character are culturally and socially determined.

A racially structured society is one in which race does a lot to determine the type of life people lead, including who they will meet, and what opportunities they will have to improve their lot. In a racially structured society your individual experience of that society, and of life itself, will be partly determined by your race. Remember the logic that if B is different from A, A is also different from B? In a racially structured society, the fact of a person being "brown" (or black, red, or yellow) has much to do with the experiences that person will encounter. So too does the fact of being white.

Being white (the focus of this book) will have an influence on experiences in your family, neighborhood, workplace, place of worship, friendships and access to power and resources. It will not completely determine your life. Class, gender, sexual orientation and a host of other social and individual differences have an impact as well. But in a racially structured society such as ours, race has a lot to do with how your life unfolds.

Monoracial and Multiracial Structures

As a matter of terminology and as a matter of values, I want to introduce the notion of monoracial structures. The term "monoracial" means "of the same race." It can refer to a person's heritage, or it can refer to a social grouping of persons of the same race. Thus we can have people whose heritage is monoracially white and other people whose heritage is monoracially black, or monoracially of some other race. We can also have marriages, families, clubs, political groups, neighborhoods, and other collections of people that are monoracial in their composition.

In the United States we generally understand monoracial people and monoracial groups to be normal. This status of "normal" is so convincing, the very usage of a term "monoracial" is greeted by many people with surprise. The term simultaneously asserts a condition (same-race origin) and an equivalence (whether white, black, red, or yellow) that usually is unspoken. The condition of same-race origin, whether of individual people or social groupings, is seen as a natural aspect of human activity. The equivalence of different racial groups implies a perspective that seldom is articulated.

What Is Normal?

The belief that monoracial (same race) arrangements are "normal" is very powerful in our society. Most white people live and work in predominantly white, and thus monoracial, settings. Many people of color cross racial lines at work, but live in monoracial neighborhoods.

Is this really normal? If we selected 100 people from around the world and set them down on Mars to start their own society, would they divide into "white," "black," and other racial groups? Probably not. It would be "normal" for people to seek each other along more personal lines. What we see today as "normal" is really a product of our specific history, not some innate drive toward racial grouping.

The power of society to define monoracial arrangements as "normal" was unveiled to me by Cessie Alfonso, my former mentor, when I was working for her diversity consulting firm. At the time I had already been married more than a decade to an African-American woman and together we had two children. Able to check nine items of the Racial Interaction Inventory (see Chapter 1), at Alfonso Associates I was one of a few white people in a multiracial organization.

In the midst of all this I somehow felt what was "normal" in my life was the monoracial and white environment in which I was raised. That's when Cessie, an Afro–Puerto Rican/Cuban woman, told me I was living a multiracial lifestyle. Like many white people, I felt that people of color were experts on race in a way I was not. But to hear from an "expert" that I was "living it" changed my perspective. Normal, I realized, was living close to the people and beliefs one values. In my life, whether by accident or through some purpose I cannot divine, these people and beliefs had come to be multiracial.

The term "monoracial" stands in contrast to the term "multiracial." People may be of multiracial heritage, and social groupings may be multiracial in character. Multiracial people are generally viewed as different from the norm. Multiracial groups are generally felt to be marginal enterprises.

Much of our thinking develops from a monoracial stance, whether that stance be as black people, white people, or people of other races. This book is an exploration of a monoracial group, white people, and the perspective that group has developed in the United States. However, I often find it useful to step out of a monoracial perspective and to look at the world from a multiracial point of view. From this angle, it is possible to consider how monoracial structures contribute toward or hinder the formation of multiracial structures.

Taking a multiracial perspective does not negate the monoracial structures of our society, nor does it deny the dominance of white culture over other racial and cultural groups. But it does afford a position from where we can discuss the development of community that transcends older monoracial formations that are firmly embedded in our national structure. Existing today on the margins of the margins, small and fragile amidst the greater monoracial forces in the United States, there is a self-identified multiracial community that is beginning to make itself heard.

Looking at Some Numbers

In order to talk about the racial structure of American society, it helps to look at some numbers. Numbers alone do not comprise structure, but they are important as a starting point. We should at least agree on some basic demographic information. According to the 2000 Census, the percentages of various racial/cultural groups in the United States are as follows:[1]

White American	69.25%
Hispanic-American	12.56%
Black American	12.08%
Asian-American	3.73%
Multiracial American	1.64%
Native American	.74%

Think about it. At 69%, it's still a very white country! All the people of color in the United States added together form less than one-third of the population. This has implications for activity directed toward racial reconciliation. Suppose, for instance, the "solution" to racial conflict was to pair every white American with an American of color, in order that they get to know one another better. As we paired off, one by one, we'd soon find there were not enough people of color to go around. In fact, when the roughly 30% of the country that consisted of people of color was paired with another 30% of the country consisting of white people, there would still be another 40% of the country, all white people, left over. We could pair each person of color with two or three white people. That would take everybody into account. But it would mean people of color would do double and triple duty.

"Seeing" Numbers Does Not Add Up

A recent *Boston Globe* poll found that both white and black Americans tend to overestimate the percentage of nonwhite racial groups in America.[2] Less than one out of six people of either race knew that black Americans are only 12% of the United States population. Almost half of those polled placed the figure at 25% or greater. Black and white Americans also overestimated the percentage of Latino/a-Americans and Asian-Americans. By implication, both black and white Americans must believe the percentage of white Americans is far less than the actual figure of 69%. Other polls have shown similar findings.

White Americans often carry this bias into personal settings. Cooper Thompson, an antiracism trainer, tells of once "doing a presentation to a group of employees at a corporation,...I thought that white people were the minority, until I actually did a head count. Of the 42 people present, there were 17 white men, 9 white women, 12 African-American women, 3 African-American men, and 1 Asian-American man—a total of 26 white people and 16 people of color."[3]

Actually, white people and people of color are not distributed evenly across the country. Some areas of the country—northern New England and the northern plains states, for instance—are much whiter than others. Other areas of the country have a much greater concentration of people of color. The local proportions of white people and people of color have a great influence on how white people and people of color interact. Living in a region that is 95% white is not the same as living in a region that is 50% white, even for white people. For people of color, the difference between an area that is 5% nonwhite and an area that consists of 50% of people of color is probably substantial. These differences may be found across regions, organizations, and between urban and rural settings. The picture becomes even more complicated when we realize that "people of color" may comprise several distinct groups, and the proportions of these groups vary across regions as well.

If we try to look at the percentage of white people in the United States population throughout our history, we run into some tricky problems. Firstly, the country itself has changed its borders from the original 13 colonies to the much larger configuration of 50 states it now comprises. Along the way, at key moments in 1803 with the Louisiana Purchase and 1848 with the end of the Mexican-American War, we have scooped up major land acquisitions and consequently taken dominion of large populations of people of color.

A second problem in estimating the percentage of white people over time is that the definition of who is white has changed. Census categories have not been constant. The racial category of white, which today applies generally to anyone of full European descent, has not always been so broadly defined. Consider the words of Founding Father Benjamin Franklin who wrote:

> ...the Number of purely white People in the World is proportionably very small. All Africa is black or tawny. Asia chiefly tawny. America (exclusive of the new Comers) wholly so. And in Europe, the Spaniards, Italians, French, Russians and Swedes, are generally of what we call a swarthy Complexion; as are the Germans also, the Saxons only excepted, who with the English, make the principal Body of White People on the Face of the Earth. I could wish their Numbers were increased.[4]

Imagine, the French and Germans not white, and Swedes being seen as swarthy in complexion! But that's how people felt back then. The Irish, for instance, were once considered to be black. During the initial wave of Irish immigration during the 1830s and 1840s the Irish struggled to establish an identity as white. This struggle, carried out at the expense of African-Americans from whom the Irish wished to distinguish themselves, has been repeated over and over as various European groups have come to the United States. In my own lifetime I can clearly remember Italians were once not considered to be white.

So counting up white people over history is a tricky business. But if we look at the definitions of white that were in place through history, it seems that there has been a steady increase of white people from Franklin's time until the recent period of 1940 through 1970 or thereabouts. In 1790, for instance, the Anglo-American population (excluding Germans, French and other Europeans not thought to be white) was only 60% of the United States as it was then comprised. Another 19% of the 1790 population consisted of Europeans not considered to be white. The remaining 20% was largely African (19%) and Native American (2%).[5]

Successive waves of immigration from Europe during the early 1800s through the 1920s created a large population of European people still not considered white Americans. Different customs and points of origin in Europe marked these groups as "different" from native white Americans. Generally, if you were foreign-born you were not considered white in America. In 1940 the immigration rate hit a low under 1% and in 1970, after a 60-year decline, the foreign-born percentage of the United States population hit a low of less than 5%. Correspondingly, in 1940 the white population hit a high of 89.7%.[6]

From colonial times until the middle of the 20th century white Americans expanded our territory and our numbers in relation to nonwhite people. Manifest destiny and white supremacy marched hand in hand from the Atlantic to the Pacific, creating a white man's country. The process was aided by a frontier mentality in which white Americans saw ourselves as surrounded by foreign and hostile cultures. By 1960 the United States was the whitest it has ever been.

Though the battle was won, the echo of those not-so-distant times still reverberates through our culture. Recently a professor at a small rural Pennsylvania college told me of a class in which she discussed race and ethnicity with her students. One female student had no difficulty discussing her heritage as an Italian-American. When the conversation turned to race, however, the student admitted she had looked at the college catalog and chosen to attend the school because she thought it was a "white" college. Running to the window of the classroom, this student pointed to the campus, exclaiming "But they're everywhere." Clearly "they" were people of color. The teacher took this moment as an opportunity and appointed a group of students to go to the college authorities and find the actual racial breakdown of the student population on campus. They returned somewhat chagrined to report there were 3,000 white students and 98 African-Americans. The class then discussed who really was "everywhere."

We'll Just Make More

What will happen when the proportion of "white people" diminishes? Will there be an attempt to bolster the numbers? Some methods for doing this seem outlandish and unlikely. Will white women participate in a breeding war? Hardly. How about closing the borders to nonwhite people, and evicting all recent immigrants of color? Some would have this, but again, it's doubtful our legal system can go that far without making the country an armed camp. Simply in dollars, it would cost billions. In human misery, even more.

But there is a way to create more white people. Since colonial times the common definition of "who is white" has expanded. Originally limited to the English, it grew to include "Anglo-Saxons," then gradually all Europeans. Today this process of expansion continues. Light-skinned Asian, Latino/a and Middle Eastern people are considered white in many instances.

Whiteness, constantly expanding and changing, has always defined itself in contrast to blackness. This contrast remains today, though even here whiteness may be making inroads. Some people feel that the move toward a multiracial identity is a way for whiteness to co-opt membership from the black community just as the black community is becoming empowered in its own right.

Now in the 2000s the country has turned another corner. The nonwhite population is increasing and the white population, as we now define it, is declining. The census bureau estimates that in 2050 the white population will be 53%, which even in historical terms will be the lowest percentage ever of white people in the United States.[7] Indeed, some of the feeling on the part of white Americans that people of color are everywhere may actually reflect a change that has occurred in their lifetime. The proportion of people of color has been increasing, and even more importantly, the images of people of color have become more common in our media.

Interestingly, the change in the proportion of white people to people of color has created different racial environments for older and younger people. In 2000, among people age 80 or older there were nearly eight white people for every person of color. Among people less than age 10, there were slightly less than two white people for every person of color. Some portion of these ratios likely reflects a higher rate of mortality among people of color, but the ratios also reveal a real "browning" of our population.[8] By the year 2050, there will be roughly one white person for every person of color. Youth, for better or worse, are in the vanguard of this change.

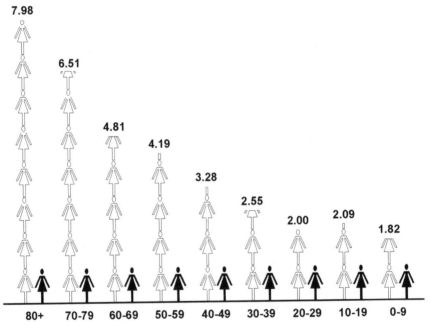

Figure 2.1 Ratio of white people to people of color in successive age groups, based on 2000 census data.

However, the definition of who is white has proven very flexible and today's definition almost certainly will change. Many Hispanic people, white Cubans for instance, are coming to be viewed as white. Asian-Americans in many cases are being assimilated to whiteness. People of partial European ancestry have also begun to be included in the definition of white. These changes take place slowly, so it's difficult to say with certainty how the current definition of white is changing. But if history is a guide, it will change and the change will be in the direction of assimilating groups now seen as nonwhite.

While this may seem to be a socially constructive process of bringing more people into the center of American society, people concerned with creating a multiracial society need to view it with a critical eye. Specifically, African-Americans, who have been here since 1619, have never been included in the expanding definition of whiteness. Their exclusion has been neither a matter of their choice, nor an historical accident. Rather, it has been one of the structural features of American society itself.

Interracial Marriage—An example

People sometimes ask me to give an example of how white people act alike. After all, aren't we all so different? What could we possibly have in common? Occasionally I reply, with a bit of whimsy, that we tend to marry each other a lot. White people marry other white people. That's stating the obvious, of course, and that's partly the point. The racial structure of our society is sometimes so obvious and commonplace that we simply take it for granted. Like watching the sun revolving around the earth every day, sometimes looking at the obvious can lead us to a new understanding. It took us Europeans several thousand years to figure out the earth actually revolved around the sun, but once we did it opened a whole new world before us.

To say that a society is racially structured does not mean this structure results only from conscious individual choices by the members of that society. Sometimes conscious decision making is a part of it. But society can have a racial structure even if participants do not consciously set out to make it that way. Past practices and historical decisions sometimes lead us in directions we do not choose of our own will. Social roles and expectations are handed down to us in such a way that they seem "obvious" when in fact they represent only one alternative among many. In a racially structured society we still make choices, but these choices are limited and guided by a social and cultural environment that leads to racially determined outcomes. Interracial marriage is one good example.

When young men and women get together on a regular basis, they become romantically attracted. When a society places no restrictions on whom a person can marry, then young people, and perhaps older people as well, will mix and mingle with one another in their selection of partners. When there are no boundaries to people associating across racial lines, many people will meet and fall in love with people of a different race.

21

The old-time white supremacists understood this clearly. White males who made laws separating the "races" were never afraid of interracial sex. Enough of our number regularly engaged in interracial sexual activity that European, African, and Native American genes are widely dispersed in the American citizenry regardless of how those citizens today may pass for black, white, or Native American. Forcible rape of women of color by white men is a well-known, if painful, historical act that seldom led to any sort of legal sanction.

What white men feared was not interracial sex, but rather interracial marriage. We feared giving interracial relationships the blessing of the state apparatus, for the entire structure of white supremacy would be undermined. White men further knew that men and women of different races would become romantically involved unless forcibly kept from free association. In the now bygone heyday of white supremacy a white man could steal the labor of a black woman. He could rape her, beat her, take her children from her, and force her to remain silent out of fear of even greater harm to her family. In that age of incontestable dominance, about the only thing a white man could not do to a black woman with impunity was to marry her. Other white men would not allow that.

Let's consider how things would look if starting today we had a truly multiracial society. How would marriages look if race were not a structural feature of society, in other words, if there were no racial preferences and barriers to marriage? People would still make individual choices according to gender preferences and other shared interests. But if race truly did not matter and if we truly were colorblind, then our choice of partner would not be based on our partner's race. The race of one's partner would simply be a matter of chance.

How Would We Look If Marriages Were Not Racially Structured?

Simple probability calculations give us a picture. If race did not matter, people would choose their marriage partners randomly in regard to race. Take a group of 10,000 people and assume each comes from one of the six racial/cultural groups listed earlier in this chapter with the 2000 U.S. Census percentages. Convert the percentages to proportions. If each person marries randomly by race, then .6925 x .6925 = .4796 gives the expected proportion of monoracial white marriages that will result. Since we assumed a starting group of 10,000 people, that works out to 4,796 people in monoracial white marriages. The probability of a monoracial/cultural Hispanic marriage is .1256 x .1256 = .0158, or 158 Hispanic persons married to other Hispanic people, and so forth.

Assume each married couple produces two offspring in the first generation. Monoracial pairs produce monoracial children and mixed pairs produce multiracial children, all of whom grow up, marry one another randomly, and produce two offspring per marriage.

Table 1 summarizes the results of the calculations. By the third generation the only monoracial/cultural group left is the white one, forming just a little over 5% of the total population (529 individuals). People have overwhelmingly become multiracial in terms of their individual heritage, and because of that, necessarily so in their marriages as well. By a fourth generation (not shown) monoracial white people would be less than 1% of the population.

Table 1
Results of random pairing by race over time
(in number of individuals)

Racial/cultural category	Generation			
	Start	First	Second	Third
White	6,925	4,796	2,300	529
Hispanic	1,256	158	2	0
Black	1,208	146	2	0
Asian	373	14	0	0
Am. Indian	74	1	0	0
Multiracial	164	4,885	7,696	9,471
Total	10,000	10,000	10,000	10,000

In America we've had about 20 generations since the first Europeans and Africans arrived. There's been ample time for us to mix and marry among one another. So how does it look today? Well, for starters, if I know you are white and married, I have a pretty good chance of guessing the race of your partner. In fact, I'd be right 97% of the time simply by guessing that your partner is also white. According to *Interrace Magazine,* that's the percentage of married white people whose partners are also white.[9]

Now, I don't mean to say interracial marriage is the solution to the country's race problem. Far from it. Marriage hasn't even solved our gender difficulties, so why should it "cure" race? Placing this burden on the multiracial community and setting up interracial marriage as a political act of social policy is hazardous and unrealistic.

Rather, the rate of interracial marriage is a measure of how the racial structure of our society is being impacted through other means. As racial barriers are reduced, we may expect multiracial families to become more commonplace. Increased contact in public, in schools, in the workplace, in places of worship, and even within extended families where some people have already formed interracial partnerships, will lead to additional partnerships being formed across racial lines.

The reverse is not probable. We are not likely to see an increase in interracial marriage independent of increased contact in other sectors of our society. In America marriages are not arranged by outside agents. Individuals pick their partners based on free association and prior contact. There is no magic hand of God or despotic hand of humankind to force people of different racial groups to otherwise marry one another. Only close, meaningful, and authentic interracial contact will foster these partnerships.

The example of interracial marriage illustrates several things about our society:

It calls into question claims that we have a "multiracial" society. Many races are represented in our society, but the status quo is one in which these races exist side by side in segregated communities and relationships.

It demonstrates an area in which nearly all white people act alike. Regardless of how different we may claim to be from one another, when we make one of the most important decisions in our lives—who to marry—97% of us choose to marry another white person.

It supports a claim that there is such a thing as white American culture. People tend to marry other people whom they see as similar to themselves. It's all a matter of how we define "similar." For most of us this means sharing common cultural experiences. The act of defining other white people as more similar than people of color is a cultural one.

It calls into question the validity of colorblindness. If color didn't matter, we'd all be shades of brown by now. We may not be thinking of color when we choose to marry other white people. Probably the idea of race seldom enters into consideration. But it seems in terms of marriage partners, we have a very strong tendency to see white.

It demonstrates that our society is racially structured. Certainly many white people find it difficult to contemplate interracial marriage. Social ostracism by other whites is one major fear. White culture is changing, but it still remains rooted in its racist past. Interracial marriage brings out the worst in white people who might otherwise pass for being "nonracist." Many other whites who might consider interracial marriage regardless of social pressure simply do not encounter people of other races in settings that encourage development of romantic involvement. We don't live in the same neighborhoods and we don't mix in public settings. Our lives are structured in a way that significant interracial contact is unlikely to take place unless we go "out of our way" to make it happen.

It provides a measure of how far we have to go. The racial structure of our society has deep roots and is not likely to change overnight. Clearly there is a lot of work to do if we want to remove racial barriers. Most Americans still view monoracial marriages as "normal." We need to question whether something is normal when it is based on placing barriers between groups.

It provides a measure of how far we have come. After all, it used to be much worse. It has only been 35 years since laws against interracial marriage were struck down by the U.S. Supreme Court in 1967. Since 1970 the number of black/white marriages has doubled every decade. Today there are 300,000 black/white marriages and slightly more than 3 million interracial marriages overall. Nearly seven million individual Americans identify as multiracial. Altogether the community of multiracial families, including those who have transracially adopted, numbers more than twelve million people. While still small, it is one of the fastest growing groups in our country, far outstripping the growth of any monoracial group.

What About Other Areas of Our Society?

Marriage is but one area of our society that is racially structured. I could just as easily have taken other areas such as work, community, friendships, or public activity and demonstrated much the same state of affairs. To those who think this exercise is trivial, perhaps it is. But I constantly hear references to how our society is multiracial, how we're colorblind, and how race no longer matters in America. And to be blunt, it's mostly white people I hear this from.

I don't want to paint all white people as racist. Certainly some of us are. But many of us are working hard to overcome the legacy of racism in the United States. Still, like the old saying, if wishes were horses, beggars would ride. We wish for a society that is not racially structured, where race doesn't matter. Sometimes we wish so hard, we convince ourselves it has already happened. Like DeMott pointed out about our media (see Chapter 1), we produce images of racial mixing, racial harmony, and racial inclusion.

But part of growing up is learning how to separate imagery and fantasy from what is real, and the reality in the United States is that we are all part of a racially structured society. This limits our opportunities for meaningful interracial contact, and even worse, it limits our ability to be the kind of society and nation we want to be. The images have a purpose. They guide us toward our dreams. But confusing images and reality will not make our dreams come true, regardless of how much we might wish it so.

Sometimes, indeed often, in our frustration to create a society that has moved beyond race, white Americans try to step out of the process. We convince ourselves we no longer are part of the racial structure. We tell ourselves either it has gone away, or those who still continue to say it exists are doing so for their own selfish purposes. We may even convince ourselves that other people are mentally or culturally incapable of living in a society where racial structure is not present.

But no single race can transcend this structure. That's what structure is all about. Either we change it together, or it continues to impact the lives of all of us. Rather than trying to unilaterally step out of America's racially structured society, white Americans need to take a close look at where we stand within it.

What Will It Take to Create a Multiracial Society?

Back in 1990 when I was working in corporate America I often spent my lunch hour visiting bookstores and newsstands. Being a prolific reader, especially of nonfiction, I perused the shelves for anything that seemed interesting. One winter's day I found myself in a bookstore on Broadway a couple blocks from Wall Street in New York City where I happened upon a then recently published book titled *Beyond Race and Gender*, by Roosevelt Thomas.[10]

The book seemed more a sociological work, but I found it sitting in the business section. The apparent disjunction probably caught my eye. Along with that, I often had conversations with my wife, a sociologist who studies both race and gender stratification in the United States. So I picked up the book and began to leaf through it. It turned out to be a discussion of "diversity" in business. Many years later the concept of diversity has spawned a small industry of trainers and consultants. Most people have at least heard the term, but at that time it was still a new concept. Thomas's book was one of the first popular works to herald this new wave of activity.

Though I didn't foresee all this at the time, I can remember quite clearly being struck by one point Thomas made in his book. Prior efforts to integrate people of different backgrounds in the business world had been flawed. The hallmark of managing diversity, he wrote, occurred when white men were brought into the process. He wasn't saying white men should control what happened. Rather he was commenting on an implicit approach by organizations in which everyone but white men were considered different and in need of integration into the organizational setting. Along the way white men were overlooked.[11]

I had never thought of it in the way that Thomas put it. At the time I knew quite clearly that white men held the power in America. I knew we also got the major share of the benefits. At the same time, I knew much of this benefit, regardless of how hard I had worked for it, was illicit. People of color and white women who worked just as hard, and often harder, did not get as much for their efforts. The game was rigged. Unlike many of my colleagues, I could see that.

Partly in reaction to this realization, I simply figured programs designed to foster inclusion, level the playing field, and create an organization in which difference was accepted were meant for everyone but the white men who basically already had things going our way. It was like compensation for everyone else. To me it felt a little cold, as if I had to set aside my own humanity because my race and gender group basically got the best of everything else. Personally I felt uncomfortable with that arrangement, but it was beyond me to change. So in my own mind I went along.

Then along comes Thomas, a black man no less, saying white men must be included in the process in order for it to be meaningful and complete. His words struck me and I was nearly moved to tears. I could be part of the process after all. This matter of diversity was not just something for people of color. It wasn't just something for women. It applied to all of us, myself included. I felt like a new kid on the playground who had been forced to play by myself because the group didn't want me to play with them. Now here was someone saying I had to be let in. If I had to give up a few of my toys to do that, I considered it a small problem, hardly worth a second thought.

Thomas ran a risk in his assertion. Might not white men, with our arrogance and intolerance for others, simply read him as validating the dominance of white males, as if to say nothing could be accomplished without us? Somehow, I realized he was saying something much more profound, and in the saying he spoke to a deep and unrecognized need on my part. This moment of epiphany led me to consider what my role might be in fostering a multiracial and multicultural society. Somewhere I had a part. Thomas had made that clear. But exactly what it was is a question that has taken me years to figure out. It's really a process, a never-ending quest in which one begins to see what needs to be done. Ultimately there is no final and complete answer, but we can develop a better understanding over time.

Some white people feel they have no role in creating a multiracial society. It's not uncommon for us to think of ourselves as finished products. We've assimilated with other Europeans and taken on an identity we've named "American." We read "American" literature, practice "American" politics, and take pride in "American" character. After centuries of assimilation, we feel we've become a distinct people in a distinct nation. Those who are different, we believe, simply have to become like us. Immigrants and people of color should try to emulate our "American" image. Our role in creating a multiracial society, according to this line of thought, is to stand as models, the finished products of a long process, and patiently help those who are trying to catch up.

This role that I've described and which has named itself as "American" is really white American. We are *all* Americans. Native Americans have been here long before us. African-Americans, too, on average have been in this country long before the average European. True, some Europeans arrived here first. But the great masses of European immigration took place after 1808, the date when forced importation of Africans was made illegal. Though a small amount of immigration, forced or voluntary, of black people has occurred since, most African-Americans today have roots in America that go back centuries. How often have you heard a white person say, "My family wasn't even here during slavery times"? Most African-American families were. So how can European-Americans hold ourselves up as different from African-Americans and Native Americans—two groups who have been American longer on average than European-Americans—and at the same time we newcomers claim to be the model of what an "American" is?

Who Should Change?

Most people realize there is some measure of racial conflict in the United States. I sometimes ask the question, "Who should change?" Should it be people of color, or white people? When I pose the question this way, most people agree that both groups need to change. Personally I think that's a fair and realistic answer. But if both groups need to change, then this means white Americans need to change. Put aside the question of what people of color need to do for a while and just consider that fact. We, white Americans, need to change. The what and how to change may not be evident, but the need and the responsibility are clear. If there is going to be some melting into a melting pot, then we all need to do a little more of it, white Americans included. Whatever the ultimate American character (and politics, and literature, etc.) will turn out to be, it's still in process.

As Roosevelt Thomas implied in his book, in the United States we cannot build a multiracial society without including white people as part of the process. It's not simply something to be done by people of color alone. We're all part of the process, and this means white people are definitely included. On the other hand, it's not something white people can do alone, either. That thought may sound simple, but it's really much deeper than it first appears. We as white Americans are able to do just about anything we want without asking for the input and approval of people of color. We can pass laws, build skyscrapers and bridges, run megacorporations, move trillions of dollars about the globe, and flex the world's greatest military muscle. And nowhere do we have to ask people of color if they agree.

Much of the time we divide among ourselves, Democrat versus Republican, North against South, that kind of thing. Because of these differences it may not be immediately obvious to us that it's still white people making the decisions either way. People of color have developed a greater presence in decision-making roles in the past few decades, and like white people they also are often arrayed on both sides of an issue. But when you get down to it, the votes, the wealth, the professional representation, the centers of higher learning, the boards of directors of the corporations, and just about every other seat of power in the country, including Congress and the Presidency, are overwhelmingly white. We may think to include people of color as a courtesy. It's no longer polite to run things like in the old days when not even that was done. But if white people ever decided to turn away from that courtesy, there is little people of color could do to change it.

When it comes to the matter of creating a multiracial society, we come to the table with some ingrained and dysfunctional habits. Here is one place where we must have the approval of people of color. A multiracial society, by definition, cannot be created by any one racial group alone. It means we each need to step out of our monoracial surroundings and work with each other to create a common set of values, understandings, and for that matter, community. In a truly multiracial society, we participate in an act of mutual creation. Any side can disown the process, leave the table, and abandon the community.

For white people (and for people of color as well) this requires a whole new perspective. It means if we sit in our nearly all-white communities, writing letters to the editor of our nearly all-white newspapers, espousing ideas we learned at our nearly all-white schools about how people of color just aren't going along with the program, we are massively deluding ourselves. And we are. Much of what passes for thinking by white people on how our society might become racially inclusive is simply a product of white people talking among ourselves. Old habits are hard to break. We've been doing business like that for a long time.

We can avoid a lot of frustration if we could just admit one thing—white people alone cannot build a multiracial society. We need people of color. We need their approval. We need their leadership. We need their consent. Now I know some white people will want to ask me what I think people of color should be doing. Maybe these same white people have their own opinions on the matter. Didn't I say white people were necessary, too? Of course I did. Sure people of color need our approval, our cooperation, and our leadership as well. It's a mutual process. That's not the point here. The point is that we, white people, can't create a multiracial society on our own terms alone. We need people of color. That's a new experience for us.

So if we are to create a multiracial society in America, white people will have a part, but the part we have will not be entirely under our control. People of color will have a part as well, and white people will not be able to say entirely what that part will be. It's likely this will be an uncomfortable role for white people, facing the unknown, taking a role where we are responsible for part, but not all, of the process. Admitting we need to change, but realizing the change is not completely ours to determine. It won't be easy for us. It won't be easy for anyone.

What Do White People Need To Do?

A couple years after reading Roosevelt Thomas's book, I found myself again in New York City, this time during the midst of summer on a hot and sultry day in an office building that lacked adequate air conditioning. Together with a senior colleague, a woman of color, I was listening to a young man, also a person of color, who was employed in an entry-level professional position at a nonprofit organization. It was just the three of us in a small office.

Though we were located only a few blocks from the bookstore where I found Thomas's book many months before, I had come a long way from the corporate world of financial services. Now part of a small, minority-owned diversity consulting practice, I was using both my business and psychology background in a way I had never done before. Our firm had contracted to provide diversity training to the nonprofit organization in whose office we sat. We were interviewing staff as a preliminary step, to identify issues and concerns present in the organization.

Typically we took turns asking questions. I had asked several questions already, and my colleague was then walking through the various social groupings that existed in the organization, asking our informant what he thought each group should do to make the workplace one in which people were more appreciative of social differences. "What should women do?" she asked. "What do you think men should do?"

The young man was giving thoughtful and perceptive responses. We had already seen several employees, and he seemed to have more to contribute in understanding and insight than had many of his co-workers. Still, it was hot and stuffy in the room, nearing the end of a long day, and I confess I was feeling a little drowsy. My colleague leading the questioning, being the senior professional, had the situation well in hand. "What do black people need to do?" she asked. I began to drift off, still listening with half an ear, ready to feign alertness. "What do Asian people need to do?" My mind had already wandered nearly beyond the office setting when my colleague asked, "What do white people need to do?"

This simple question is not one white Americans have asked ourselves, at least within my living memory. Sure we've done things. We've been on both sides of the issue, racist and antiracist. Many of us have worked to dismantle the racial inequities of our society, even as our racial brothers and sisters have sought to perpetuate them. But this work—and here I'm speaking of the antiracist activity—has been carried out with a vision of racial justice and equality intended to benefit people of color. We've often taken charge of the process, but stood outside of it at the same time. Our actions were not directed at ourselves, and particularly they were not directed toward understanding our unique role in a larger, cooperative process.

The question of what white people need to do to create a multiracial society is both timely and new. It's not one that assumes white people automatically know what to do. Nor does it suppose the answer is as simple as white people just stopping our racist ways. Rather the question asks how white people, as part of the multiracial mix in America, can take an active role in freeing all of us, white people included, to create a society structured not by race, but by our recognition of our common humanity.

This sort of question, seeming simple but inviting a broad social response with major implications for our society, takes time to answer. A multitude of voices contribute to the process. No single person can give the definitive picture. It is the sort of question whose answer builds upon the contributions and insights of many people, each perhaps inspired by the partial answers offered by those who have spoken before. It is within that context, in respect to those who have spoken before, and with anticipation of those who will speak in the future, that I offer some partial answers.

Whatever white people must do, it seems clear we will not all do it at the same time. Social change never happens that way. Rather, some white people will take leadership, and indeed some already have. Other white people will remain locked into their old, and in many cases, racist ways. It is worthwhile to pursue an agenda that seeks to convert racist whites into nonracist or antiracist whites. It seems just as valuable to develop a body of white people who are interested in looking at new approaches to creating a multiracial society. The status quo is no longer serving us very well. We need to seek new answers if we're ever to realize this higher purpose and dream of a multiracial society.

White people need to stop believing we must control the whole picture. Often this belief is a subconscious one. We need to test it. It's one of our historic blind spots. We need to become a little more humble and focus on our own role. Certainly we need to address the social inequalities of our society as they bear disproportionately on people of color. We should offer help, assistance, and resources to people of color if they ask. But let's not lose sight that we need to work on our own house. We're no longer responsible for maintaining the entire town. We have a part, a significant one, but we don't have a monopoly. Nor should we.

Marimba Ani, in her monumental critique of European society, has pointed out that European cultures often take a universalistic stance.[12] This stance is one in which we purport to speak for all of humanity. We announce principles that, we believe, apply to all groups equally. We interpret the behavior of other cultural groups as if they are motivated by the same forces that motivate us. In the process we overlook how we are simply one cultural group among many. In the United States our "universal" point of view that claims to speak for everyone is often a white American point of view that speaks from the standpoint of white culture. We need to avoid confusing issues and claiming to speak for everyone when we are actually coming from a more limited cultural stance.

Does Everyone Want a Multiracial Society?

No, of course not. Many white people want to remain encapsulated in a white society. If there is a problem with this, it rests in the fact that white society has not allowed other racial/cultural groups the same privilege. Freedom and liberation movements by people of color often aspire toward autonomy, i.e., the ability to decide one's own fate and the fate of those who share a culture of color without interference from white culture. Other efforts by people of color have provided an inclusive vision of a multiracial society in which all races partake. Either way, the resistance these movements have fostered against white culture as the central and controlling force in our society has been, and continues to be, the main source of energy for dismantling the racially structured society we have in America.

We need to accept leadership by people of color. Had not people of color resisted white supremacy, there would be very little resistance at all. White people have always provided some measure of resistance to the racist aspects of our society, but it has been the effort by people of color in pursuit of their own freedom and liberty that has led the United States to change its laws and change its ways. It has been the leadership by people of color that today allows us to even talk about creating a multiracial society. This does not mean white people cannot lead. But it does mean that we must also learn how to listen and how to follow.

It was listening to a person of color on that hot summer's day that led me to an insight, sent me on a journey, and led me to write this book. This young man, who was of mixed Asian and European ancestry, was speaking plainly. His answer, though disarmingly simple, let me know I had a gargantuan gap in my knowledge of race, of difference, and of my own experience. He created a dilemma for me about an issue that seemed both very foreign and so close to home it was part of my very being.

Unknowingly, he woke me up, both literally that day and figuratively since that time. He led me to research what other people had said, and in that research I found a strange state of affairs. Many people of color had spoken of the same need as he did. Sometimes they had done research and developed elaborate and convincing explanations of their view.

White people seemed to never even think about it. Some recognized its importance, but they were few, so few they seemed like marginalized oddballs, do-gooders, and troublemakers who would never gain the attention of a serious audience. Yet the more I looked, and listened, and learned, I began to wonder why so many people of color identified this need and so few white people did. Even white people who had spent their lives working for racial justice seemed to have a blind spot here. Even in the face of overwhelming support from people of color, most white people were opposed to the advice embodied in this young man's comment.

"What do white people need to do?" my colleague asked.

"Just be a little more aware of their whiteness," he replied.

3

Remedial Education for White Folk

When I first heard that white people needed to be aware of our whiteness I was woefully ignorant—though not of race, for anyone living in American soon develops a large repertoire of racial understandings. I was ignorant of whiteness. I also had a lot to learn about racism.

Ignorance is not the same as stupidity. To be ignorant means a person has the ability and opportunity to learn, and has ignored that ability and opportunity. I consider myself an educated person, of at least average—if not above average—intelligence. Certainly I had the ability. As I was soon to find, there are ample resources like books, videos, discussions in the media, and organizations that talk about race and racism from the standpoint of creating a society that is not racially structured.[1]

Being surrounded by other white people who shared this ignorance, people who otherwise were often very educated, I did not notice the lack of my knowledge. Only when I began to consider in earnest what it meant to be white, and what it would take for white people to help create a multiracial society, did I begin to see what I had been missing. I found the average person of color knew more about it than I did. Things that surprised me were often accepted as common knowledge among friends and acquaintances of mine who were not white. Things like the "one drop" rule (that states to be considered white a person cannot have any black ancestors), or the extent of suspicion innocent people of color raise when in predominantly white neighborhoods, or the impact of institutional racism—these things seldom crossed my awareness. When they did, I saw them as actions by individually bigoted people who had nothing in common with me. Even the fact that our

34

society is racially structured—something now glaringly obvious to me—was often hard to see.

White people who want to build a multiracial society need to overcome a deficit in our education. We need remedial programs. I'm quite aware of the irony of suggesting remedial education for white people. The traditional model offers remedial education to people of color who seek to participate in the predominantly white mainstream. I am using the concept exactly the same way, but applying it to white people who want to participate in creating a multiracial society. Despite the humor, I'm quite serious. Before we join the larger community, we've got some catching up to do.

In this chapter I want to discuss some basic concepts. You may wish to either skim this material or read it closely. Some of it is general background, laying out a foundation for other discussions in this book. Some of it is particular to the white experience in America. Either way, you should have a feel for the concepts of this chapter if you want to follow the rest of the book.

Physical and Social Reality

Humans deal with both physical and social reality. By physical reality, I mean the concrete, measurable circumstances we encounter in our environment and the needs they create within us. This includes things like the way matter and energy act as described by the laws of chemistry and physics, the need of food for sustenance, the need for shelter from the elements, and the need to avoid physical injury. Each of these circumstances, or needs, is universal. They are not dependent on the particular social group in which we are members.

Social reality refers to how we form our understanding of customs and practices of our social group, how we are accepted within that group, and how we share a view of our world with other members of the group. The "group" in this case can mean a family, an organization, a culture, or a society. Our social reality is composed of all these groups, which vary in size and overlap each other in our lives.

Physical reality varies on its own while social reality varies according to people's views. In other words, if everyone agreed underpants should be worn outside their clothes, then society would care and everyone would feel normal and comfortable doing it. That's social reality. If everyone agreed the weather should be 80 degrees outside in January in New England, physical reality wouldn't give a hoot.

We spend our lives managing both physical and social reality in order to meet our needs. When our needs fit the reality, regardless of whether that reality is physical or social, then we feel comfortable. When there is a problem in the fit, we notice it. If the problem is big enough, we take action. In terms of physical reality, we generally do not notice when a room is at a "comfortable" temperature. When it is too cold, we turn up the heat and when it is too hot, we turn on the air conditioning. If no air conditioning is present, or heat in the case of a cold room, then we may leave for a more comfortable setting. Or if we must stay, we do our best to ignore a situation that still intrudes on our consciousness.

When things are going well in our social world we don't tend to think about them. We may even take them for granted. But when problems arise, again we try to correct them. We often anticipate problems that might arise and take steps to head them off. This may mean being courteous and considerate to others, trying to meet expectations and demands placed on us by others, and seeing that we do not unnecessarily intrude on other people's interests. We also act upon our own needs as they arise, seeking cooperation and support from others.

Seeing and Believing

The tangible nature of physical reality makes physical reality easier to see. Social reality, though harder to grasp as a concept, is quite potent in its effects. Social psychologists back in the 1930s demonstrated that people readily produce and believe in a common social reality. One experimenter placed individuals one by one in a dark room with a single point of light placed 15 feet in front of them. The light was stationary, but people invariably experienced the "autokinetic effect," an optical illusion in which the light appears to move. The experimenter asked each person to estimate how far the light moved, and after several "trials" each individual settled in on an average estimate of how far the light moved each time.[2]

Then the experimenter placed individuals into groups of three and again asked for individual estimates. The initial estimates of each individual varied widely from others in the group. But over time the group members eventually converged in their estimates and "agreed" on how far the light moved. This little experiment shows that social reality can be extremely strong and convincing, even to the point of bringing people to agree on what they perceived physical reality to be.

Managing our social reality is a major task, and it is social reality that is one of the main concepts under discussion in this book. Even though social reality is dependent on people holding common views, that does not mean it's unreal. How people perceive their social world has very real implications. It helps us define what is natural, comfortable, expected, and acceptable. Often it is our social reality that is most important to us. Strictly speaking, if we only sought physical comfort we should avoid life-threatening situations as much as possible, but dramatic as it is, human experience is replete with examples where people have given up their physical lives for social things, like family, religion, and nation.

The ideas of "fit" and "comfort" are simple. You may want to point out that people place themselves in uncomfortable situations intentionally, whether it be something physical like mountain climbing, or social, like working our way into a group that is hostile or disinterested in our presence. This simply calls for a broader definition of comfort, one that contains an element of free choice over our actions. Jumping into ice cold water as a member of a polar bear club is one thing. Some people, odd as it may seem, actually do this for the thrill of it. Falling into ice cold water unintentionally is quite another thing. Being thrown in against one's will is yet another.

Culture

Some people think of culture in terms of food, clothing, and works of art. Some people think of culture as what happens in art museums, symphony halls, and opera houses. Other people take a broader view of culture, and it is that broader view that I am using here. Culture, in this sense, refers to the shared customs, practices, meanings, and understandings among a group of people. The group may be a small group, such as an organization, or a large group such as might exist in a geographic region or nation. It may comprise a subset of a larger population that has similar characteristics or living circumstances. In this latter sense, we hear terms like "culture of poverty," "gay culture," "male culture," and "organizational culture."[3]

Cultural Membership(s)

Some people approach the notion of culture as if any single person must belong to one, and only one, cultural group. Since I was raised in New Jersey, for instance, and that is very different from being raised in Mississippi, Iowa, Maine, or Oregon, I might claim to come from a different culture than persons raised in those regions. Other white people use ethnic origin in the same way. Since we are of some combination of European origins such as Italian, English, Polish, Irish, etc., we view ourselves as distinct from people who have a different European ethnic background. According to this type of reasoning, being Italian-American is a very different experience from being Irish-American, which is different from being English-American.

Often this sort of reasoning is used to demonstrate there is no such thing as white culture. If we have these cultural variations by region or by ethnic background, how can such a thing as "white culture" exist? How can we claim shared cultural meaning to being white? Ironically, this concern is seldom raised in discussing other types of culture, though the concern is of the same nature. Along with white culture, how can we assign meaning to the other types of culture (poverty, gay, male, organization) mentioned above, if either region or ethnicity is so overpowering as to preclude any other type of cultural identity or formation? Which of the two—ethnic origin or region—is greater, and does one override the other? What do we say of someone of both Italian and Irish heritage who was born in New Jersey, moved to Mississippi at age five, then to Maine at age eleven, and finally attended high school in Oregon? This type of experience is not uncommon for military families.

Rather than trying to prove that one source of cultural identity makes another impossible, as if only one source can apply in a person's life, a more reasonable approach is to look at a variety of cultural influences, of which region and ethnic origin are two. Cultural identities and cultural experiences may be found in other aspects of our world. Gay culture, straight culture, male culture, female culture, and any number of organizational cultures all may form part of our lives, each influencing and modifying the experience we have of ourselves as individuals and social beings.

People sometimes take the notion of "white people" and begin to break it down into the different types of white people they can identify. Often they do this along ethnic lines. This process is one of taking a large group and then finding distinguishing details among the members of that group which demonstrate that smaller groups exist within. We might take each of those smaller groups and break it down even further into smaller groups, repeating the process until we are left at the point of distinguishing each and every individual as uniquely defined. We are all individuals, after all.

This same process can be applied to any large group, not just white people. Take a large business organization, such as AT&T. We can divide it into divisions, departments, subunits, etc., until we arrive at a unique description of every employee in the company. But it's doubtful this will render AT&T nonexistent, despite our discovery of the unique individuality of each person in the organization.

Whiteness is a large social formation that has cultural characteristics. So, too, do other racial/cultural groups, each of which can be subjected to this process of division and subdivision in the same way that "white people" can—or AT&T for that matter.[4] Everyone of us can describe our existence at several levels of analysis. We are truly all individuals, unique and precious. We are all the same under the skin, humans who are part of one and only one universal human race. In between those two, somewhat contradictory, descriptions there is a middle land of group memberships that include socially ascribed statuses like race and gender, along with a profusion of self-selected group memberships.

Cultural Practices

If you and I talk together and I nod my head up and down as you are speaking, you would probably see that as an indication that I agreed with you, and that's what it would be. I might not even be thinking about the gesture of head-nodding itself. It's just something I do because that's what I have learned as part of my culture.

When I was living in a multicultural boarding house with other graduate students, I often met foreign students who had just arrived in the United

38

States for their graduate education. Thus I clearly remember Raju, from India. Raju was a very friendly man. We would talk about various things and as we did he would offer a wide and embracing smile so convincing and sincere that no one could doubt the goodness of his feelings. But I had the distinct impression he disagreed with me.

Eventually I realized as we talked, even at the same time he was smiling, he would shake his head from side to side like Americans do when we say no. The friendly smile on the one hand, and the shaking of his head from side to side on the other hand, left me with the impression he was feebleminded, smiling at everyone but not comprehending what was going on.

I knew very well Raju was not feebleminded, so I began to question him about his head gesture and found out in his culture that was how one indicated agreement. Several years later I saw a documentary on culture that discussed this very gesture, called a head wobble. It resembles the American gesture of shaking the head from side to side to say no, but not exactly. The head wobble is used in India and other places just as we use the head nod, up and down, to indicate agreement. I had never run across this specific gesture before, and when I did, I (mis)interpreted it according to the closest thing I had encountered before.

Not Just the Food

Culture is more than the obvious differences of food and dress, music and language. It makes itself felt in thousands of ways. Cross-cultural trainers can produce hundreds of stories like mine, illustrating how ingrained, unconscious habits in one culture lead to misinterpretation in another culture. Some educators distinguish between surface culture and deep culture.

Surface culture includes visible elements such as food, dress, language, art (literature, dance, music, storytelling, drama, etc.), and holidays. Multicultural celebrations often involve the display and exchange of elements of surface culture among cultural groups.

Deep culture, unlike surface culture, contains values, beliefs and attitudes that permeate virtually every aspect of a person's life. One educator, for instance, identified twenty elements of deep culture: ceremony, courtship and marriage, esthetics, ethics, family ties, health and medicine, folk myths, gesture and kinesics, grooming and presence, ownership, precedence, rewards and privileges, rights and duties, religion, sex roles, space and proxemics, subsistence, taboos, concepts of time, and values.[5] Any one of these elements comprises a vast range of experience. Unlike surface culture, we are generally unaware of deep culture. But, deep culture provides the very social and communal framework in which we live.

Purpose of Culture

Every day we greet others in our social world. The act of greeting involves mutual acknowledgment of each other's presence, with some demonstration of goodwill and lack of threatening intent. In my native culture I customarily do this by shaking hands, or by giving a wave of the hand if passing by. Other cultures have different methods. In some cultures, people bow to one another. In other cultures they hold up their hand, palm facing outward. In still other cultures a kiss is used. Many greeting gestures doubtless exist among cultures, whether these cultures be ethnic, organizational, or otherwise.

The greeting gesture solves a problem. How do we, as individuals moving about our social world, indicate our readiness to be social, to interact as needed, and to be nonthreatening? And how do we receive indication from other individuals that they are in the same state of mind? It may seem trivial, but this is a very important thing to know. Perhaps the easiest way to point this out is to ask what happens when we greet someone and they do not reciprocate. We're likely to take it as a sign of hostility, a potential threat, or an assertion of power on the other's part, as if to say we are so unimportant as not to be bothered with. This may lead us to spend some time wondering about the implications of the other person's state of mind. If this is a person we have to work with during the day, that person's lack of willingness to interact with us could have serious consequences for us. Throughout our day every mutually acknowledged, and thus successfully completed, greeting gesture assures us that all is well between us and that person.

Now there are actually two problems to be solved here. One is in the greeting that indicates a willingness to interact in a nonthreatening way. The second is in how this message will be conveyed. Do we use a handshake, a bow, a palm gesture or some other method? Suppose every time we met someone, we had to figure out what gesture to use. We would do a little dance, each trying different gestures until our meaning was conveyed. This would quickly become a problem in itself, taking an inordinate amount of time to convey a simple message. Fortunately, our culture tells us what to do. Indeed, it is in the shared understanding of what gesture to use, and the shared understanding of what the gesture means, that much of the idea of culture can be found. As members of a shared culture, we can use our greeting gesture, like a handshake, and move with relatively little effort through a large number of people, exchanging greetings.

Culture allows us to form habits and these habits, once formed, become unconscious. That's their role. They allow us to get to other

40

things in our lives that require our conscious attention, like working at our job, or pursuing personal and family needs. We don't have to think about the thousand little things that allow us to communicate and coordinate our actions in a social environment because we have already learned them as part of our culture.

We learn our culture *in situ*, as part of our living experience. Some of it is formally taught in schools, some is conveyed by parents and other adults, and some is simply learned through observation. Often the learning is not given as explicit lessons, but rather found in the reactions of other people to our youthful activity. A few years ago my family was at a cookout at a friend's house. We were among a multiracial crowd and people were comfortable with this. My son, then age five, was talking to my wife and me as we sat at a table within earshot of several other people also having conversations. My son, pointing to another child, said "the little white girl" as a descriptive reference. Though done in innocence, his simple reference to the "white" girl stopped conversations, including our own. Following an awkward moment of silence among the adults, we shrugged it off as a child's unintentional misspeaking and went on with our conversations.

Now I could say a lot about this incident, about how perhaps it should not have had that effect on the adults, how whiteness is not named in our society, or how I, as a person who studies whiteness should have been nonplused. But the point here is that my son learned something. He got a little cultural lesson on what happened when he named whiteness in a mixed-race crowd. What that lesson was, I'm not exactly sure, but I am sure that's how many of our cultural lessons are learned.

Over time these little cultural lessons add up and we develop an understanding, generally an unconscious one, of things like norms, social roles, characteristics of different groups, social status and power, and virtually everything else that comprises the cultural experience of our specific social environment. Within that cultural world we go about meeting our other needs, forming relationships, obtaining food and shelter, protecting ourselves and loved ones from hardship, avoiding pain and seeking out things that are fun. All these we see as real problems needing real solutions and that is where our conscious thoughts are directed. We give very little thought to the cultural learning we have mastered that allows us to interact meaningfully with others and manage the complex social rituals of our social world. Our past cultural learning has already solved those problems. Our cultural knowledge rests below our consciousness, helping us constantly, but consuming little of our conscious attention. That's its role.

41

Cultural Location and Change

Culture does not describe any single person. When we talk about a culture, many people may be presumed to participate in the shared understandings that comprise that cultural experience, but the culture does not define the entirety of any one person's experience. People encounter a number of different cultures in the course of their lives. Some, such as organizational cultures, are localized. Others, like national cultures, are widespread. Any one person will partake of several cultural experiences.

A person may be centrally positioned in a culture, privy to all its understandings, fully immersed in its values and benefiting from the rewards such participation may bring. Other people may be marginally located within the same culture, and as a result may not participate as fully as someone centrally located. Cultures themselves may flow, one into another, such that the centers of two adjoining cultures may be apparent, but the boundary between them less so. Looking at regional cultures in the United States, the Yankee culture of New England is clear, as is the culture of the South. As people travel from Boston to Atlanta though, they will experience a gradual transition from one culture to the other, and no place will they find a clear demarcation that tells them when they have passed beyond the influence of one culture and fully into the realm of the other.

Cultures also change. Closely related cultures may undergo assimilation, and a single culture may become differentiated into two or more cultures. These processes take time, but in the course of history they become evident. No culture remains static and unchanging.

Race

One recent night I found myself in a country field away from the normal glare of the more urbanized setting where I live. In the dark sky I could see many more stars than I could at home. As a child I used to stargaze with my family, identifying constellations and planets, so it was a small pleasure to do this once again. As I looked at the heavens, I spotted a dim cluster of stars at the corner of my vision. When I turned my eye to view it directly, the cluster disappeared. Moving my eyes to the side, again I could see the same cluster, but whenever I tried to focus on it, the cluster vanished. I could only view it out of the corner of my eye.

This is not so strange as it may seem. The periphery of our eyes contain more rods, the nerve receptors that allow us to distinguish subtle shades of black and white. The center contains cones, which allow us to see in full color. Under the viewing conditions that night, the rods were better suited for detecting the star cluster.

Looking at race is a lot like looking at that star cluster. From the side of our vision, it seems clear, but when we begin to examine it critically, it always seems to disappear. Under scrutiny there is no single way of defining race that is completely logical. All definitions of race suffer from some sort of contradiction. I am not going to resolve these contradictions. The best I can do is point to them. But I will say that some people think that because we cannot define race in a logical, noncontradictory way, race does not exist. From there they conclude that race has no effect on people's lives. That conclusion is unwarranted.

What the Race Experts Say

Is race a scientifically valid concept? Let's see what the scientists say. Anthropologists study physical and cultural differences among humankind, and anthropology has long considered the scientific validity of race. The American Anthropological Association (AAA), says "the concept of race is a social and cultural construction, with no basis in human biology." As far as our genetic makeup, they tell us "the data also show that any two individuals within a particular population are as different genetically as any two people selected from any two populations in the world." They add "the continued sharing of genetic materials has maintained all of humankind as a single species."

As to differences, "physical variations in the human species have no meaning except the social ones that humans put on them." Finally, they "conclude that present-day inequalities between so-called 'racial' groups are not consequences of their biological inheritance but products of historical and contemporary social, economic, educational, and political circumstances."[6]

Clearly the scientists no longer believe in "race." The AAA recognizes that we still need to look at race as part of "the cultural and political fabric of the United States." So corrective measures need to consider "race," even though it has no biological validity. But they call for its eventual replacement with "more non-racist and accurate ways of representing the diversity of the U.S. population."

Biological Definitions

Biological definitions treat race as a fixed property of the individual. These definitions go back to the early 18th century when European scientists first began to consider how humans could be classified according to their physical differences. Physical features, in particular skin color, but also hair texture and the shape of facial features like the nose and lips, were used to create classification schemes in which people were divided into a small number of racial categories such as Mongoloid, Caucasoid, and Negroid.

Prior to this time, the prevailing thought among Europeans was that environmental differences accounted for physical differences. Dark-skinned people were dark, it was believed, because they lived near the equator. It was just a matter of time, many thought, before the progeny of light-skinned people in the tropics, such as English people in Barbados, would darken and the progeny of dark-skinned people in colder climates, such as Africans in Massachusetts, would grow lighter. After a few generations, when this and other anticipated changes did not emerge, European scientists began to look to biology to explain racial differences.[7]

What the European scientists sought to explain was not simply physical differences in skin color, but also social differences. Europe had universities, emerging nation states, Christianity, the printing press, technological advancements in military might, and global navigation. Countless other social differences existed. Compared to Europeans, other people seemed not only different, but less advanced in things Europeans understood as important. Biological theories of race, just like the older environmental theories, sought to account for these social differences as well. Ultimately the biological theorists did not simply create discrete groups. They arranged the groups hierarchically with Europeans always occupying the top of the hierarchy.

Social Definitions

Biological definitions of race held sway through the 18th and 19th centuries. By the time the 20th century rolled around, some "scientific" experts had developed classification systems that named hundreds of "races." These experts often testified in court as to who was what race, and what that implied about the social and personality characteristics of the person in question. Much of our common thinking about race today can still be traced to these theories. But beginning in the 1920s scientists again began to challenge the prevailing view of race. The challengers portrayed race not as a matter of biology, but rather a creation of culture. Biologically, these scientists held, we are all the same "under the skin" but we live in societies that use physical characteristics and cultural differences to assign stereotypes to different groups. People may believe these stereotypes have a basis in biology, but they do not.

The new breed of scientists went further to say racial stereotypes are used to justify unequal treatment among groups, giving rise to prejudice, discrimination, and whole societies structured along racial lines. At the societal level, racial differences are written into the laws, which in turn grant rights to some racial groups while denying them to others. Once society has become structured by race, the changes become frozen in place and difficult to overcome. Confusing these social and cultural processes with biologically based explanations of difference simply serves to perpetuate the social differences.

Comparing Social and Biological Explanations

Social theorists say that race is a "social construct," meaning the notion of race is developed from our social and cultural outlook. Accordingly, it does not represent any essential or eternal biological characteristic of the individual. Social theorists characterize biological theories as "essentialist." An essentialist theory holds that racial difference cannot be changed because it is part of an individual's physical nature.

An example of essentialist theory today is the belief that IQ is determined by race. When researchers talk of "heritability factors" and seek to demonstrate genetic differences along racial lines, they are espousing an essentialist point of view. Another example of an essentialist view is one espoused by Malcolm X in the 1960s, that white people are devils. Prior to his trip to Mecca, Malcolm X implicated all white people in his assessment. After having met white people outside the United States who were not racist, Malcolm X revised his understanding to a socially contructivist position. In his new incarnation as El-Hajj Malik El-Shabazz, he believed that while virtually all white people in the United States were racist in their social and cultural outlook, it was not a biologically determined fact they would always be like that. Under more favorable conditions, in theory at least, white Americans might be able to transcend our racist ways.

Group Differences in IQ

It's a common finding that white Americans as a group score significantly higher on IQ tests than do black Americans. Does this prove that white Americans are more intelligent? Even if we accept the validity of the concept of IQ and the possibility that it is significantly influenced by heredity, the case for innate differences in intelligence between racial/cultural groups is seriously flawed. Measures of IQ can distinguish between individuals within the same group. A naturally intelligent person will score high in his or her group, regardless of the conditions the group has encountered. But when we compare different social and cultural groups as a whole, we have to consider members of a group may have received a positive or negative influence on their IQ.[8]

Consider a simple experiment. Take a group of 200 infants. During their childhood, call half of them low-IQ, tell them no one from their group has ever been President of the United States, chronically underfund their schools, and to keep it interesting, give them a daily sprinkling of lead paint chips in their diet. When they reach age 18, give both groups the same IQ test under identical conditions. Would you expect the high-IQ group to actually score higher? Probably so. Would it prove the high-IQ group has an innate genetic superiority? Probably not.

Social theorists point out that no single set of "racial" characteristics can be used to divide people into discrete groups. Skin color varies along a gradient from very light to very dark. At no point can we draw a clear line to create two groups without ending up with a large group of people who fall in between. Other characteristics, such as hair texture, vary in the same way. People can be positioned along a gradient, but assigning them to discrete categories always involves a large group of people who fall through the cracks.

The situation becomes even more complicated when more than one physical feature is used. Shades of skin color vary in one pattern across humankind. Shades of hair color vary in another, and different, pattern. Hair texture, nose shape, and lip thickness all have their own unique patterns of variation in the human population. Biological theorists have difficulty specifying which features are most important, and in what combination they should be used to define groups. On top of that, biological theorists bear the burden of explaining why things like skin color and hair texture, which seem relatively superficial after all, are related to differences in behavior and character. The latter differences are much more complex and subject to endless cultural variations even within the same "racial" groups.

Biological theorists of race reply that social constructionists go much too far. Differences in skin color exist, and often are as clear as "black and white." Skin color and other physical features are only indicators of a shared genetic history that probably expresses itself in other ways. Some medical professionals claim that certain diseases appear at different rates among people of different "races." These diseases sometimes have genetic causes. Indeed, this is probably the one claim of biologically based racial difference that has a shred of scientific credibility. Yet geographic origin is really a more accurate way to identify genetic differences in susceptibility to various diseases. That some diseases are common to people of a given region is no more surprising or noteworthy than the fact that some diseases run in families. Yet no one tries to infer that such families are sub-intelligent, or prone to violence, or superior rational thinkers. For that matter, things such as skin color and shape of facial features run in families, too. Again, they have nothing to do with people's character or capabilities.

Race and Culture

More than once I have spoken to persons born and raised in the United States, who, in their country of origin, are considered to be "black." These persons have told of going to various parts of Africa, where they are told by the local populace that they are "white." When they return to the United States, they become "black" once again. This miraculous racial transformation happens without any effort on their part. Other people simply see it that way. Americans have one definition of race. Africans have another. If people were to travel about the world, particularly people of combined African, European, Asian, and Native American heritage, they would be racially defined in a dozen different ways, depending on where they are on their hypothetical trip.

Race is not something we are born with. Rather, we are "racialized" by our society. Having looked carefully at much of the evidence, I take the social constructivist position. Race is a matter of culture. Biology has a role to play, but it is minor compared to the social and cultural elements that shape our experience and understanding of race. It is our society and our culture that tell us what our race is, and what the implications are of being that race.

Some people believe that because race has been disowned as a scientific (i.e., biologically based) construct by many scientists, that it has no reality at all. Because race is a fiction, they feel, we should not acknowledge it in any way. We should not talk about it. We should not recognize it as a point of difference. We should not treat anyone "differently" because of race.

This view ignores the fact that how we are racialized by our society has a significant impact on our lives. Skin color, as a biological fact, may not make a big difference, but as a socially observable phenomenon that allows us to assign people to categories, skin color has a substantial impact. This process of assignment is so pervasive and ingrained in our culture that simply saying it should not be so is unlikely to change it.

Denying that race exists even as a social phenomenon also overlooks a long history of regional and cultural differences among people of African, European, Asian and Native American origin. These are broad cultural groups, infinitely diverse within. Nonetheless each have a shared character that distinguishes them from other groups. The French are quite different from the English, who differ from the Swedes. But there is a common European heritage in which their cultures are similar to each other and collectively different from African cultures.

The visual apparentness of skin color and other racial features; the large regional differences in culture; and the history of European expansion, conquest, and domination have all come together in the United States to give race a specific and enduring character that has shaped our culture, our society, and our nation. It is regarding the character of race in the United States to which this book is addressed. Our history is one in which European-Americans have racialized ourselves as white and concurrently, racialized other groups variously as black, red, yellow and brown. The specific details of the process are many, and the individual "races" that our society has designated have changed over time as well, but the process of racialization in the United States has been with us through our history,[9]—and the dominance of white Americans has been an equally constant element of that process.

It becomes possible to speak of a white American culture, or a black American culture, etc., because these groups have developed from dissimilar cultural origins, whether they be Africa, Europe, or North America or Asia. These groups have also shared common experiences in America that were not shared by other groups. Whites controlled the political structure. Africans faced forced importation and slavery. Native Americans lost their native lands and faced genocide. Asians were imported in waves as cheap labor and, denied citizenship by law, settled America from West to East, contrasting with the more commonly visible European "march to the Pacific."

Racial groups in the United States provide a vector for assimilation. The United States has been a melting pot, though not quite in the simplistic way it often is portrayed. For example, the concept of "Italian" people first achieved public acceptance not in Italy, which comprised many separate and semi-autonomous regions in the late 19th century, but rather in the United States. To the native citizen of the United States, a person from Sicily appeared and sounded much like one from Naples, Rome, or Venice. In effect, they all looked "Italian" here, and that's what they became. Some people today like to discredit the suggestion that there is an Asian-American identity by pointing to the fact that Asian-Americans consist of Japanese, Chinese, Koreans, and several other distinct cultural groups. But the notion of Japanese American is already an amalgamation. Japan is one of the most ethnically diverse nations in the world, with over 200 ethnic groups. In the United States, Japanese American is understood to be a singular identity. The process continues and now in the 1990s an Asian-American identity is beginning to make itself felt.

Various ethnic groups have assimilated in the United States, but not all of this assimilation has been of Europeans toward a central American identity. Indeed, the melting pot conception of the first half of the 20th century was myopic to the point of being incorrect. Our history has been one of various ethnic groups assimilating, and being assimilated to, racial groupings. The dominant group has often played a decisive role in the process. Europeans intentionally divided kidnapped Africans into multiethnic groups so that no single ethnic group could prevail in its language and customs—and thereby create an organized community capable of resisting enslavement. In time, due to this forced social maneuvering, Africans experienced the greatest degree of inter-ethnic assimilation of any racial/cultural group in the United States.

European immigrants faced many pressures from native white Americans to adopt white American ways. Generally presented as a process of "Americanization," this included charitable, coercive, and legal processes. Native American groups faced a more brutal attempt by white Americans to Americanize them in the boarding school programs of the early and mid-20th century. Forcefully separated from their families, and removed to institutions often at great distance, they were severely punished for displaying any sign of their native cultural heritage in speech, dress, or social practices.

Today nonwhite racial groups continue to confront common issues in dealing with white Americans as white Americans, whether it be as the "model minority," encountering "English only" movements, being characterized as "pimps" and "welfare queens," or trying to obtain national (tribal) sovereignty. These issues follow racialized lines, sweeping up many different ethnic groups into a larger process in which their interests are commonly impacted, and thus become a common point requiring defense and counteraction. The process of racialization is not simply one-sided. Cultures of color have built upon their cultural base and the continued need for defense against the dominant culture. In some cases this has lead to rich and shared traditions.

Race As a Cultural Formation

In the United States, racial groups contain various ethnic groups. Racial groups are large social/cultural structures that have cultural characteristics. They change in scope over time, particularly as ethnic groups that comprise them also change. African-Americans, for instance, experienced a long history in which they were highly assimilated as a racial group due to their early history of forced ethnic merging. Today the United States is seeing increasing immigration of ethnic groups of African descent (e.g., Nigerians, Ghanaians, Jamaicans). The racial group of "black" in the United States is becoming more ethnically differentiated. At the same time, black immigrants are being racialized into an already existing image of African-American. Asian-American, Native American, and Latino/a-Americans are all undergoing transformation as well, assimilating to some degree to their racial centers, and contending with countervailing—and often contradictory—forces that would assimilate them to the "mainstream" society at the same time.

What Are Hispanics?

Social scientists often define race as a social categorization based on skin color and other physical attributes. This definition is fine when we discuss whites, blacks, Asians, and Native Americans, but most Latin American and Caribbean countries have a mix of people of various races, including particularly people of combined European, African and Native American heritage. To describe someone as "Hispanic" or "Latino" in appearance may invoke stereotypes among non-Hispanic-Americans, but it has little value as an actual physical description. An Hispanic can appear to be black, white, or mixed in any number of ways. Not uncommonly, these variations appear within the same family.

On the other hand, Hispanics in the United States share much in common with other "racial" groups. They originate from a common geographical area of the world, though admittedly after a few centuries of assimilation from original immigrant and indigenous groups. Hispanics share a common history of being structurally located (oppressed) in our political structure. They are creating institutions directed toward recognizing and addressing their common interests. And surveys indicate both Hispanic- and non-Hispanic-Americans consider "Hispanic" to be a "race." All in all, Latinos/as form a broad cultural group similar in many respects with other broad groups in the United States that have a racial character.

White Americans also face change. The political structure of the United States, always a white enterprise, has undergone modification. Virtually every European nationality now has a history of assimilating to whiteness, even as the process continues for new immigrants. Light-skinned Asians and Latinos/as are being accepted as white in some parts of the United States.

On the other hand, European-based culture is nearly 400 years old in the United States, and the notion of the white race has been around for at least 300 years of that history. White American culture is real, both in its presence and its consequences. With roots to the past, it continues to evolve. Today it remains the dominant culture of the United States.

White American Culture

Americans in general, and white Americans in particular, are among the most individualistic people on the planet. As Diana Dunn of the New Orleans-based People's Institute for Survival and Beyond has pointed out,

> We have to recognize first that there is a white mainstream normative culture and how that culture keeps us from developing authentic relationships with people of color. It's one of the hardest things for us to see as whites because one of the most important values in white culture is individualism. It's hard to view ourselves as a collective. Until we view ourselves as a collective, we can't begin to change that collective.[10]

We seldom think of ourselves as a collective entity, yet it's important to do so. It is within our collective and cultural process that we find the means to understand what it will take for white people to help create a multiracial society.

Let us assume for the moment that white people did act in a collective way. You may not feel this is true. I am certainly not saying it is true in all cases. But sometimes it is helpful to suppose a state of affairs just to get the conversation going. Looking at white people as a collective group, let's ask: When do white people need people of color? White people have power and resources already. We do not have to bargain for them. White people have a cultural heritage from Europe. White people have a large population and an absolute majority in votes. White people have technical skills. White people control institutions. Whenever a white person wants to do something, he or she can do it without reference to people of color. The only time white people need to include people of color in a meaningful way is when we want them included, and even then, white people almost always set the terms for inclusion. We almost never include people of color because they have to be reckoned with as a source of power, because they control significant resources, or because they bring a unique perspective to the process.

We are living surrounded by a big veil of white culture. Virtually all our physical needs, including those of safety and security, can be satisfied behind this veil. So, too, can most of our higher needs of growth and development. We can pursue a lifetime career without ever having to work for a person of color, or seek their approval in an application process, licensing process, peer review, or other milestones of advancement. We can busy ourselves with the nearly infinite range of human activity, and we do, all within the confines of white society.

Recall that culture is a means of solving problems. The problems, once solved, are relegated to the habitual and unconscious realm of our lives. "Why fix it if it ain't broke?" we say. Why stir up trouble? Few people are so unoccupied they want more to do. Most of us are involved full-time simply doing what we have already been given, or taken on, as our daily routine. Within the vast collection of white people in the United States, a group that numbers nearly 200 million, we as white Americans have plenty of room to develop ourselves, pursue our needs, achieve personal growth, and live our entire lives seemingly without reaching any social horizons.

But is it possible a horizon is there? Is it possible that in the vastness of all this activity, we are still isolated? Is there a cultural wall around us, this big white veil of which I spoke? Are white Americans, who on the surface are a very outgoing people, actually ingrown in a way we cannot immediately see? Let me ask some more questions along this line. Do we do great things, or do we simply define the things we do as great? Are we so innocent, or do we simply name the terms on which innocence is granted? Does our nation's history only contain significant achievements by white people, or has it been whitened? Are these questions you feel you can ignore? Are you tempted to say, "Who cares?" "It's not my problem." "So what?" "Race doesn't matter?"

Living surrounded by the big white veil as we do, white people don't have to care. It's not our problem, at least in the sense that we can do more or less what we want without having our race be a limiting factor. Because of this, it's easy to feel race doesn't matter. Not only do we feel this way as individuals, we are surrounded by other people, thousands upon thousands, even millions, who feel the same way. We compare notes, share experiences, make speeches, and write books, all of which tell us that racially speaking, everything is comfortable and cozy, and anyone who doesn't feel that way has some other ax to grind for personal advantage. We talk to our friends, our neighbors, our religious leaders, our colleagues at work, and they all affirm our basic outlook. Since race doesn't matter, it's rude to even notice what race we are.

It's literally hard for white people to see this. My wife watches TV and finds black people are generally shown in negative stereotypes. Little programming exists that presents them in a more positive and accurate light. I have a hard time seeing it. When I tell her so, she is mildly incredulous, since it seems so visually obvious to her. But to me, it seems as if there are more black people on television all the time. After all, isn't there always a black doctor or lawyer popping up in every new and popular television drama?

But over time, I've noticed an interesting phenomenon. People newly immigrating to America come here with an image of African-Americans as lazy, ignorant, stupid, and dangerous. It doesn't matter what race the new immigrant is. Jamaicans and Africans, Latinos/as, Asians and Europeans all have this image of African-Americans in their heads even as they step "off the boat" onto our soil. How can this happen? How can people who have never met an African-American in their lives come with a preformed notion of what African-Americans are?

The answer is simple. They've been watching our media. We export our television programs and movies throughout the world. The same media that show buddy pictures of black people and white people getting along in relationships seemingly unaffected by race, also show African-Americans isolated in their own element, ignorant, lazy, stupid, and dangerous. I still have trouble seeing this. It's been too much a part of my life, an ever present part of my surroundings, for me to step back and experience it from any view other than that of white culture. Yet I'm forced to admit it's there.

Newly arrived immigrants come with another interesting image, and this one applies to white Americans. We may feel we're individuals. We may feel we are diverse in our ethnic and regional heritage. We may feel we have a million ways to differentiate ourselves, and that each of these ways is more important than race. But our own media tells a different story, according to immigrants. It is only after arriving, often to their surprise, that they realize white Americans are diverse. From our media portrayals, to which they have been witness, they arrive here believing all white Americans are the same.

4

Colorblindness, Personified

From the Margins to the Center, Historical Development

> In view of the Constitution, in the eye of the law, there is in this country no superior, dominant, ruling class of citizens. There is no caste here. Our Constitution is color-blind, and neither knows nor tolerates classes among citizens. In respect of civil rights, all citizens are equal before the law.
>
> —John Marshall Harlan

So wrote the United States Supreme Court Justice as he raised his lone voice in dissent to the court's decision in *Plessy v. Ferguson*. It was this case in 1896 that legally blessed the policy of "separate but equal," initiating a lifetime of racial isolation and subjugation that lasted, in law, until the *Brown* decision on school desegregation in 1954.

Exactly 100 years later, another white man was to speak. Unlike Justice Harlan, this man, let's call him Robert, was not famous. He was simply a member of a focus group I was facilitating on race relations. I had asked the group to consider the question, How does it feel to be white? His halting words capture a sense of the times in which we now live.[1]

> Personally, I'm very content with what I am. Maybe as an individual I don't really relate it feeling white. I don't in my mind get to that, to that level. It may be purposely, because I do see a lot of maybe injustice towards individuals from other individuals which is racism, possibly. I'm not, you're not really sure because you don't know what's behind the, the mind who's up to it. I just don't find myself placing that kind of exposing, "I'm white. How does it feel

to be white?" I really never thought about that. I think it's tough for everybody, okay. It's too, a couple who has to work to support a household, whether they're black or white, okay, or Asian or whatever they are....So, I find that it doesn't really enter into my particular feelings toward the color or anything like that. I'm an individual.

At other moments in the group this individual pointedly identified himself as colorblind. Despite what we see in the news and despite characterizations of the country's "race problem," millions upon millions of other individuals in the United States believe in the idea of colorblindness. We've come a long way since Justice Harlan's time. Back at the turn of the last century white Americans openly proclaimed their belief in the superiority of the white race. Justice Harlan was virtually alone in his defense of the colorblind principle. Now, 100 years later, the idea of colorblindness has become the orthodox view among most Americans.

Today, even in the face of sensationalized reports of white supremacist groups, colorblindness has become the dominant philosophy of race relations. It is spoken by people on the street. It is blessed within the media. It is proclaimed by groups working to reduce racial conflict. It is espoused by virtually any politician running for office. Even racists find themselves forced to use colorblind rhetoric if they have any hope of reaching the mainstream. Thirty years ago, John Wayne, the actor and American icon, publicly announced, "I believe in white supremacy until the blacks are educated to a point of responsibility."[2] Though questionable even then, today such a comment from a major public figure is unthinkable. Colorblindness has become elevated to the status of mom, apple pie, and the American flag.

Is colorblindness all it claims to be? Remarkably, given the ubiquitous nature of colorblindness as an espoused philosophy, there is very little in the way of academic and scholarly work that looks at the colorblind perspective. One might easily find dozens of books written on the beliefs and activities of white supremacists as such. Few, if any, books exist describing the activity and beliefs of colorblind people.

Colorblindness deserves a closer look, if only as the now-dominant approach to race relations. But there are other reasons as well. Colorblindness, as a philosophy, often arrays itself in opposition to multiculturalism. It seems particularly resistant to talking about whiteness. Why this is so is something that a book on whiteness needs to consider. Finally, colorblindness, while voiced to various degrees by all Americans, is voiced most strongly by white Americans. Americans of color frequently regard it with a suspicious gaze. This seems peculiar, since colorblindness characterizes itself as a benefit to the racially oppressed.

Defined simply, colorblindness says that our racial and ethnic group membership are irrelevant to our treatment. Consequently, we should not take race and ethnicity into account when forming impressions and making decisions. To do so is illegitimate. Recognizing race and ethnicity leads to discrimination, either against minorities or against the dominant group.[3] From this stance, colorblindness opposes racism wherever it can see it, and, in doing so, stands against racial categorization, upholds individuality, emphasizes our common humanity, and works toward achieving "one people" status.

To people like me who were raised in a colorblind household, it seems as if colorblindness is a simple, obvious, and natural perspective. Surely if we're not going to be racists, colorblind is what we must become. But while ostensibly a simple concept, colorblindness manifests itself in at least four ways, as (1) an idealized goal, (2) a legal theory, (3) a culturally based set of beliefs, and (4) a political theory. Furthermore, while it appears obvious and natural to many, it is a response to historical conditions, both shaping and being shaped by those conditions.

As an Idealized Goal

Colorblindness has always been implicit in American thought. Among our history's greatest ironies is the creation of the phrase "all men are created equal." Penned by Thomas Jefferson, these inspiring words from the Declaration of Independence were understood, both then and now, to mean that race and ethnicity were not sufficient reasons to deprive men, though perhaps not women, of their rights. In the parlance of the Revolutionary era, the Rights of Man were God-given and universally granted. This ideal has remained in American thought to the present day, creating much tension in our culture when it is held up against the ways in which not just race, but gender, class, and other social differences are used to create inequality.

As a Legal Theory

Though long inherent in American thought, true colorblindness as it is understood today began to appear much later in our legal system. The earliest steps were taken after the Civil War during Reconstruction with the XIII and XIV Amendments ending slavery and guaranteeing citizenship privileges to all persons born or naturalized in the United States. In the Civil Rights Bill of 1875 "citizens of every race and color" were guaranteed the "full and equal enjoyment of the accommodations, advantages, facilities, and privileges of inns, public conveyances on land and water, theatres, and other places of public amusement."[4] Needless to say, this law was undone, in fact if not by actual repeal, during the Jim Crow era initiated 21 years later by the *Plessy v. Ferguson* decision.

The modern era of colorblindness in the law began after World War II. Following in the path of the war, though not strictly a matter of legislation or judicial action, President Truman integrated the armed services by executive order in 1947. This was followed by a series of decisions by the courts removing the requirement that only white persons could be naturalized citizens (1952), ruling that segregated schools were inherently unequal, hence unacceptable (1954), and freeing persons of different races to marry (1967). Civil rights and voting rights acts were passed by Congress during the same period, again removing race as a source of different and unequal treatment. Now in the 2000s the theory that law should be colorblind is broadly accepted.

The Escape Clause to "American Freedom"

One of the great ironies of American history is that Thomas Jefferson, author of the words "all men are created equal," later wrote a highly influential book, *Notes on the State of Virginia,* in which he argued that black people are inherently inferior to white people. Jefferson's book, the only one he ever wrote, appeared shortly after the Revolutionary War during a pivotal time in our country's history.

The war had created a tension between the reality of slavery and the principle of universal freedom. Prior to the Revolution it was widely believed the degraded position of Africans in America was due to environmental influences. Slavery made people act like slaves, people believed. Following the war, American thought, under the reach of Jefferson's monumental influence, began to define blackness as inherently inferior. By 1800, white Americans believed that inferiority was an innate property of Africans themselves. Now seen as subhuman, black people were thought deserving only of slavery. Universal freedom applied universally—to white people.

As a Culturally Based Set of Beliefs

Beginning in the 1920s, anthropologists leveled a critique against the prevailing notions of race as a biologically determined characteristic of people. At the time, race was used to explain virtually every aspect of difference between cultural groups, from skin color to personal character. Led by Franz Boas, the culturalists questioned prevailing classification schemes of race, some of which included hundreds of racial groups. Culture, the anthropologists said, controlled the character of peoples, not biology. Ethnicity superseded race, which was relegated to a minor role describing the external physical features of groups from differing geographic origins.

Over time the anthropologists prevailed. Scientific opinion no longer held that race alone could explain the diverse nature of humankind. Sociologists still retained the concept of race, but it was understood to reflect a social category more than a biological one. Because people thought that race mattered, the sociologists believed, it did. The specter of Hitler and Nazi atrocities based on racialist thinking led many at home in the United States to reject the validity of race for creating models of social relationships. By the end of World War II this viewpoint was commonly accepted in educated circles. From there it spread amongst the enlightened public, gradually making its way into the thoughts of everyday people. Today the notion that ethnicity is more important than race passes not only as scientific thought, but also as one of the dominant underlying assumptions of mainstream culture.

As a Political Theory

The post World War II era inaugurated the civil rights movement, which rode upon and amplified many of the changes occurring in the legal and scientific communities. African-Americans, previously "invisible" to many white Americans, began to organize their resistance to Jim Crow. This movement, led by people of color and joined by many white Americans, began to bring the structural injustices of the Southern system of segregation to light.

Throughout our nation's history it has been black resistance that has awoken white consciousness of racial injustice. There have always been white people who have spoken of how black people are content, content as slaves, content as illiterate serfs, content to live in segregation. Slaves had it easy, many believed, compared to the white wage worker. This thinking prevailed during the 1940s and 1950s just as it had before, and just as it continues in modern form today.

The civil rights movement did not create a new resistance to racial injustice so much as it refined and focused the resistance that had always been present in the black community in ways that became undeniably visible to the white community. No longer could white people say a few malcontented Negro men were causing trouble. Whole communities were rising up, and women and children were often on the front lines, right before our eyes on the television cameras, now as never before visible to the nation.

The liberals in the civil rights movement believed in colorblindness with a passion. Many, both black and white, felt if they could only strike down racist laws and change the hearts of our misguided elders, we would learn to live together. Race would no longer matter. In the late 1960s, when racial strife in this country was worse than anytime since, with race riots, Vietnam, and assassinations, the shadow of a race war clouded the thoughts of even middle class white communities. Still many felt at heart it was only a matter of time until the United States would overcome its racist past. Some felt it already had.

Concentration Camps? Not in Our Country!

By the end of the 1960s racial tension permeated out society. Lois Mark Stalvey, a white middle class woman working for racial justice at the time, pondered the experience of German citizens who, living next to the concentration camps, failed to halt the extermination of Jewish people and others defined as social outcasts in Nazi Germany. Stalvey saw an analogy to events in the United States, writing:

> Somewhere, right now, there is surely an insane black man ready to commit an act as unspeakable as those of Lee Harvey Oswald or Sirhan Sirhan or James Earl Ray. And somewhere there is a skillful white demagogue becoming aware of how effortlessly he could exploit white fear and convince the white majority it is "necessary" to intern those we fear. He could persuade us so easily to trade our morality and our freedoms for our "safety" and his power. And we would be, all of us, ten miles from Dachau.[5]

I recall, as a college freshman that year, glibly talking with other students about the possibility of a race war. It all seemed very real at the time. Looking back, one might wonder if Stalvey's prediction has come true. We are building prisons at an unprecedented rate, mindlessly spending billions to employ mostly white men in a process of incarcerating mostly young black men.

In the early 1970s colorblindness as a political philosophy passed from the hands of liberals into those of neoconservatives. The law should be colorblind, they agreed. Ethnicity, not race determines character. Conservatives began to argue against race-based remedies for past discrimination, i.e. affirmative action. Using terms like "reverse discrimination," conservatives tried to remove explicit discussions of race from the American agenda. In a laissez-faire approach to race relations, they felt the major work had been accomplished. With colorblind laws now on the books, the country should forget about race and move on to other matters. Indeed, a continuing preoccupation with racial redress would put white people at a disadvantage, and that was not a desirable outcome.

A Big Step

When I was young, in the 1960s, I saw many examples of my elders converting to a colorblind way of thinking. Some I witnessed through the media and some I saw close at hand. People who previously had no doubts that white people were more intelligent and capable than people of color, and who accordingly would never approve for membership, hire, or live next to a person of color as an equal, realized that even in their most kindhearted and conciliatory moments they had been wrong. They recanted. Often they

58

described how after years of living differently, they now saw we are all one and color should not make a difference.

I have nothing but respect for the courage these white elders displayed. Their conversions were real and sincere, offered by people whose entire childhood and adult lives had been structured to tell them differently. Yet they overcame their past learning and responded to some higher purpose.

Looking back, we sometimes imagine that white supremacy meant hatred at all times for people of color, but just as often it expressed itself in a condescending kindness. A young black boy might be counseled in a friendly way to forsake academic learning and dreams of becoming an attorney, doctor, or scientist because it was beyond his ability. A kindhearted white teacher might take on the serious and unpleasant task of dispelling these dreams, believing ultimately it was better for the child of color to adjust realistically to his or her world.[6] A white person of similar mind might hire the same child as a gardener, or his sister as a maid. Those who recanted their views knew this kindness, as much as hatred, was part of their mistaken beliefs.

In the intervening years, we have witnessed the enshrinement of colorblindness as a principle in our society. This has been an historic step. After three centuries of white supremacy, in three or four short decades we have moved closer to our ideals as a country. Given our history of race relations, we should think carefully before undoing this accomplishment.

Will It Bring Us a Multiracial Society?

Colorblindness has been a noble response to the previously dominant philosophy of white supremacy. It stood against a proud and openly acknowledged racism and defeated it.[7] Now colorblindness is king. At least two generations have been raised to adulthood under its banner. What was once a matter of conversion, often through a process of painful self-reflection, has now become simply an unexamined way of life to which we are socialized.

Colorblindness has played an historic role usurping white supremacy. Little could be done to make the United States a country no longer structured on race, when most white people thought it only right and natural that white people were superior. But the colorblindness of today is not the same as the colorblindness of the mid-20th century. No longer the revolutionary, it now rules in its own right.

Like many revolutionaries turned ruler, colorblindness is troubled and confused by the fact that not all our problems, in this case our racial problems, have disappeared. Unwilling to acknowledge its victory, colorblindness continues to wage war against the old-style white supremacy as it understands it. If we still have racial troubles, colorblindness reasons, it must be because the enemy was never truly defeated.

Little wonder that colorblindness becomes upset when multiracialists accuse it of fostering the very thing it worked so hard to defeat—racism. No longer the agile, dedicated warrior, the aging colorblind behemoth simply does not understand how this usurper can accuse it of consorting with its old enemy. The multiracialists are conscious of race, and racial problems still exist. The multiracialists look like the old enemy who was never defeated and must be opposed.

But the multiracialists—which really consists of a motley collection of multiculturalists, radicals, antiracists, academics, social activists, and people in interracial relationships, not to mention a small proportion of white people and large proportion of people of color regardless of what other political views they may hold—have been critical of colorblindness. It has become powerful, they say, and that power has become corrupt. Better to fight the explicit unabashed racism of the past, they say, than to fight the surreptitious closeted racism of the present.

Multiracialists do not argue against colorblindness as an ideal goal. But they claim when examined for its particulars, when colorblindness is espoused as a strategy in the here and now of our racially structured society, it masks a white perspective that has little hope of achieving the noble condition implied by its name. Colorblindness only makes sense from within the big white veil. Rather than packing and getting ready to make the long and arduous journey on the road to a multiracial society, a society no longer structured by race, colorblindness sits blindly in the middle of a racially structured society and tells itself it has already arrived. No journey is necessary.

Though multiracialists hardly speak in a single voice, the complaints they bring against colorblindness strike many notes in a common chord:

Colorblindness denies that race makes a difference in people's lives. This is colorblindness in its vanity. Convincing itself that its final goal has been achieved, colorblindness says we are all the same under our skin. We all have the same chances and opportunities in life, so there is no need to dwell on race. When people of color do not achieve, it's not because of race, but rather is the individual failure of the people involved. Unwilling to look at race, or even to name it, colorblindness is sometimes unable to spot racism as well.

Colorblindness enforces a taboo against talking about race. We all avoid conflict at one time or another. In short-term social encounters we may simply step aside. In long term relationships, we avoid discussing sensitive topics. Sometimes we believe talking about a source of conflict exacerbates the conflict itself, so we avoid the topic alto-gether. Colorblindness enforces a taboo against talking about race. This partly stems from a desire to avoid conflict and partly from a belief that acknowledging race in any form creates the problem in the first place. Not talking about race may avoid short term conflict, but in the midst of a society that is racially structured, to say talk creates the problem will keep people from discussing what is needed for solutions. If simply not talking about race is the solution, how would we know? The "problem" of race is only solved when people of all racial groups feel it is. White people, for instance, cannot unilaterally say that because things are okay for us, racially, that things are okay for other racial groups. We need to check with people of other racial groups and see how they experience it. Yet how do we share that experience if not by talking about it? And if you believe talking is the problem, how do you distinguish between a genuine racial concern experienced by someone of another racial group that they need to talk about, versus a problem that was created simply because someone started talking about it?

Colorblindness believes color consciousness must be racist. White supremacists are color conscious. They see themselves as white and they see other people as black, red, and so forth. In its heyday, nearly all white people were white supremacist, at least to the extent of seeing themselves as white and simulta-neously as superior. Color consciousness then, has become the mark of the enemy to colorblindness. Today colorblindness opposes any sort of color consciousness, particularly from white people but also from people of other racial groups. There is a point of confusion here. It's not color consciousness that is important, but what is done with that consciousness. Black people during slavery were certainly conscious that they were a people, they were black, and this had consequences for their lives that they shared with other black people. In other words, they were color conscious, just as whites were. But color consciousness on the part of black people did not mean they believed in black supremacy. White abolitionists were equally color conscious, but for at least some, this did not mean they attributed superiority to whiteness. Some were deeply ashamed of being white. Indeed, their consciousness that they were white, that they were part of a people, and that being white people had consequences for their lives led them to work hard to change the racial structure of society at that time. Because colorblindness equates color consciousness with racism, it also believes that speaking about race, and especially about one's own race, is racist.

Colorblindness sees other racial groups but is blind to mainstream whiteness. When racial problems arise, colorblindness attributes them to other racial groups. It blames nonwhite racial groups for bringing up race, for being unwilling to assimilate, and for being historical victims who are now unreasonably embittered and hostile. It sees as "whites" those white people who are white supremacist. Everyone else is assigned to a raceless category as just plain humans. This invariably includes colorblind people and also invariably includes the central assimilated group of people who comprise mainstream American society. It's within this group that colorblindness finds good characteristics, and these good characteristics are all held to be individual properties of individual people.

The phrase "colorblind white people" is an oxymoron to colorblindness, yet the central, mainstream culture of the United States is still very white. This is not an accident, but rather a product of our national history. This is also something colorblind people cannot permit themselves to "see" because it involves naming race, generally in this case their own race. Furthermore, these same colorblind white people share a cultural heritage with white supremacists as people of European descent. This shared European heritage forms much of the mainstream culture that often is taken as the norm, as background, and assumed to be something "everyone" knows. But it is not "American culture" in the fullest meaning of that term. It is simply the dominant culture, which is itself predominantly white.

Colorblindness believes we will all assimilate into the mainstream. American culture is not simply the assimilated center but also the unassimilated margins. Both margins and the center comprise one system and this system has a racial structure that colorblindness does not acknowledge. Preferring to see ethnicity only, colorblindness views the formation of the mainstream as a process of all excluded groups moving equally to the center. If movement falters, it must be the fault of the group.

Our history shows us a distinctly different story. Assimilation has come to groups in order of their "closeness" to the Anglo culture of the original English settlers. European groups, through a progression from western Europe into eastern and southern Europe, have been the ones to assimilate to the mainstream. Other racial groups have not. Indeed, at times in our national history, both African-Americans and

Native Americans have been forcefully separated from the mainstream after having made inroads toward assimilating.

By the same token, the assimilation of European groups is remarkable given that these groups, while in Europe, fought fiercely among themselves and often harbored century-long prejudices toward one another. Not everyone can be central to a society. In the United States presently assimilated groups formed a common bond as whites that simultaneously required that nonwhite groups be excluded. Margins must exist, and without people of color in this role, the remarkable unity of European peoples in America probably would not have been achieved. Had people of color been allowed to assimilate, then center and margins would have been defined along other, nonracial, lines.

Colorblindness says we are only individuals. Actually what colorblindness says is that "we are all individuals," which is true, but colorblindness acts as if "we are only individuals," which is false. We are all individuals. We are all the same (which colorblindness admits as well). In between being completely unique as individuals and completely identical as human beings, we are all members of social groupings, be it men, women, white, black, red, yellow, brown, mixed, gay, straight, middle class, upper class, lower class. Our social group status does not define us exclusively. Nor does our common humanity. Nor does our individualism. Each of these contributes to our experience and our nature. To single out one and hold it above all others is arbitrary and misguided.[8]

Individualism is sometimes elevated by colorblind people to near cult status. This generally is characteristic of white American culture. Self is very important. Our vocabulary shows it. We have self-concept, self-esteem, self-analysis, self-confidence, self-defense, self-control, self-consciousness, self-assurance, self-assertiveness, self-sufficiency, self-satisfaction, self-discipline, self-identity, self-interest, self-worth, self-reliance, self-expression, and self-regard. I'm a white American myself and I have the deepest respect for rugged individualism and the sanctity of the individual. But sometimes I believe all this talk about self is a little self-righteous if not outrightly selfish. Other racial groups place a relatively greater value on family and community. Why don't we have a bunch of words like community-concept, community esteem..., well, you get the idea. The problem when colorblindness sees only individuals is that it is blind to racial structure, which sometimes acts beyond the scope and awareness of any single individual.

63

Colorblindness believes intent, not effects, are important. The focus on intent is one that gives benefit of the doubt to the perpetrators of racism and places the burden of proof on its victims. Intent is something located within individuals. Institutions, on the other hand, do not reflect the individual intent of people. Rather, they act according to the cultural and political inclinations of groups under whose control the institutions operate. These inclinations may be unconscious and they almost always are historically determined. Institutions operate in patterns set up in the past and only change slowly over time. Even when individuals have moved beyond these past historical conditions, the conditions continue operating in the institutional here and now. These patterns may be unintended in the individual sense, but they support and maintain a racially structured society nonetheless.

What Racism?

In today's society it is illegal to discriminate. The colorblind norm also assures that open discrimination will be condemned. Shortly after we were married, my wife and I went apartment hunting in the mid-1980s in New Jersey. I contacted a landlord through a want ad. On the phone he agreed to show the apartment, insisting my wife and I see it together. When we arrived outside the apartment building, the landlord, a middle-aged, stooped, balding white man with an eastern European accent, introduced himself and ever so apologetically said he had left the key with the downstairs tenant who had left unexpectedly. He anticipated her return any moment. We waited patiently. After 45 minutes, my wife insisted we depart. I still wanted to take the landlord at his word. He was ever so patient and sure the tenant would return. But he seemed equally agreeable with the fact we were leaving. Never having been in this situation before, it took me a long time to figure it out. My wife, having looked endlessly for an apartment in a similar area a couple years prior, had already undergone countless patient and polite subterfuges staged by white people wanting not to rent to a black person. Does one fight this, and without any proof? To this day I cannot prove the intent behind the landlord's act.

In many cases it is possible to cover up racist actions, even intentional racist actions, under the guise of some other intention. Most cases of discrimination are not openly and outrightly apparent, especially from the standpoint of intentions. Surreptitious discrimination exists nonetheless, and its effects are just as damaging to its victims. Indeed, they are more harmful in that victims have no means of challenging discriminatory action. Racism can flourish forever in this guise, and even a small number of overtly racist white people can do considerable harm under the assumption of innocence that colorblindness makes available to them.

Colorblindness believes people are either racist or nonracist.
When colorblindness sees racism as individual intentional acts only, it
denies the complexity of the human condition. We all have prejudices,
often from influences beyond our control. We may both love and hate
something. We may be working to overcome our prejudices and be the
victim of them at the same time. We may be unconscious of our prejudices. We may be saintly among people of our own race, but overtly
racist toward people of other racial groups. The simplistic division of
people into racist and nonracist denies all these subtleties and encour-
ages people to espouse a purely ideological and politically correct line
of being free of racism. Colorblindness gives no support to people
who want to work on their more complex, real, and human feelings
that result from living in a racially structured society.

Color is beautiful, and colorblindness can't see it. Racism is ugly,
and race itself is an outmoded concept. But there is something insult-
ing and condescending in the notion that the solution to racism is to
blind ourselves to color. Does this mean when we see color, we automatically think it's bad, automatically treat it as a negative, run from it,
and interpret it as inferior? The answer seems to be yes, that is exactly
what colorblindness assumes. Colorblindness spends a lot of time literally trying not to see color. Colorblind people even have trouble
naming skin tones. Some people literally convince themselves they cannot observe color differences. From almond to alabaster, coffee to
cream, chocolate, pecan, pink, and ivory, the color of our skin is full of
variety and beauty. And all people, even white people, have the capacity for seeing beauty in other people. If we truly are over our racism,
how can we be so cynical to assume that looking at color will cause us
to become, once again, unmitigated racists.

Radical Colorblindness

Most Americans endorse the ideal value of colorblindness. When it
comes to colorblindness as a political, legal, and cultural expression, people
hold to it in various degrees. Some believe colorblindness should be applied
selectively. Some believe it should apply generally but people are not perfect
enough to do it. Some seem to go a little bit further, acting as public colorblind standard-bearers. To myself I have named this last group the "radically colorblind."

Radically colorblind people take an explicitly named "colorblind" stance
in public conversation. Recall the statement by Robert, the focus group participant quoted at the start of this chapter. Robert was one of three people
in the seven-person group taking an emphatic stance on colorblindness.

While seemingly noble in their intent, this subgroup acted as enforcers of a narrow, ideological position. At one point Helen, a middle-aged white woman and a minister, suggested that white and black people should talk about race, and discuss each other's feelings about being black or white in America. Robert replied that when white and black people socialize, they generally do not talk about how they experience race.

When Do We See Color?

Marian Groot, of the Women's Theological Center wrote of a revealing experience:[9]

> A few years ago when my parents were visiting me, I introduced them to a Nigerian neighbor who was studying in the U.S. During the course of the ensuing conversation, my father said, "We're colorblind." I don't remember anymore what that was in response to, but I do know that it was not the first time I heard him use the term.
>
> What suddenly occurred to me was that I have only ever heard white people use the term colorblindness when we are in the presence of persons of color or when the subject of race happens to come up. I suddenly realized that the only reason white people use the term at all is because we are in fact noticing color. Most of the time, when white people are surrounded by other white people, we aren't noticing color at all. We don't think about the fact that we're white. In fact, it's when we're "on our own" that we're blind to color (our own). When we are in the presence of people of color we will notice color—theirs, not ours.

Helen politely persisted, saying it might make a difference if people talked to one another. Robert repeated he was colorblind and he found when talking to people that we are all individuals. Helen tried one more time to say that maybe talking about how people experienced race might open a path to genuine communication and caring relationships. She was then met with a chorus of replies from all three "colorblind" participants. Speaking rapidly on top of one another they emphatically and rhetorically (there was no room for her to actually reply) questioned Helen. Why talk about race, they asked, as if she had not already explained this. We should be colorblind they told her. It turns people off, they said, and clearly they were quite turned off by Helen's modest suggestion. As the radical colorblind cohort worked itself to a pitch, an amazingly ironic exchange took place.[10]

> ***Betsy:*** ...or why do you have to do that? What do you think about being a minister? Now I think that would be more interesting, as opposed to, I think that's, that to me is something that, that's how problems start. That's the reason why in the United States you have the problems with the blacks, because they ask that question all the time. What does it matter? What...

Gerald: They bring up the fact that color exists.

Betsy: Why?

Robert: That's correct.

Somehow, at the very height of their defense of "colorblindness," this radical colorblind cohort saw a color. It was black and it was to blame. The color white was never named. Helen, having heard all this, made another half hearted try, but then gave in to the apparent will of the group. The colorblind cohort continued to assert their view in an animated, somewhat agitated fashion for a couple more minutes. They told Helen it was socially inappropriate to talk about race and color. The only authority the "colorblind" participants offered for this belief was their own self-cohesive agreement. Though Helen had previously been an active participant, she now remained silent for about 15 minutes and did not bring her idea up again for the rest of the group session.

Radically colorblind white people tend to police expressions of racial consciousness among white people in general. Radically colorblind white people blame the racial structure of our country on racially conscious people and groups. When radically colorblind white people name a color, it is usually "black" and seldom "white." Radically colorblind white people also tend to give a high value to individualism, elevating it to near-cult status, while denying that society is also racially structured.

Colorblindness—Reconsidered.

Colorblindness gave itself an impossible task. Successful at what it did, turning the tide against white supremacy, it continues to oppose all change rather than admit its methods alone cannot dismantle a structure that has been in place for 400 years. This is asking too much for any single philosophy. Even white supremacy has taken several different legal, cultural, and political forms, many now forgotten and some newly emerging today.

Colorblindness is the first dominant racial philosophy to move us toward becoming a multiracial nation. It will always be a part of that forward movement. That it should confuse its role in part of the process as being the process itself is perhaps forgivable. Like any old warrior, we owe it homage, yet we cannot afford to fight the battle we've already won.

When we are colorblind, we have trouble seeing racial structure, unconscious racism, and positive aspects of color. We censor dialogue on these topics. We deny human complexity, dividing all people into racist vs. non-racist categories. We can only create multiracial structures if we first convince ourselves that the structures are multiracial by happenstance. We fail to affirm ourselves as a racial/cultural group, European-Americans, and we are suspicious and jealous of other racial/cultural groups that do so.

Taken to an extreme, radically colorblind people may become arrogant and condescending. Unable to see race, the colorblind white American cannot see racism. Colorblind white people take the ideal of colorblindness and interpret it in political, legal, and cultural ways that fail to recognize we live in a racially structured society in which white culture, with roots deep into the past, still holds the cultural memory of white supremacy.

People of color don't buy it. Nor should white people who want to move on in creating a multiracial society. Listen to a young black Duke University graduate student, "Colorblindness is not colorblindness. If we were at the point where colorblindness really actually meant colorblindness, then maybe I wouldn't have a problem with it. But let's just be up front about the fact that colorblindness means be white, act white, dress white, talk white. Let's deal with that. That's my perception. That's why I think this whole colorblindness business is a sham. I'm not colorblind and no one who deals with me or interacts with me is colorblind."[11]

We want to be colorblind as an ideal, all of us more or less, of all racial and cultural groups. But we as white Americans need to be a little more open in our thinking about colorblindness as a political concept, along with the taboos and censorship that radical colorblindness creates. We need to do something about cultural colorblindness that keeps us from seeing color in all its manifestations, including its beauty. Our legal system needs to question the interpretation of colorblindness as a legal concept, and measure this against the ideal concept to which we might all aspire.

Dr. Martin Luther King Jr. is often quoted saying in 1963, "I have a dream that my four little children will one day live in a nation where they will not be judged by the color of their skin but by the content of their character." Children, we are fond of noting, are born colorblind. They don't learn racial distinctions until around four years old. When children of color begin to learn about race, they sometimes tell their parents straight out, "I want to be white." The parent of a child of color must work with his or her child and give the young child of color the support he or she needs to participate in a society that still privileges white people. Both my kids went through this stage. Other parents tell me the same thing happened with their kids. It's not a matter of having a white dad or mom. Black children in monoracially black families do the same thing.[12] The kids, when they begin to see race, get the message that white is better. To a child's eye, it is.

We need to see our society with the honesty of that child, but with an adult eye to changing it as well. Four years after his famous quote above, Dr. King said, "Whites, it must frankly be said, are not putting in a similar mass effort to re-educate themselves out of their racial ignorance. It is an aspect of their sense of superiority that the white people of America believe they have so little to learn."[13] Indeed, even in 1967, I remember, most whites were talking colorblindness, and I haven't seen much change since. Dr. King was speaking to that mainstream colorblindness in its arrogant mode, colorblindness believing it had the ideal answer, with the politics, the laws, and the culture to put it into effect. We were still trying to do it all on our own.

We need to relax a little. We need to let go. We need to be ready to move to another mode of seeing if that will better move us to our goal of becoming a multiracial society. Our elders dared to change when they moved from a comfortable white supremacy to a new and uncharted colorblindness. We need to dare as much today. We need to listen to people of color. We need to follow their leadership.

There is only one place in the country "where white people are routinely bossed around by blacks and where black leadership is very, very evident and well regarded" say sociologists Charles C. Moskos and John Sibley Butler.[14] That place is the United States Army. No other large institution has had the same level of success creating a multiracial community. Race relations in the Army are not perfect, and the authors admit it. But experience counts, and in terms of developing a multiracial culture, the Army is indeed the institution in the United States that has made the greatest progress. In 1995 black personnel constituted 27% of the Army compared to 17% for the Navy, 16% for the Air Force, and 15% for the Marines. The proportion of black generals in the Army was three times greater than the best of the other services.

Multiculturalism is too soft to meet the Army's needs, say Moskos and Butler. It's "black and white," the aged, seminal polarity that has defined race in this country that we need to attend to. Multiculturalism has diluted the black-white focus on integration, and black people often are lost in the process. Gains made by black people in civil rights have benefited all marginalized groups. But as these gains have been institutionalized in our society, other marginalized groups have crowded black people out.

In the institution of the Army, it's different. Black people are welcome. In fact, they're participating in a significant act of integration, as are white people and people of other races. Multiculturalists are off the mark, too, say the sociologists, in their approach to affirmative action. Creating double standards will not work. The institution needs to understand its mission and set the standards it needs to perform that mission. A single standard of qualification applies to all people.

The Army promotes from eligibility pools of personnel, as do organizations generally. In the Army way, you must pass the tests (however they define it) and then you advance. The Army looks to draw a racially representative group of people to advance. They draw from those who pass the tests, and if it is not racially representative, they work with the applicant pool to bring those in need up to the standard. This is supply-side, not demand-side, economics. Work with the pool to maximize everyone's chance to qualify, rather than creating a double standard. This is slow, determined work that only pays off when done on a large scale, consistently over many years. Labor pools take time to develop. The Army has taken that time.

Not all is perfect. Black people still have a hard time getting through the rank of major to that of colonel. Black generals talk candidly about their belief that blacks still have to work harder and perform better than whites to gain the same opportunities. But it's a damn sight better than anyone else is doing. If any institution of similar size has a better story to tell—or even one remotely close to that of the Army—they should tell it. The Army approach stands contrary to multiculturalism in the non-military sector of the country, whose demand-side approaches and multi-tiered qualifications by race lead to integration that does not include African-Americans as central. It's enough to make a neoconservative, post-*Bakke*, I-don't-have-a-race, white male consciousness sing.

Only the Army isn't colorblind. It's "race-savvy," say Moskos and Butler. Awareness of race is used to further nonracist goals, they explain. The Army philosophy holds that just and harmonious race relations are essential to completing its mission of combat readiness. This is recognized throughout the system. EEO and diversity-type positions are temporary assignments because racial awareness is incorporated throughout the operations in the ranks. The Army is not flying blind. They have conducted the largest research effort on race relations since the civil rights era. Research and an ingrained, race-savvy organizational culture drive the Army's movement to a multiracial organization.

White Army personnel have come to live within a multiracial world, unlike many in their cohort outside. This centering of a multiracial perspective draws from an institutionalized belief that American culture is both black and white. It is, in fact, "Afro-Anglo American," or just American for short. People, the sociologists say, whether black or white, incorporate some of the other in their own racial and cultural definition. Once inside the Army, culturally at least, you'd better learn to like mulatto.

Mend It; Don't End It.

The Army is committed to making their organization colorblind in the ideal sense of the term. This is a view of colorblindness that a majority of people, both black and white, support. Unlike radical colorblindness, though, the Army favors a color awareness similar to that among multiculturalists in the non-military sector, but with some key differences in policy and program. Creating real, viable multiracial settings takes this kind of awareness. But colorblindness, maybe even radical colorblindness, has its place. Put it up against real old-fashioned white supremacy in a solidly white world, and it can be a true counter-force for good.

In the summer of 1993 my family vacationed in Cape May, New Jersey, a southern New Jersey resort town popular to ocean vacationers since Victorian times. Cape May is a generally well-to-do, predominantly white town, the type that makes me racially cautious. It's a town where a family of color might expect to be greeted courteously on many occasions and by thinly disguised racism on a few. In a town whose income depends on tourists, most realize that racism is bad business. But a racially conservative culture is also present enough that people living beyond the white veil sense a need for caution, a need to go slow.

So Long As the Service Is Good...

Sometimes our eyes "see" what our mind is reluctant to acknowledge. In our society, people generally expect white people to be in the company of other white people. I recall once entering a restaurant in Westfield, New Jersey, dressed in a business suit. The hostess smiled, took a menu, and began to turn with a gesture toward one of two separate dining rooms. In the moment the hostess made her gesture, my wife appeared behind me, dressed in similar business attire, but looking very much the African-American woman she is. The hostess registered a fleeting moment of surprise, then recovering, adjusted her body and gesture midstride to show us the other room. It was just that clear. I imagine she kept one room for white people, and saved the other for a multiracial crowd, for as we ate, she seated both black and white folk in our area. We had a good dinner. As we left, I peeked in the other dining room and basically confirmed my suspicion. Just white people there. Be that as it may, she placed us in the right room after all. I'd much rather hang with the multiracial crowd than be the cause of discomfort to a bunch of self-segregating white people, provided our service and dining experience were both receiving attention. It seemed to me they were.

One morning we went to a dockside pancake house on the bay that, I'm pretty sure, catered to local white people. There wasn't a person of color in the dining room when we arrived, but there were no white people, either. The place was empty. I don't remember the hostess's expression. It was probably neutral or thinly pleasant. I do remember it felt like a very white place, as if she was giving off vibes of distancing like some white people do around people of color. There was a waitress—another white woman—in the dining room and no other personnel present. The hostess escorted me and my family to the far side and very back of the dining room and placed us in the booth in front of the swinging kitchen doors, the only spot in the room that was hidden from view of the front entrance. She plunked us down, gave us menus, and disappeared.

71

As we were sitting, I taking in the obvious—I mean, the woman had barely tried to cover her tracks in placing us there—I remember thinking, "We're Americans. This isn't the way we're supposed to be treated." I decided we weren't going to take it. The waitress had entered the kitchen shortly after we arrived. When she came out I asked her with proud annoyance, "Can we change tables?" Midstride, this woman, sincere, blond, buxom, full-boned, and boisterous, responded without a moment's hesitation, "You can sit anywhere you want to!"

So wholehearted was her reply that it nearly lifted us to our feet. We moved as one family up to the front-most booth, back in the sunlight, with a beautiful view of the inlet. Needless to say, we had a good meal. I still remember that waitress and I always will. She was colorblindness personified, in its most heartfelt expression defeating white supremacy.

I am often thankful to be an American, but I am less often proud. There's been so much confusion in the past between the meaning of being American and the meaning of being white that I'm reluctant to give myself wholeheartedly and unabashedly to either identity. But that waitress, a white sister, made me proud we shared a race and proud to be American.

Separate-but-equal segregation lasted a lifetime. The "equal" turned out to be a lie. The colorblind perspective began as a small movement at the height of the separate-but-equal state and now has become the dominant philosophy. Today a multiracial color consciousness has begun to take shape under the wide-reaching colorblind state. This new philosophy might be named "together but different." Under the now departed separate-but-equal philosophy, people lived separately, but found out the "equal" condition wasn't true at all. Under a together-but-different approach we may just find that we will live together, but in the end, the "different" condition may become equally untrue.

5

How Did It All Begin?

Mainstream education teaches us a Eurocentric history, telling stories of white men, and much less often white women, as they conquered and settled America. Ironically, this Eurocentric history gives little insight into the evolution of white people and white culture in the multiracial setting of the United States. For instance, Europeans have been around for thousands upon thousands of years, but white people, that is, people who have understood and named ourselves as white, are of much more recent origin. In fact, the original English settlers in what is now the United States did not think of themselves as white at all. The notion of white people, and a white race, was to be made in America.

How did it all begin? And if these early people were not white people, who were they? Recall in Chapter 3 we discussed that culture is a means of solving problems. Once solutions are developed, they become an ingrained and unconscious part of the culture. In looking for the foundations of white American culture, we need to ask what problems were present as this culture developed, and how the solutions led to the creation of white as an identity.

1607 – 1622: Forging a Common Identity

The first permanent English settlement in the United States,[1] as every school child is taught, was established in Jamestown, Virginia, in 1607 by a private group of investors, the London Company, seeking to develop a profitable enterprise. Colonists were not simply exploring, nor were they simply individuals in search of personal opportunity, though individuals indeed had these motives. The settlers were held accountable to a corporation that financed their effort and wanted a return on its investment. Individual motivations were secondary when they conflicted with corporate goals. The investors wanted the colony to succeed, and this provided the initial step in the creation of a white identity.

The Jamestown settlement faced, as did all early English settlements in America, a basic problem of survival. There were four possible outcomes to the settlement effort: (1) the colony might survive and grow; (2) it might dissolve as settlers assimilated into Native American culture; (3) it might disband and the settlers return to England; or (4) it might perish. Many years earlier, in 1585, the first English attempt at settlement had failed and the settlers did indeed return to England. In 1587 they tried again. Two years later the colony could not be located by returning supply ships. Whether the settlers perished or assimilated into Indian societies is a question historians still debate, though the assimilation theory has gained support in recent times. For English investors, the "problem" of creating a self-sustaining culture in the Americas was not at all simple.

For the settlers, the picture was mixed. Individual settlers did not necessarily share the need of the investors to see the colony grow. Even if that was their initial motivation for embarking on the journey to America, they might soon change their minds when facing unanticipated circumstances. Certainly no one wanted to perish. But returning to England or assimilating into the existing American Indian cultures might appeal to individual members of the colony.

Colonists comprised a mixed lot of individuals, ranging from an elite group who exercised control of the colony on behalf of the London investors, to the larger body of commoners. In England elites and commoners did not form a single identity group. Rather, the commoners faced oppression from the elite, who often spoke of the English poor as "brutes" and "savages," and exposed them to harsh treatment that degraded and dehumanized their existence. These practices were undoubtedly carried on in the early Virginia settlements. The notion that the English common settlers should necessarily join together with the elite as "Englishmen" (or any other sort of common identity) against the indigenous people they found in the American wilderness is not something that can be presumed to have arrived with them from Europe.[2]

Yet in time they did. Consider their alternatives. Many settlers chose to run off with the Indians. How many is not certain, but the option of "going native" appealed favorably when compared to staying in the colony as poor laborers facing harsh conditions. Colony officials seemed incapable of growing their own food supply, relying instead on infrequent shipments from London, and forcing Indians to trade corn. Conditions were so severe in the winter of 1609/10 that colonists lived in holes dug in the ground. In desperation some unearthed and fed upon corpses of dead comrades. One man killed his pregnant wife as she slept, salted, and ate her. Only 60 of 500 settlers survived until spring. Colony officials instituted martial law and the London Company continued to replenish the colony population, so the colony continued despite poor supplies and an astronomical death rate.

White Indians

"Thousands of Europeans are Indians," said one colonial observer, echoing an oft mentioned phenomenon, "and we have no examples of even one of those Aboriginies having from choice become Europeans!"[3]

Indian tribes in the Northeast readily sought and adopted captives into tribal and family positions, replacing lost relatives. Some later rose to status as chiefs. Rape, a capital crime among Indians, never befell captive white females, who were to become sisters and daughters. Captives on the trail were given equal provisions and new footwear. Entering their new village, they ran the gauntlet, where the blows, often more symbolic than real, beat the whiteness from captives. Women of the village then forcefully scrubbed the captives in a river. When dry, they attended a ceremonial induction, with the chief speaking before the assembled town. One captive described his resulting experience: "All the family was as kind to me as if I had really been the nearest of relation they had in the world."

On occasions when family or white officials reclaimed white captives, the captives balked, and most refused. Many were forced to return to white culture, only to refuse personal contact with their "saviors." Several escaped back to Indian ways. Indian relatives cried when forced to part with adopted whites. Some were known to make regular visits for years after to recaptured relatives living in white settlements.

Historian James Axtell wrote, "They stayed because they found Indian life to possess a strong sense of community, abundant love, and uncommon integrity—values that the English colonists also honored, if less successfully. But Indian life was attractive for other values—for social equality, mobility, adventure, and, as two adult converts acknowledged 'the most perfect freedom, the ease of living, [and] the absence of those cares and corroding solicitudes which so often prevail with us.'"

Little wonder then the allure of Indian villages where people lived in well-fed comfort. Indian tribes accepted English runaways, despite periodic skirmishes that took place between both peoples. English officials showed a proclivity to belligerence and the ruling elites took steps to punish those who left. When Powhaten, the regional Indian leader, refused to return escaped colonists in 1610, a force of colonists raided a nearby Indian town, killing fifteen people, burning their homes, destroying their corn crop, and capturing the queen of the local tribe and her children. Upon journeying back, the English discussed the matter and "it was Agreed upon to putt the Children to deathe the which was effected by Throweinge them overboard shoteinge owtt their Braynes in the water."[4] Later, when the colony governor complained that the queen was spared, the expedition's leader, weary from a day of bloodletting, had her stabbed to death in lieu of the more traditional burning alive.

The following year a new governor took time to oversee the execution of recaptured settlers who had gone to live among the Indians. Using a variety of means that included hanging, burning, breaking upon wheels, staking, and shooting, the hapless souls, deprived of their multiracial deliverance, were made an example to others. The same governor one year later took Powhatan's daughter, Pocahontas, hostage, demanding the return of more runaway colonists. Powhatan, to his credit, resisted, and eventually a peace was made.

If running away to the Indians was not a solution, neither was returning to England. Settlers, often without their knowledge beforehand, were given one-way tickets. Effectively, the poor among the settlers could not afford the passage back and were faced with either perishing, or surviving and growing with the colony. For a decade the colony stumbled along, looking for a source of quick profit. Real gold was not to be found, but gold of a sort was discovered in tobacco. Preliminary crops were grown in 1616, and the next year, 1617, production rose by 700%. A boom was under way, and even the marketplace and streets were planted. Typical of boomtown economics, tobacco itself became the local currency. Production rose 250% in 1618, and from there increased more than tenfold over the next decade. By 1621 a recent arrival wrote home, saying, "any laborious honest man may in a shorte time become ritche in this Country."[5]

Colonists flocked to Virginia in what came to be named the Great Migration. Hungry for opportunity, they expanded throughout the tidewater area, encroaching on Indian lands and straining relations. After 1618, as part of a liberal revision of colony laws, colonists were given private grants of land. Several hundred signed up as tenants, giving half their produce to the company for seven years after which they owned their 50 acres outright.

In England, land ownership, associated with elevated status and rank, lay beyond the reach of common people. Content with making their fortune in Virginia, English colonists sharpened their prejudices against the Indians. The death penalty for running away, no longer necessary, was removed. Finally, in 1622, fifteen years after the first English landing at Jamestown, the Indians launched a massive coordinated attack, killing 400 of the 1200 settlers then in Virginia. The Indians did not distinguish between the poor and the elite English, and the poor took the majority of the losses. By then it became apparent the initial "problem" of the colony had been solved. Both poor and elite settlers had joined together in a common identity group.

The non-elite occupied a lower rank, but they were elevated above the native population at whose expense they acquired land, and from whose wrath they sought the colony's protection. Thus the cradle of white American culture was crafted not by individuals (though many were important), and not by government (though it played a role), but rather in what's become a typically white American phenomenon: by a corporation, the London Company, seeking profit in a new world.

Meanwhile, late in 1620 the Pilgrims, of Thanksgiving fame, established Plymouth colony, now part of Massachusetts but then separate and the first in New England. Over the next several years other Puritan colonies were established in New England, each being somewhat independent.

One early effort, though Anglican and not Puritan, took place in the spring of 1623 when sixty colonists set up nearby in Wessagusset. Fearing competition in the fur trade and a lack of proper Pilgrim morality by the newcomers, Miles Standish arranged a meeting with Indian leaders at Wessagusset, (notably not Plymouth, his own colony). He and the Pilgrims murdered the seven Indians present, claiming the Indians intended to attack Wessagusset. Three colonists also died.

The Wessagusset colonists subsequently refused the proffered "protection" of the Pilgrims and disbanded due to the now very real threat of Indian hostilities. The Indians themselves were bewildered, naming the Pilgrims "Wotowquenange," meaning cutthroats. Perhaps they were further dismayed by the head of their chief impaled on a stake above the Pilgrim's fort in Plymouth. In England, others wondered how Englishmen had become savage in the New World.[6]

1623 – 1669: English, Indeed, but Not Yet White

The London Company, ironically, failed to reap the profits of its efforts in Virginia. Occasionally idealistic and evenhanded in their project, the Company sought to diversify the Virginia economy and even attempted to integrate Indians within the colony. Their noble plans died after the 1622 massacre in which the leading Company proponent of integration on hand in Virginia, George Thorpe, was among the first to fall. The Company, together with Thorpe, was blamed for the devastation and a review disclosed that settlers were dying by the hundreds. Of the 7,289 English settlers who had arrived in Virginia by the year 1625, over 6,000 were already deceased. The King disbanded the Company and placed the colony under control of the crown.

In actuality, effective control rested not with the King or Company, but rather with people in Virginia itself. And the profits, of which there were plenty, remained in their hands. Frontier boomtown Virginia produced as much greed, degeneracy, and corruption as ever seen in North America. With land plentiful and the tobacco market exploding, a man could become as rich as the labor he commanded. But how to command that labor?

In England, laborers sold their labor in annual contracts with employers. Renegotiating each year, they chose their boss. In Virginia, those who were not tenants were often indentured servants who agreed to work without wages for room, board, and passage to Virginia. Seven years was a common term, though shorter or longer contracts existed. Sounding good in theory, this arrangement became a living hell for many a man and woman. Conditions were horrid, often brutal, and most died. Fed little more than cornmeal and water, and perhaps meat once per week, servants worked long hours, suffered beatings (up to 500 lashes) and were sometimes victims of unrevenged murder by the very masters who sat as judges in the courts to which they might appeal for relief.

Physical deprivations aside, servants came to suffer a fate no laborer in England faced. Their contract took on a life of its own, becoming a piece of property for sale from master to master. Given the high death rate, servants were often part of estate settlements, and agreements with one master were forgotten by the next. No one could keep track of who owned what and whom. Any person lacking written proof was subject to servitude, and unscrupulous masters contrived all sorts of methods for extending a term of service. Petty crimes or alleged debts owed the master became excuse for adding years. Englishmen and Englishwomen were bought and sold, traded in settlements, and even gambled away at cards. The winners won big. By the mid-1620s an elite had emerged, and they ran the show. The courts, the laws, the economy, and the wealth were in their hands. Not even freemen were safe. For speaking against the governor in 1624, Richard Barnes had his arms broken, his tongue bored through, was forced to run a gauntlet of 40 men, struck by each, physically thrown out of town, banished, and made to post a bond to assure his good behavior as he left the colony.

Most colonists were neither servants nor freemen, but rather tenants-at-halves. The elite took exception to this, seeing no reason why they should only collect half a worker's proceeds when they might collect it all. The 1622 massacre provided an excuse. Half the survivors were forced to retreat to the Jamestown vicinity, losing their access to the land they farmed as tenants. The Indians had struck intentionally during corn planting season and food was scarce. A crucial supply ship from England sank before arrival, and famine arose.

The colony elite responded by banning all planting of corn near homes and settlements on the pretext it might provide cover for Indians. Colonists were further prohibited from hunting, lest they be taken captive. Laborers starved on gruel when waterfowl abounded within sight. The only access to food lay across the Chesapeake Bay where friendly tribes traded corn. Only the elite had the boats, and they cornered the supply, selling it at the highest prices they could obtain. Displaced tenants who previously grew their own food and tobacco for export had to sell themselves into servitude, or starve.[7]

78

By 1625 the elite of Virginia controlled a far greater proportion of the colony's wealth than the elite in England controlled in their home country. And in Virginia, the principle wealth consisted of people.

Individual servants continued to run away to the Indians, but colony officials and opinion makers relentlessly portrayed Indians as barbarous and uncivilized. For several years they adopted a policy of genocide and deceit. One notable example in 1624 took place when a colony official celebrated the completion of a "peace" treaty by serving poisoned wine to members of the tribe, killing 200. Another 50 were dispatched by weapons.

The prospect of an integrated English-Indian community fared no better in New England than in Virginia. Thomas Morton, a gentleman and free spirit, found himself left in Massachusetts as part of a temporary colony while the colony's founder sailed to Virginia to sell several of his indentured servants. Morton convinced the remaining indentured servants to rebel against their overseer and join together as free men in a settlement. Unlike the Pilgrims, Morton admired the humanity of neighboring Indians and the richness of the countryside. He named the new settlement Ma-re-Mount, meaning mountain by the sea.

The settlement, to the Pilgrims' dismay, began trading profitably in furs, teaching the Indians how to shoot, and interacting with the natives in such a way the Pilgrims thought the devil himself was loose among them. They dubbed the settlement "Merry Mount," whose members, they said, were given to "drinking and dancing about [a Maypole] many days together, inviting the Indian women for their consorts, dancing and frisking together like so many fairies."[8] In 1628 the Pilgrims and Miles Standish, once again, caused Morton to leave and the community disbanded. Quickly suppressed, the demise of Ma-re-mount stood as a boundary marker for European-American culture. An integrated English-Indian society would not be tolerated.

Indians were to forever remain outside of English society, though many short-term alliances existed through time. In 1637 the Puritan colonies joined forces against the Pequots who stood in the way of the colonists' expansion. Assaulting the Pequots' main fort, the English set it afire and formed a circle about the perimeter. As Pequot men, women, and children fled the inferno, the English cut them down. The Narragansett, allies of the English, criticized the English style of total war as wicked, saying "it is too furious, and slays too many men."[9] The English sold their captives into slavery in the West Indies. Sales of Indian captives proved to be a profitable enterprise throughout the colonial period, often paying the costs of the various English-Indian wars.

In Virginia the Indians struck the colony again in 1644. Though causing considerable damage, they were outnumbered by the now much larger colony and soon defeated. The resulting treaty set boundaries between

English and Indian, foreshadowing the reservation system. No Indians were permitted in the colony, and colonists were prohibited from Indian territory. The defeated Indians acted as a buffer against stronger tribes in the interior, and served further as a resource for tracking down and returning runaway English servants.

Despite ruthless exploitation by the Virginia elite, by the mid-1600s a fair number of freemen began to emerge. Though boom times had passed, the tobacco market, now huge, continued to provide the colony with exports. European-Americans now began to live longer, though why is not entirely clear. Servants fortunate enough to complete their service and secure their freedom might obtain some land of their own.

Family life in Virginia was hard to come by. Women, though present from the earliest years, were scarce. Those women who were in the colony were often widowed, since men died quickly.[10] Some women accumulated fortunes, passed from husband to husband, and marriage became a means for ambitious men to rise rapidly in society. Adding to their wives' fortunes, they expired, leaving another man to repeat the cycle. Nonetheless Virginia remained largely a society of single men. Servants were forbidden to marry without their master's permission. That permission was seldom granted since marriage distracted a person from the unrelenting regimen of toil. More importantly, English custom dictated that a wife was controlled by the husband and outside authorities must work through his means. The planters, intent upon exploiting women's labor directly, found marriage obstructed their purpose. Sex outside of marriage, known as fornication, was punished severely. Pregnant women were made to serve an additional two and one-half years for the labor denied their master during their pregnancy. Children, having no labor to offer, were a burden.

The Great Awakening

In the mid-1700s the Great Awakening, a wave of religious revivalism, swept the colonies. In Virginia, "almost invariably, when it came, *it came when and where whites were in extensive and intensive contact with blacks*." Taking its most pronounced form among Baptists and Methodists, the surviving records show "virtually all eighteenth-century Baptist and Methodist churches were mixed churches, in which blacks sometimes preached to whites and in which whites and blacks witnessed together, shouted together, and shared ecstatic experiences." African-inspired spontaneity and world-views informed services, heightened emotionalism, and deepened the spirituality of all.[11]

Most black church members were slaves and many white members were slave owners. Often both attended the same church. The consequences between servant and master could be dramatic. In 1772 Brother Charles Cook was suspended "for burning one of his Negroes." He repented before the mixed congregation and later began to preach. Ultimately he was accepted as a teaching elder before a congregation with a large black membership.

Blacks took part in all aspects of church functions, at various times bringing charges against other members, both black and white, and other times serving on committees to investigate and resolve charges by other members. Blacks were among founding signatories of church charters. Church morality grew from a lived experience of community, cautioning masters against brutality and servants against theft. Owners were forbidden to break apart married couples held as slaves. Some churches even determined that slavery was a sin. Owners freed slaves and supported abolition.

By the end of the century, the Great Awakening waned. White members began to separate themselves from black. But for half a century at least, the religious experience of the common person in Virginia was deeply multiracial, far more than is common today.

Yet sex outside of marriage was frequently practiced, as a recent analysis of court cases demonstrates. Historian Theodore Allen identified 304 cases of fornication, adding,

> In 140 of those 304 cases, the identity of the male partner is known. In all, 17 were owners, 2 were overseers. Of the remaining 121, 67, including 2 African-Americans, were freemen, the great majority of whom had been bond-laborers [servants]. Some 54 were bond-laborers — 31 European-Americans, 22 African-Americans, and 1 American Indian.[12]

In addition, eight of the women were African-American. One was a free-woman, as were three of the European-American women. The rest were servants. Allen points out that sex with masters and overseers may have been coerced. Furthermore, servant women may have sought freemen as a means of escaping servitude via their lover's purchase of their freedom. But 54 women and their male partners risked and suffered great penalties for no apparent gain beyond the rewards of sensual love and companionship.

The statistics shed light, too, on the role of African-Americans of this era. Black people first arrived in Virginia in 1619 (before the Mayflower, as noted by historian Lerone Bennett Jr.). Beginning with 20 black men and women at Jamestown that year, African-Americans grew to number 1,600 in Virginia by 1675. This was 5% of the total population in the colony of 32,000, or roughly the same as the proportion of black people in Wisconsin, Nebraska, or Massachusetts today.

Blacks coming to Virginia often came from West Indian or Spanish territories, and sometimes from England. They might be expected to speak some Spanish and English. Many were already Christians. These first African-Americans lived together with European-Americans. Both groups probably recognized a cultural difference between European and African, but it mattered less then, in many ways, than it does today. Africans and Europeans alike endured common and oppressive use as the unpropertied class of labor. They worked together. They ate together. They lived together. They ran away together. Despite the early prohibitions of the elite, they clearly slept together and had children in common. Nor were these exceptional cases. The record abounds with examples of African and English joined in mutual human involvements.

Even the planter class was integrated. There was a black middle class, however small, and like the Europeans they got there the same way—by owning European people on limited-term contracts. Consider the Johnson family. Young and black, Anthony Johnson made his way to America from England in 1621, just two years after the first Africans landed in Jamestown. Thirty years later he received 250 acres as reward for bringing in five indentured laborers, including some who were English and Christian. John Johnson, his son, imported eleven English and Christian men and women in 1652 and received 550 acres next door to his dad. Richard Johnson then brought in two additional laborers.[13]

Another African-American freeman of the time, Anthony Longo, reacted in a characteristically English way when summoned to testify in court. Telling the official "shitt of your warrant," he and his wife threw the man out of their house. Like many of his English brethren, he eventually paid a penalty for contempt of court, but his attitude suggests he was certain of his social standing.[14]

To the elite, black or European, it didn't seem to matter much. Your task was either to labor at the bottom of society or support the propertied interests. Black people and English people shared common work, housing, political office holding, servant holding, religion, love, marriage, family, and fate.

Among the laboring class, African-Americans and European-Americans ran off together, at some risk to the Europeans who might otherwise pass into the predominantly European class of free laborers and propertied persons. Antagonism between black and English did not seem to exist. According to Allen, "in none of the hundreds of cases of the oppression of bond-laborers and the resistance by them have I found any instance in which European-American bond-laborers expressed a desire to dissociate their sufferings and struggle from those of the African-American bond-laborers."[15]

Not all was equal. The English, particularly the elite, had a strong preference for things English. They discouraged interracial and intercultural activity in which English social norms were not dominant. Here the seeds of slavery had already germinated. But though slavery existed in the Americas under the Spanish, the English were slow to develop the practice. The very notion of slavery as lifetime servitude that passed from one generation to another in perpetuity took a generation or two to appear in Virginia, another entire generation to come into common use, and two more generations to become completely and only associated with African labor. By the 1640s some blacks facing judicial punishment began to receive different sentences from European-Americans, some being newly enslaved for life and others having no additional time given because they were already in lifetime servitude. Unlike the English and other Europeans who had some minimal protection from their home countries, Africans were completely alone at the mercy of fate and the Virginia elite.

Indians, too, were enslaved, but colony officials had to be careful not to antagonize neighboring tribes too much. Often enslaved Indians were sold to the Caribbean. Virginia remained, as always, an English settlement, yet African-Americans, unlike Indians, existed within the culture and community. Other people were present as well, including Portuguese, Spanish, French, Turks, and Dutch.[16] European-American laborers remained the preferred source of labor. Life was becoming better as people in the English settlements lived longer. But the increasing number of freemen began to outpace the available land, which was held in parcels of thousands of acres by the old planters. Many freemen were forced to move to the outskirts of the colony, and after 1640 virtually none were able to rise, as before, into the ranks of the ruling class.[17]

By that time the elite were using whatever devices they could to subject the population—English, African, and other assorted persons alike—to their insatiable need for cheap labor. The planters developed new ways to extend the terms of service of those whose labor they controlled. Lifetime servitude was considered an ideal method, but a problem still existed even for property owners who wanted to enslave black people as their English brethren were doing in Barbados. Could Christians enslave Christians? Certainly enslaving Moslem heathens was all right, but keeping fellow Christians in bondage was more problematic. The problem had many facets. Many blacks were Christian before reaching the United States. Others converted when here. If conversion meant freedom and equal treatment with European-American Christians, it would likely become quite popular. Slave owners might try to keep those they enslaved from receiving religious instruction, but this was contrary to the teaching of Christianity. How could it all be sorted out? Not for the better, as it turns out. And it took a bit of a ruckus before things jelled in a grim state of affairs.

The Reverend Morgan Godwyn, in Virginia on behalf of the Anglican church in 1667, saw passage of a law there saying the baptizing of slaves did not result in their manumission. The church figured to take care of the lives of men and women after their departure from this earth, while leaving to the kingdom of man those affairs of earthly presence. The Anglican church developed this line of thought into the 1700s, clearing the religious path toward racial enslavement of "black" people by a people soon to be named as "white."

1670 – 1705: The Birth of Whiteness

In 1670 the Virginia colony made it illegal for any "negro or Indian," free or not, to purchase Christians.[18] The owners of European-American labor, it seemed, were destined to be themselves European-American. Not only were Indians and African-Americans given a setback, so too were English freemen who held no land, for in the same year of 1670 the colony elite told them they could no longer vote.

Less noticed, but portent, in 1670 the first self-described white people appeared in the form of a meddlesome Protestant sect known as Quakers, led by George Fox. In Virginia, Quakers were less welcome than Africans. According to historian Terrence W. Epperson, "anyone bringing Quakers into the colony or hosting Quaker meetings was to be fined one hundred pounds sterling."[19] Little wonder, too, because the Quakers were preaching to slaves when George Fox toured Barbados and Virginia in 1671.[20] He and other Quakers left a trail of correspondence discussing the need to spread the Christian message among blacks and "*whites*."

Prior to this moment the English in the colonies always called themselves either "English" or "Christian." They repeatedly distinguished themselves from Indians, "heathens," and blacks whom they called by various names. Legislation often made reference to one group or another, so it certainly was not a matter that they failed to take note of differences. But nowhere did they call themselves "white." Fox's writing categorized different cultures of humankind, and he placed Europeans and European-Americans together in the white box, saying "And so now consider, do not slight them, to wit, the *Ethyopians,* the *Blacks* now, neither any Man or Woman upon the Face of the Earth, in that *Christ* dyed for all, both *Turks, Barbarians, Tartarians,* and *Ethyopians;* he dyed for the *Tawnes* and for the *Blacks,* as well as **for you that are called *Whites*...**" He also wrote, "So that you may see that there was a Church of God in *Egypt,* in *Babylon* and *Ethiopia,* who were Christians, as well as **among the *white* People, so called by the *Blacks*.**"[21] There is a strong suggestion here that Quaker missionaries settled on the use of the term "white" after hearing it used by "Blacks." The contrast of "white" to "black," seems obvious. Thus the term "white" may have come into use from several sources. But at least one original source for the term "white" was from those whom "white" people called "black." We were named as a people early on by African-Americans.

In the meantime, something happened in 1676 that made the propertied and ruling class wet their pants. One hundred years before the American Revolution a critical transformation took place in European-American culture in Virginia. It started after a multiracial group of patriots kicked the butts of the proto-white elite.

Called "Bacon's Rebellion," it consisted of "a peculiar coalition of frontier planters, poor tenants, indentured servants, and enslaved Africans [who] overthrew the government of Virginia and torched Jamestown, the colony's capital."[22] Nathaniel Bacon broke the peace of thirty years between English and Indian, starting an unauthorized war with the Susquehannah and Occaneechee on the frontier. A property owner, member of the Assembly, friend of ruling Governor Berkeley, and somewhat of a social entrepreneur, Bacon took up a concern with the large landless class of poor laborers in the colony.

Out on the frontier, Nathaniel Bacon and his co-conspirators may have felt less accountable to the central and culturally restricted interests of English American society. Richard Lawrence, a ringleader with Bacon, was described by a contemporary as throwing his learning and ability away "in the darke imbraces of a Blackamoore, his slave: And that in so fond a Maner,...to the noe meane Scandle and affrunt of all..."[23]

Seminole Wars

Long before the Vietnam War the United States became mired in an equally protracted, costly, and ultimately unpopular war against the Seminole Indians in Florida.[24]

The Seminoles were a multiracial nation who first formed in 1566 when Calusa Indians fleeing Spanish oppression joined migrating Creeks in Florida. As the Spanish and later the English fought and defeated Indian tribes in the Southern colonies, the remnants fled to the Seminoles' ranks. The tribe also became a haven for African-Americans who freed themselves from slavery, and white people who found their own culture oppressive.

Although the Seminoles occupied some lands desired by white settlers, it was their proclivity for harboring runaway slaves that angered white Southerners. The Seminoles steadfastly refused to return their black comrades to enslavement. Instead, they moved into the interior swampland of Florida and resisted repeated attempts by the U.S. Army to remove them. The second Seminole War of 1835 – 1842 lasted longer and cost more than any Indian War before or since. Eventually Northerners became infuriated when they learned that Southerners were pursuing the war to support their pro-slavery claims.

Some factions of the Seminoles surrendered and were transported westward to reservations, suffering greatly in the process. Others remained in Florida, never yielding. During World War II they refused to register for the draft on the grounds they were still at war with the U.S.

The wealthy colonists feared this class of men and women. It mattered little they were fighting Indians. To organize landless laborers in an armed force threatened the propertied elite. Governor Berkeley understood the masses were moved by the "hope of bettering their condition in a Growing

Country."[25] Containing largely Europeans, but Africans too, this was the class created on a broken promise. Since the time of Jamestown, settlers had been given land in reward for their risks and their labor, and as an inducement to remain hostile to assimilation with Indian cultures. But now, trading on a remarkable buildup of indentured labor in the colony, speculators cornered the market on land. For poor laborers, land ran out. The landed elite in the Virginia Assembly, still in need of labor, extended the time of servitude for indentured Europeans and created longer terms as punishment for runaways.[26]

Attacking the Indians was the way new lands had been gained before, so Bacon's rebellion started simply as an expression of a pattern already established in the earliest years of the colony. But the propertied elite in the Assembly were afraid. Guns in the hands of the masses would never do. The elite now wanted them disarmed immediately.

It was not to be. The governor charged Bacon with treason whereupon Bacon took his 500 men and marched to Jamestown. Taking the capital, he burned it, chasing Governor Berkeley away. Bacon, at this key moment, died—some say mysteriously, others say of dysentery, or by imbibing too much brandy. Governor Berkeley secured the services of the King, returning with an armed naval escort and a standing detachment of troops. Captain Thomas Grantham, a leader of royal troops, reported:

> I met about four Hundred English and Negroes in arms, who were much dissatisfied at the Surrender of the Point, saying I had betrayed them, and thereupon some were for shooting me, and others for cutting me in pieces. Most of them I persuaded to go to their homes, which accordingly they did, except about Eighty Negroes and Twenty English which would not deliver their Arms.[27]

Captain Grantham was indeed being deceitful. Taking first those who left, then forcing the remaining hundred to surrender or be blown apart, he sent them all back "to their Masters." The forces of the crown restored themselves, but Berkeley was unpopular, to say the least. Only 500 of a possible 15,000 men-at-arms in the colony supported Berkeley in the end. His well-to-do loyalists wanted to confiscate rebel property. So determined was he to grievously punish the rebels, the Crown sent three commissioners who soon took control. Berkeley was packed home to England where he died shortly after, having become gravely ill during the passage. From there, political power passed through a series of appointed governors.

The propertied elite were left to face the problem of a multiracial class of armed free men who were without opportunity in a land of promise—a recently defeated but still aggrieved underclass that no longer believed in the American dream. The planters needed labor, there was no doubt. So they turned to racial slavery. Already at hand, slavery and the differential treatment of black people were elements of Virginia society.

The planters took another step and made an implicit deal with poor European-American people. If they went along with the slave system, supporting and upholding it, poor European-American people would have a floor under which they would never fall. Freed by a 1670 law from ownership at black and Indian hands—more of a possibility than a real likelihood—European-Americans were now freed from suffering under lifelong European-American ownership. As it moved to degrade Africans to chattel slavery, the upper class (which now effectively excluded blacks and Indians due to the same 1670 law) loosened its grip on poor European-Americans. Together these actions created an implicit commonality among European-Americans we now call whiteness.

From 1619 to 1675, a period of 56 years, the African presence had grown to only 5% of the colony. In the 40 years following Bacon's Rebellion, the percentage of Africans climbed to 25%, growing much more rapidly than the expanding colony itself. By 1700 when the market for indentured servants subsided, the market in African labor was booming.

According to Ronald Takaki, "Four years after Bacon's Rebellion, the Virginia Assembly repealed all penalties imposed on European-American servants for plundering during the revolt, but did not extend this pardon to black freemen and black indentured servants."[28] Takaki also points to many other changes in the aftermath. Over the next three decades, slaves were denied freedom of assembly and movement. Masters were allowed to have no slaves but their own on their property for more than four hours at a time. A militia was authorized to monitor movements of slaves. Blacks, free and enslaved, were disarmed. Freeing of slaves was prohibited unless the master shipped the freed black people out of the county. Free blacks were denied the right to vote, the right to hold office, and the right to testify in court.

"Christians" (soon to be whites) were allowed to abuse blacks with impunity. Blacks were whipped for raising their hands against proto-whites. European-American people, especially women, were banished for having multiracial children. Their children were enslaved for 30 years. All property owned by slaves was confiscated and used to tend to the needs of poor European-Americans. By 1705, when new slave codes were enacted, "black" and "white" had become very real.

Ten years after Bacon's Rebellion, property owners kept slave and indentured laborers in separate housing, contrary to earlier practice. A French Huguenot traveler observed at the time, "a Christian twenty years old or over, cannot be a slave [indentured servant] for more than five years, whereas Negroes and other unbelievers are slaves all their lives."[29]

The term "white" now came into its own. By the early 1680s Colony Governor Lord Culpeper wrote English authorities suggesting black labor be made more available since "Blacks can make [tobacco] cheaper than Whites..."[30] Implicit in the term "white" is a willingness toward the assimilation of other non-English European-Americans into the dominant culture, bounded by the exclusion of black people. Still, the word "white" itself did not appear in legislation until late in the century. Historian Terrence W. Epperson discusses the moment of its appearance:

> The institution of white identity can also be traced with particular clarity in Virginia's evolving legal code. The first use of the term "white" does not occur until 1691, in a law designed to prevent "that abominable mixture and spurious issue" which would purportedly arise from intermarriage between any "English or other white man or woman" and any "Negro, mulatto, or Indian man or woman bond or free". It is no coincidence that "white" first appears in miscegenation legislation, where the assertion of racial difference is particularly crucial. Note also that white is used here only in conjunction with English. Later in the act the phrase "English woman" is repeated twice without the modifier white. The first unambiguous legislative use of "white" without the modifier "English" does not occur until 1705, again in miscegenation legislation. This law levied a fine of ten thousand pounds of tobacco against any minister who might "presume to marry a white man with a Negro or mulatto woman; or to marry a white woman with a Negro or mulatto man.[31]

It took a quarter century, a full generation after Bacon's Rebellion before the term "white" became institutionalized. By the time it happened, even free white people and free black people—for "white" and "black" they were now—were not free to marry each other. Perhaps the change was slow because the upper class needed time to adjust to the notion that they shared a common identity in any form with the rabble. For the elite to name themselves as a collectivity that included the poor was not something they were likely disposed to doing. In the aftermath American culture changed. It created a racial unity that cut across class lines, and made race, not class, the most prominent structural feature in the dominant society. By that time, at the start of the 18th century, the Virginia colony had become 100,000 in number.

Clearly the propertied elite won and African-Americans lost. Whether poor white people gained or lost is much more questionable. In return for freedom from ultimate enslavement by our rulers, our ancestors gave up their community and common purpose with African-Americans. The life of European-American servants remained unrelentingly brutal under the profit-hungry planters. One poor soul in 1680, too sick to work and expected to die, was made to dig his own grave rather than divert time from other laborers in the field.[32] In return for values of freedom and opportunity for themselves, our ancestors accepted into their worldview that they had a right to deny freedom and opportunity to people of color. By doing so, they opened a willingness to placidly accept any debasement so long as their African-American brothers and sisters were degraded one step more. In effect, the farther down the elite could push black people, the farther, too, they could push whites, leaving just enough space for poor white people to feel they had the better end of the deal. When poor white people could be trusted with guns again, they would point them to the frontier where more land lay ready for their racialized exercise of freedom and opportunity. The culture, for better or worse, avoided changes it may not have survived. The problems of labor, of class warfare, and frontier expansion had all been neatly solved. And the culture that emerged under the solution named itself white.

1706 – 1780: The (White) Rights of Men

In the traditional Eurocentric telling of our history, modern Americans celebrate the increasing freedom in our condition. But it really didn't happen like that at all. Not when we consider all Americans.

Looking back at the 17th century, the plight of lower-tier white people was modified at two significant points. First, poor European-Americans in the early Jamestown settlement were elevated above indigenous Americans. The culture avoided loss of laborers, who might return to the homeland or go native in their new and plentiful country. Lower-tier European-Americans were paid off in land and rights. Indigenous Americans were relegated to a subservient role, forced from their lands and murdered or enslaved.

Second, following Bacon's Rebellion 60 years later, European-American culture created a subservient tier of African-American labor. Never again in our history was there to be a significant multiracial labor movement. Again, poor European-Americans were elevated, and again they got land and rights, along with a new identity as "white."

A pattern was emerging. As poor white Americans gained political rights, indigenous Americans and African-Americans were being denied rights. *And it was the latter that made the former possible under the existing culture.* Not everybody cared for this deal. Since it was aimed at the lower-tier European-Americans, the response of European-American laborers was pivotal. Although most white Americans took the offer of increased rights and property, a few continued to develop family and community ties with people of color.

The movement toward whiteness represented a cultural migration by European-Americans in a direction that mitigated some of the more ruthless aspects of their exploitation by English elites. It also represented a progressive abandonment of African-Americans and the cultural bonds that must have been forged in the early years. This did not happen easily. The change required was great, and real people in real roles and relationships could probably accommodate only so much in the way of new thinking. The movement toward whiteness, begun as small changes in the breeze, took many generations before it became a gale. The 18th century reflected this transition. During the first 60 years of the century, give or take a few years, several trends were evident. They were not consistent. Rather they sometimes contradicted one another, existing almost in an equilibrium of opposing tensions.

It's Not What You Do. It's Who Does It.

From 1800 to 1860 European immigrants flooded the United States, including nearly three million Irish. The Irish were permitted citizenship—an important right denied by law to all nonwhite immigrants between 1790 and 1952—but socially were considered not white. Some considered them black.[33]

The Irish displaced free Northern black Americans from their traditional working class occupations, among men: as coachmen, draymen, stevedores, scavengers, porters, waiters, bootcleaners, and barbers; and among women, as maids, cooks, scullions, and washerwomen. More than simple economic competition was at hand. The Irish needed to establish the social fact of their whiteness, and they could only do that, as the language of the time bluntly put it, by doing "white man's work." Black Americans desperately sought to work for less but were barred from working at all.

White workers called strikes and rioted if blacks were hired. Frederick Douglass, ex-slave, was told in a New Bedford shipyard "that every white man would leave the ship in her unfinished condition if I struck a blow at my trade upon her." Black women and child employees in a Brooklyn tobacco factory were driven to the top floor as white rioters set fire to the ground floor, not relenting until the owner promised to hire only Irish. In Cincinnati, a trade association publicly tried their president for hiring a black youth. Far from exceptions, these events were the norm.

Southern slave owners working through the Democratic party sought the votes of free white labor. Together they succeeded in forcing free black workers "to the ranks of the destitute."

According to Winthrop Jordan, "it seems likely there was more [interracial sexual mingling] during the eighteenth century than at any time since."[34] Some historians suggest this was largely a matter of white men having forced sexual relations with women of color, but according to Lerone Bennett Jr., many white women, so many as to be a majority of the instances of interracial sexual union, cohabitated with and married black men. In one Pennsylvania case a black man and white woman were cited for having a bastard child. The court records show "the Negro said she intised him and promised him to marry him; she being examined, confest the same." The woman received twenty-one lashes and the Negro was threatened with death if he repeated the offense.[35]

Countless other stories appear in the records. Slave and master, free woman and freeman, black, mulatto, and white, all possible combinations were present. At times surreptitious and other times open, these relationships tell of a complete range of expression, from abusive to loving, from forced to consensual, with doubtless many gray areas in between and at times even within the same relationship. Clearly European and African-Americans did not consider one another so different in these matters.

Running beside this very human mingling of emotions and drives was an official attitude of disapproval. Laws against miscegenation were passed in the Southern colonies during the end of the 17th and beginning of the 18th centuries. Intended to disrupt the blending of peoples taking place, which jeopardized the slave system, these laws frequently singled out white women. Early on, white women having mulatto children were enslaved themselves, along with their children. These measures were dropped when slave owners began to force and entice white women to marry enslaved black men as a means of procuring the permanent servitude of the women in question.

No matter what measures the legislatures took, however, the problem of interracial relationships persisted. Even members of the elite participated, though others of their class looked on their actions with personal distaste. The difficulty, from the standpoint of those who wished to prevent these unions, was that racial prejudice and racism were not yet fully ingrained in American society. Certainly there was differential treatment under the law. But black and white people still responded to a common humanity in one another that counterbalanced the institutional measures aimed at separating European-American from African-American. You can't legislate morality, it's been said. The failure of 18th century legislative attempts to separate the "races" are good examples of this point.

Nonetheless, lawmakers and the elite had their effect. By the mid-1700s the term "white" was used clearly, unambiguously and unapologetically in reference to the dominant European-American culture. It was equally clear that black people and Indians were not white, and accordingly, not part of the dominant mix. White American culture, in turn, pictured itself as English, and its institutions were decidedly English in origin and custom. But if red or black skin proved a near insurmountable boundary, white skin was already a ticket to acceptance. One did not have to be from England to enjoy the benefits of seamless inclusion in white American culture, however "English" it may have considered itself. Consider the lament of a Swedish visitor in 1745:

> I found in this country scarcely one genuine Swede left, the most of them are either in part or in whole on one side or other descended from English or Dutch parents, some of them have had a Dutch, German or English father, others a Swedish mother, and others a Dutch or English mother and a Swedish father. Many of them can just recollect that their grand-fathers or mothers were Swedish. In general there is such confusion in their lineage, that they themselves can't tell, if they spring from English or Dutch, Swedish or German parents.[36]

Not just Dutch, German, and Swiss, but also French, Irish, Scot, and Scots-Irish joined the mix. During the 18th century, white American society began to come into its own. According to Gary B. Nash, by the second decade of the 1700s thousands of non-English Europeans began to flood the colonies, leading to a proportion of cultural newcomers that exceeded even that of the great waves of European immigration during the 19th and 20th centuries. The emerging culture gave rise to a social fad, whereby "European aristocrats would never tire of touring the colonies and setting down the characteristics of the people they saw—so different from what they knew in Europe."[37]

Differences, indeed, were emerging. The English colonies lacked a class of nobility. In the 1600s some noblemen had arrived, as had many more men of lesser rank. But few matched the greatness of men still in England, and in the 1700s even fewer of the middle and upper classes chose to settle in the colonies. Lacking a nobility seasoned through generations, the elite in the colonies also were deficient in a spirit of *noblesse oblige* by which men of rank considered the general welfare and felt a duty to provide for those inferior in class.

Colonists also lacked a concept of limited good, bred within European peasant societies in which land was parceled out sparingly. During the 1700s colonists began to develop a spirit of egalitarianism, spurred on by one thing they had in plenty: land. Provided the Indians could be dispossessed—and the previous century's experience proved they could—a man might hope to grow as big as his ambition would allow.

Though class differences existed, the common white American considered himself the social equal of any person. A captured British officer held at the house of an American colonel during the Revolutionary War commented on the manners of three "peasants" (his very un-American term for three common Virginia white men) who called upon the colonel regarding the milling of their grain. They made themselves quite at home about the fire, spitting and removing their muddy boots. When they left, the British officer remarked about the liberties they took. The colonel explained the spirit of American equality. "No doubt," he said, "each of these men conceives himself, in every respect, my equal."[38]

For white Americans, things could be good in the colonies. Three or four generations prior, their grandparents had been coerced and maneuvered to sell out their brethren of color. The living memory of those events faded, and now the grandchildren reaped the benefits, having forgotten the cost. White Americans fared well compared to commoners in Europe. Touring England in 1772, Benjamin Franklin observed the nobility "living in the highest affluence and magnificence" next to the "extremely poor, living in the most sordid wretchedness, in dirty hovels of mud and straw, and clothed only in rags." How fortunate the New Englander, Franklin wrote, who had food and shelter and a vote in his government.

But Nash points out what Franklin failed to acknowledge. The true American society was more than white people. Red and black men and women lived in misery as bad, and often worse, than Europeans, and it was on the backs of those red and black people, on their land and labor, that the egalitarianism of white American culture was to be found. Placed side-by-side with the whole of American society, the comparative wretchedness of European culture disappeared.[39]

It was not even clear all of Franklin's white Americans were doing as well as he claimed. The sunny farms of New England may have provided a living, but in the cities of Boston, New York, and Philadelphia public relief of the poor and propertyless became a growing burden. As the spirit of the country became egalitarian, the wealth of the country moved upward into fewer hands.[40]

A century and a half before the Revolutionary War, the London investors who established Jamestown had a vision of community interest that never grew in the native soil of Virginia. A few years later New England was settled by men and women who placed community beyond the individual in all aspects of life. In the intervening years, the Virginia model of unfettered individualism in pursuit of economic wealth won out. The Puritan fervor had diminished, and white Americans both North and South were jealous and resistant to government and authority, unless it could be persuaded to support their individual interests. To the small citizen, this meant no government was the best. The wealthy citizen favored government wise enough to protect his (for women were not generally among the propertied class) property, award him contracts, and provide him access to cheap and plentiful land for his speculations. Either way, individualism grew strong, aided by the fact each man was armed and able (in theory) to strike out on his own in a country of cheap land, moderate climate, and plentiful resources.

In the meantime, the thinkers of society, having solved to their satisfaction the notion that all who are Christianized are equal after death, turned their attention to matters of life. Secular matters came to the fore. The natural state of man (for again, women were secondary) was to be free, and—in some of the most famous words ever written—"all men are created equal." Brothers in Christ, according to Jordan, had become Sons of Liberty.[41] Yet if all brothers were equal in the eyes of Christ, it was glaringly apparent not all enjoyed the liberty to which men were entitled. The bondage of Africans and African-Americans appeared to many to be a sin. To others less inclined to divine interpretations, slavery was at the least an egregious affront to the evolving philosophy of the "Rights of Man."

Then, leading up to the Revolutionary War, a new word appeared in the language: *prejudice.* Arising in both the propertied elite and among the white laboring class was the view that associated not slavery, but blackness itself with debasement. The Marquis de Chastellux summed it up very well in his impressions on a visit to the English colonies near the end of the Revolutionary War. He compared the slavery in America to that practiced in ancient Greece and Rome. Until then, most European-Americans doubtless felt that slavery was simply one of life's misfortunes that befell politically undefended people. But slavery in Europe could be transcended and slaves, if freed, could enter society and eventually assume a position among other masters.

In America, the Marquis noted, "it is not only the slave who is beneath his master, it is the Negro who is beneath the white man. No act of enfranchisement can efface this unfortunate distinction."[42] Collectively, a perspective was starting to grow within white culture that was eventually to assume that freedom alone, even if granted, would not bring African-Americans and European-Americans into a common society. White people would remain supreme.

Yet the prevailing sentiment in the Northern colonies asserted that all men are equal, not only in God's kingdom, but man's. The character of the "black slave"—for surely these two terms were now being mingled in white consciousness as a singular image—was not inherent in the slave, but in slavery. Conditions created by one class of men over another, and environmental differences created by God, fully accounted for the character of the "black slave." Blackness, in other words, was different socially, culturally, and politically, but there was nothing in the biology of being black itself that lent itself to one form of character over another.

In the early and middle part of the 18th century the notion that color could be a basis for slavery struck many European-Americans as somewhat nonsensical. One writer reflected this view: "Some have been so grossly stupid as to assign colour as a mark for servitude. This, if it could prove anything would prove too much. It would establish it, that all complexions but the fairest should be, in some degree deprived of liberty. That all black persons should be slaves, says Montesquieu, is as ridiculous as that law of a certain country, that all red-haired persons should be hanged."[43]

White Slaves

Suppose you were a man with few scruples who could earn more than a year's pay by traveling to the North and kidnapping a white person off the street. Returning to the South you sell the person into slavery. In the process, the victim had no right to summon witnesses, no formal hearing, and the official who judged the victim to be an "escaped slave" earned twice the fee than if he had found the victim innocent of such status.[44]

How could a "white" person be a slave? Southern law enslaved the children of enslaved mothers. Over time some slaves had as little as 1/64th portion of black blood. They looked white, to the astonishment and dismay of Northern visitors who often remarked on their presence. In fact, had they been free, Southern law would legally consider them white since 1/8th measure of black blood was considered sufficiently small that such a person was legally entitled to a white identity and all rights associated with it.

The Southern planter oligarchy ruled the U.S. Congress prior to the Civil War. The Fugitive Slave Act of 1850, which legalized the scenario posed above, was simply one example of their assault on poor white people. Zealous in their defense of slavery, many wanted to extend it to the North, to all poor people regardless of color. Northern Republicans and abolitionists raised a commotion, and many a poor white person feared slavery might become a very personal issue to them. Historians frequently have puzzled how a war to free oppressed blacks did not lead to racial equality. The answer, in part, was that the war was as much to preserve white freedom (which was also being eroded) as it was to free enslaved black people.

European-Americans could be articulate about freedom and liberty because it was very much in the air. Many causes spurred such talk, not the least of which was the practice of using black people to keep the white colonials, including even their elite, in their place. Earl Conrad describes this practice of the English back home in England succinctly:

> …as slavery spread, the English adopted a different attitude. They decided that the way to control the colonials was to have them in their debt. So long as the New World was retained as an agrarian and dependent region, remaining one continuous, large-scale plantation, control could be maintained. With the merchants, planters and slavedealers answerable in court for their debts, England would be dominant, the slave trade could continue indefinitely; Liverpool and London would go on prospering.[45]

When the King heaped on a few excess taxes, it didn't help matters much. In one of the most glorious chapters of our nation's history, we fought our Revolution and won our nationhood from England. Though promoted by a group of wealthy, self-interested slaveowners, the philosophy and emerging political structure of that time has shaped the modern world. Yet much was left undone. The basic hypocrisy in fighting against English tyranny based on universal principles of liberty, while holding other people enslaved, was openly discussed on all sides. After the war was over, the example of 5,000 black patriots fighting in the ranks of the Continental Army and the exhilaration of national birth led many to free their slaves, over 60,000 in all.

1781 – 1860: The Birth of the White American Character

Many historians and writers have said the American character was forged in the years following the American Revolution. Named the "Federal Period," this was a time when the new country sought its own identity. White American culture and society had always identified strongly with the English. Though different in many ways from Europeans, white Americans clung to the character of European ways as they understood them. This came to include embracing a self-definition of white, civilized, and free that set itself against an image of Indians as not white and not civilized, and black people as not white and not free. In the midst of a multiracial country, the dominant culture had become monoracial. Yet problems in this definition persisted.

The colonies had always seen a multiracial space existing on the fringe of the dominant white culture. European, African, and Indian blended their lives in a thousand different ways—culturally, historically, psychologically, socially, and genetically. In any age and time, from 1607 to the present, this blending has taken place and some portion of white Americans has always taken part. A new country beckoned with a new way of living. The allure of living simply as humans with the people with whom one shared space was strong. In the spirit of the recently completed Revolution, it was not always easy to demonize Indians and dehumanize black people. For people they were understood to be.

By the end of the Revolution, the basic structure of white American culture was in place (see fig. 5.1).[46] Individual opportunity had become a core value, particularly when individuals sought economic gain. This was based on a relationship of power and control that white culture and its institutions held over communities and cultures of color. Universal human rights were granted to people (read as men) in white culture, reflecting the egalitarian "Rights of Man" philosophy of the Revolutionary era.

White culture also opened itself to assimilating people from many different backgrounds, *provided they were not too different*. Whether a person had a claim on "universal" rights and whether a person could assimilate to the dominant culture was a matter that was open to question in many cases. The boundary between white culture and cultures of color was often hazy and

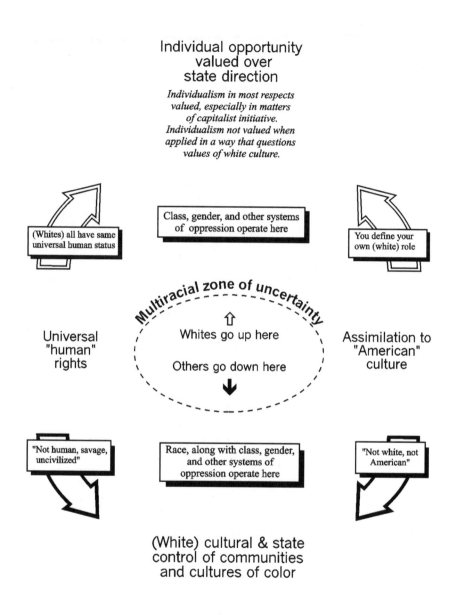

Individual opportunity
valued over
state direction

*Individualism in most respects
valued, especially in matters
of capitalist initiative.
Individualism not valued when
applied in a way that questions
values of white culture.*

(Whites) all have same universal human status

Class, gender, and other systems of oppression operate here

You define your own (white) role

Multiracial zone of uncertainty

⇧
Whites go up here

Others go down here
⬇

Universal "human" rights

Assimilation to "American" culture

"Not human, savage, uncivilized"

Race, along with class, gender, and other systems of oppression operate here

"Not white, not American"

(White) cultural & state
control of communities
and cultures of color

Figure 5.1 Social and historical structure of white American culture.

porous. Could an Indian be a white man? What if he were a farmer living in a village surrounded by orderly fields and orchards? Many Indians, in fact, lived this way. What if he became Christian? What if he held a significant portion of white parentage in his bloodline?

And a black person, what if he were free, self-supporting, and working as an artisan in a Northern state where he was entitled to vote? Suppose he were mulatto, with one white and one black parent. And what of white people who preferred to live among Indians, or slave owners who wanted to give their slaves the freedom the owners themselves treasured so much? What of religious congregations where people, black and white, worshiped together as their grandparents had? Between white culture and cultures of color there existed a large multiracial zone of uncertainty.

The Revolutionary War did not end oppression. Nor did membership in white culture. Men oppressed women. The rich oppressed the poor. The native white Americans oppressed new immigrants from Europe. Often this oppression was ruthless. But those standing outside white culture faced racial oppression as well. So the matter of where one stood was a question of great consequence to any person living in the United States. It was this very question that became problematic during the Federal Period. White American culture might have opened its boundaries a little. Certainly there were people of color whose lifestyle in every way prepared them to enter. Or it might make the boundaries more rigid. Either way, the situation was unstable.

As the Revolutionary War was ending, the glaring inconsistency between the "Rights of Man" philosophy and the fact of slave ownership caused much anguish and hand-wringing among white Americans. Furthermore, what did it mean to be an American? The colonists had considered themselves English, but having fought a war to gain independence from England, an identity as English was now out of the question. But America had been known in Europe and the colonies as the New World in which many races met and mingled with one another. It was a mulatto, mestizo mix. And the term "American" was commonly understood to mean Indians, not white people! What to make of it all?

Not one to be daunted was Thomas Jefferson, a walking contradiction in terms as slaveowner who opposed slavery. Not only that, it was Jefferson who penned the words "all men are created equal." Thinker, statesman, revolutionary, and Founding Father, Jefferson was perhaps the most influential white American of his time, save for his fellow Virginian, George Washington.

On "scientific" matters, Jefferson's opinion was highly regarded, and in 1781 – 82 he wrote a book called *Notes on the State of Virginia*. Proclaiming on the one hand the evils of slavery, Jefferson condemned African-Americans as an inferior, subhuman species on the other. According to

Jefferson, black people were oversexed, lazy, criminal, stupid, and they smelled bad. Black and white people could never get along, and the nation would some day pay in blood if it did not solve the problem of Negroes in its midst. All in all, Jefferson echoed modern racist opinions about racial difference. In fact, this modern thought came largely from his work and influence.[47] In the intervening years, it seeped into white American culture to the point that it formed an underlying, and often unconscious framework.

Black Americans were dehumanized. The thinking that had seemed so incredible a generation prior now took sway. Color united with biology, and the very fact of being black, in the eyes of white Americans, removed the holder of that distinction from the human race. Blacks were still deserving of consideration, but only that granted to dogs and horses, not people. Winthrope Jordan describes the common feeling of the time: "The proper color of man was white: the Negro was simply not measuring up to a standard which was not, after all, excessively high, since white men universally had no difficulty reaching it."[48]

It was in this era that we find the birth of the schizophrenic character of white Americans. Before the Revolution, most would acknowledge the humanity and the contribution of black Americans to the nation, and admit the possibility of multiracial family and community so long as the values of "English" culture remained dominant. The change to the "American" character required that these things be repressed. As a new nation unfolding its sails, it was first necessary to throw black people out of the boat. Rights universally belonged to men. If the right to liberty belonged universally to men, then to deny a class of people their right to liberty could only be done if they were not part of universal mankind. By the time the good ship of universal American liberty left port, only white people were on board.

As much as this thinking has driven the white American psyche, it has always been contradicted by the overwhelming evidence of the humanity of Americans of color. This has become the dark family secret of white Americans, with all the dynamics of loyalty, shame, guilt, anger, and on the part of outsiders, incredulity and bewilderment that surround such secrets. It is just as much a part of our character as our fanatic thirst for liberty and freedom. Like twins from the same egg, created in the same moment and part of each other's being, the love of American freedom and the hatred of Americans of color became ingrained in white American culture.

In the years between the Revolution and the Civil War, these basic themes were played out in a thousand different ways. By the beginning of the 19th century, African-Americans, who in many cases had recently and forcefully been evicted from what became white churches and other white settings, began creating their own institutions. The black church arose in this era. The contributions of black patriots who fought in the Revolution were forgotten. In some towns their names were chiseled from monuments commemorating the late war. Newly entering immigrants from Europe, such as the Irish, used violence and mob action to push upright, hardworking, self-supporting free African-Americans from the trades they had practiced for generations, proclaiming the right of white people to do the work.

In Philadelphia lived James Forten, a wealthy Revolutionary War hero and self-made individual who exemplified freedom, initiative, and responsible citizenship. But his sons, black like him, were locked out of the trades, and all his influence could not see to their future. Integrated neighborhoods gave way to segregation. To live with black neighbors and to work in the same trade with black people made one suspect of being black. It wouldn't do.

European thinkers began to design scientific typologies, dividing the world into "races" such as Caucasoid, Mongoloid, and Negroid, thus proving to themselves the superiority of white people. Images of black people as monkeys and apes became common, supported by scientists who were little more than charlatans. In the Northern states, free black men were denied the vote even as the property requirement for white men was relaxed. In the South laws made it nearly impossible for an owner to free his own slaves.

The term "American" by 1815 had come to refer not to Indians but to white people.[49] In a few years' time Native Americans, such as the Cherokee, including even those who had assimilated into white society, were uprooted and sent on the "Trail of Tears." Everywhere, people of color who were making it in America by hard work and dedication to basic American principles found that wasn't enough. It came to naught. White Americans, elevating ourselves to near God-like status by our recent Revolution, could find nothing better to do with our position than to hurl thunderbolts and destruction upon our fellow Americans of color below. The multiracial space that had always existed began to shrink and harden into a color line.

By the 1850s white Americans had pushed the envelope as far as it could go. One historian has identified these times as perhaps the most miserable ever experienced by African-Americans.[50] The United States Supreme Court completely threw out the notion that a black man could even be a citizen, saying black people had no rights that a white man had to respect. Whiteness, citizenship, and "American" character, it had all come together in a deeply rooted and perverted way. Some stood on the opposite side of the schizophrenic chasm, the great cleft that had arisen in the formidable white glacier. John Brown, in pursuit of a humanity most white Americans did not realize they had lost, forced the issue at Harpers Ferry. Crazy like the rest of us, his major sin was to shoot white people in the name of those who were black.

It wouldn't last, though even today we suffer for it. One simply cannot destroy the humanity of others and keep their own at the same time. The energy it takes to convince oneself otherwise is potentially cataclysmic, like trying to contain a lit stick of dynamite in a paper bag. You may not see the fuse burning, but eventually it makes itself known. In 1860 that pent-up energy exploded and white American culture learned what would happen when self-hatred and self-aggrandizement could no longer be contained. Literally tearing itself apart the (white) nation gave the Western world its most destructive, and technically innovative, war of the 19th century. After the war, the slaves were freed. And in time, perhaps, historians will find this is when, as white Americans who had forsaken our own humanity, we truly began to free ourselves.

6

Looking at White American Culture

Who Owns a Culture?

Culture does not emerge from nothing. It is shaped by history and people, passed down over time to future generations by their ancestors. White Americans think of our ancestors in terms of a direct line of genealogical descent leading ultimately to our unique and individual person. My family tree, for instance, includes my paternal grandfather, many grands ago, arriving in America in 1635. His wife's family had already been here a generation prior. Five generations later another grandfather in my direct line of descent fought under George Washington in the Revolutionary War. I am descended from a man whose brothers were known to own enslaved Africans. That my own grandfather of that generation was not himself a slave owner like his brothers may have meant only that he could not afford the two years' workingman's wages it cost to purchase a slave. My mother's family arrived after the Revolutionary War, though one side came before slavery ended. They were part of the great wave of European immigrants coming to America in the 19th and early 20th centuries.

Scottish and Welsh on my mother's side, and English on my father's, my family is firmly and deeply rooted in the history and evolution of white American culture. If ownership of culture is passed to us by our ancestors, and ancestry is genealogical, then I am unquestionably an owner. White American culture is my culture. What you say about it is personal. What rights and glories it has achieved are mine to claim. What evils and crimes it has committed are mine to atone for. It is my heritage. Speak of it, and you speak of my family. Claim it, and you claim a personal connection to me.

There is another way to the question of ancestors and cultural ownership. Rather than bloodlines, we can speak of ancestors as those who came before us in the past and shaped our way of life. Their connection to us may not

102

be by direct genealogical descent, but in creating the cultural surroundings into which we are born, usually in association with those from whom we are directly descended, these people in fact have created us as the people we are. When it comes to accounting for our personal being in the world, this concept of ancestry is characteristic of cultures of color. In fact, it is the more common conception of ancestors among the various peoples in the world. Ancestors, in this sense, have a spiritual connection to us. They shape our experience, and we honor their presence as the foundation of our lives.

Where Are Our Ancestors?

"It is peculiar to white people, Europeans, that we equate ancestry with genealogy," says Meck Groot of the Women's Theological Center in Boston. Other cultures have a deeper, more spiritual connection with the past and those who came before. Groot offers the example of the Chinese character for respect, which teaches us respect is achieved when the heart acknowledges the wisdom of twenty generations. In her own family, she calculates, twenty generations took 600 years and included 1,048,576 direct ancestors. Such a large number surely means white Americans today have many ancestors in common.

Christianity, according to Groot, replaced our tribal ancestors with other figures. Abraham, Issac, and Joseph are not our true fathers. As Europe was Christianized, tribal holidays celebrating the repeating cycles of seasons were replaced by celebrations marking historical events in linear time, such as the death and birth of Jesus. In the process we moved away "from indigenous spirituality and from a sense of wholeness in which the material and the spiritual were intricately connected."

White culture often lacks respect for the earth and for humanity. Says Groot, "I do not mean to give the impression that everything was wonderful in our pagan past. Some tribes were passive. Some were aggressive. There was good. There was bad. But there was an understanding that the material and spiritual realms are connected, that our elders had wisdom to teach that had been passed down orally for generations. There was respect based on the wisdom of twenty generations."[1]

White Americans do not speak of our "ancestors" in this non-genealogical and spiritual way. Nevertheless, we do experience some of our culture in this fashion, as handed down by a distant set of founders to whom we feel a personal connection, even though they do not include people from whom we are personally descended. These founders of our culture are venerated. Stories are told of their exploits. Children are taught their wisdom. Warriors fight great battles to defend the sanctity of the concepts created by these semi-legendary figures of the past. Our very present, our dreams, hopes, and aspirations are bound to them in a deeply spiritual way. We even gave them names. We call them Founding Fathers.

It was the Founding Fathers who assembled the four legs of the platform on which white American culture stands today. These four legs are, first, a view of human rights as universal and God-given; second, valuing the rights of the individual over that of the state; third, the assimilation of white people to the culture; and fourth, the dehumanization of people of color. Each of these themes was present in our culture before the Founding Fathers crafted a new nation. Each of these themes has been only imperfectly realized since that time.

Even in the historical period of national creation, the Founding Fathers argued among themselves about which themes were important. Contradictions, such as that between slavery and freedom, or between governmental power and individual action, existed and continue today. But these four themes form part of our consciousness as a culture, or as our mythology would have it, as a nation. It is, as many have observed, a sort of civil religion that unites the "American" people. These four themes work together in such a way that we really cannot understand one without understanding how the other three affect it. The civil, national, and even spiritual heritage of white American culture has woven these four themes into a holistic worldview. Treating any one theme in isolation is not possible, regardless of whether that treatment is done intending to understand, enhance, change or dismantle the theme in question.

Some white Americans experience difficulty acknowledging that our culture is based in part on the dehumanization of people of color. This leads to one of two reactions, both of which involve disassociating oneself from the notion of white American culture itself. The first reaction is aptly summed up in a statement I've often heard from white Americans, that "my family wasn't even here when slavery took place. Why should I be blamed for that?" Clearly nobody today can be blamed for slavery. The "blame" in this case is cultural. White people enslaved black people. If you are white, you inherit a culture and a heritage, and hence some responsibility, for the historic circumstances of slavery. By claiming his or her family was not here, the white person is saying that ancestry, and thereby cultural ownership, is a matter of bloodlines and genealogy. Since the person's family can be proven not to have been in the United States during slavery times, the person feels excused from any sense of ownership for that cultural event.

If you are one of these people, that's all well and good provided you always play by the same set of rules. But I'll bristle if you turn around and claim a personal investment in the American civil religion of the Founding Fathers. After all, your family wasn't exactly here for that either. My family was here, on both counts, slavery and freedom, and we have ties by blood to each. I wonder how some people feel entitled to take one part of my heritage, the Revolutionary War and freedom, which is the best part after all, and claim they share it equally with me. The same people reject another part of my heritage, slavery and racism, implying that I, and not they, are completely responsible for its present manifestation. I can't separate one part of my family's experience from another, nor can history separate one part of the culture from the other. How is it these newcomers feel entitled to make this separation?

We Can All Be (White) Americans

To be fair, it's because in large part we teach it. A central theme of white American culture is that "anyone" can become an American. Historically, this has been a myth. In fact, the Founding Fathers put the nix on people of color becoming Americans in 1790, when the first ever session of Congress, newly created under the United States Constitution, passed a law saying only "white persons" could become naturalized citizens of the United States. This law ruled the land until 1952. Some exceptions occurred, true. Black people already here were made citizens in the Fourteenth Amendment in 1868. But immigrants from Asia and Africa were denied citizenship.

Historically, the legal fact of citizenship was available only to "white" immigrants. Even those persons of color who, nominally classified as white, achieved citizenship still suffered at the hands of the United States government. During the Depression era into the 1950s our country deported 500,000 people of Mexican heritage, half of them legal citizens of the United States.[2] If anyone can become (and stay) an American, this has only been true in very recent times. Many will dispute that it is true even today.

The belief that anyone can become American is not a generalized phenomenon, but rather is rooted in the specific cultural experience of European nationalities coming to the United States. These people had to meet both legal and cultural requirements before they truly became accepted as "Americans." It was not an easy process, but it was possible and many passed the test. The 19th and 20th centuries proved to be periods of assimilation of huge numbers of disparate national groups. The culture stretched, accommodated, and incorporated people vastly different from the original English who settled Virginia and New England, until the very fact of being an English immigrant seemed oddly out of place among the Italians, Irish, Poles, Jews, and millions upon millions of others aspiring to become "Americans."

Herein lies the second way in which white Americans try to avoid acknowledging that our culture is based in part on the dehumanization of people of color. We simply name ourselves Americans. Our ancestors from Europe "came to America," where they became "Americans" and learned "American" values of freedom, democracy, rights of the individual, and a society based on the common man. There's nothing in this self-definition that says anything about whiteness. By naming ourselves as American, and only American, it is possible to avoid the whole matter of naming ourselves as white at all.

This is a complicated and insidious bit of perfidy. People of color nowadays are American, too. In terms of citizenship, "American" no longer means strictly white. But this is like getting off on a technicality. The Founding Fathers clearly intended the idea of "American" to apply to white people only. "Americans" were those white people in the United States, in contrast to those who stayed in Europe or journeyed to other countries. "Americans," according to the Founding Fathers, were definitely not to be found among the Africans, both slave and free, who lived here. And when white people in the United States decided they were "Americans," the indigenous people of the same region lost this title.

The American-as-white image is deeply embedded in our society. So much so that it is hard to sort out what is really American, in terms of cultural elements that apply to all American citizens across all racial groups, and what is simply white American, i.e., limited to a more specific expression among American citizens of full European descent. This confusion of imagery, white as American and American as white, permeates our educational system. It is only of late, since the 1970s, that American education has begun to recognize the presence and accomplishments of other racial/cultural groups in the American mix. This process, under the banner of multicultural education, is still partial and much in dispute. Business as usual continues to portray our history and our character as white. Imagine a "typical" American and most people will see the image of a white person.

Who Is White?

Court cases have been fought over the very question of who is, or is not, white. And, in general, whether or not one is seen as white can have an impact on one's life. Yet there is no simple definition. Rather, many definitions are in use, and no one definition fits all.

Often people believe if you "look white," then you are white. Light-colored skin and European features, such as blond hair and blue eyes, define whiteness in this case. However, many Latinos and some African-Americans "look white," yet define themselves otherwise.

Another set of definitions use parentage, or "blood" to determine who is white. If both your parents were white, then you are. In some definitions a certain fraction of your ancestors is required to be white, e.g., three out of four grandparents or seven out of eight great grandparents.

Purportedly scientific theories use terms such as "Aryan" and "Caucasian," based on now discredited systems of racial classification. Nonetheless, the terms linger on and some still give them credence.

All racial classifications are cultural in the sense that they are socially constructed, with no credible foundation in biology and genetics. However, there is also a "cultural" definition of whiteness that says if you act white, you are white.

Historically, many European groups had to give up their Old World ways to fit this definition.

Finally, some definitions, including the one used by the United States government for statistical reporting, looks at the individual's country of origin. Some groups limit their definition to people originating from northwestern Europe. Others, like the government, include all of Europe, along with parts of the Middle East and North Africa.

In our most enlightened moments we celebrate the multiracial character of America. Most Americans, of all colors, identify with the civil religion of freedom, equality, and democracy, but white Americans often relate to this identity in ways that other racial/cultural groups do not. Firstly, we see this definition as a complete expression of our political, cultural, and national being. It is enough to be "American," we believe. There is no need to further describe ourselves as white. People who identify with a racial/cultural group, we believe, are not and cannot be as truly American as we are. To become American, one must leave such group identifications behind.

Secondly, we believe that in relation to people of other racial and cultural groups, we are the original core from which the definition of "American" has come. We have an origin myth that says white Americans, on our own, created a political structure, a national character, and a culture that was open-ended. Because it was open-ended, people from throughout the world have been able to come to the United States and, once they learned the rules, enter into our society as equal participants. But as the progeny of the founders of the "American way," even though we remain generous in extending our nation and culture to others, we retain a sense of ownership and ultimate authority on who and what is American.

Somewhere along the way we forgot the barriers the Founding Fathers and others placed in the way of people of color becoming American. Instead we developed a myth that newly immigrating European groups became (white) American by working their way up the ladder. First generation families made great sacrifices to come to these shores. Their children worked hard to live up to American values and their children's children finally became Americans in the fullest sense. Like many myths there is much truth here. It was hard, hard work becoming American. The only advantage European immigrants had, small as it might be, is that—already being white—it was not impossible.

Few people have worked harder than African-Americans in building this country. If participation in the national identity of American were compensation for hard work, African-Americans would long ago have achieved status as paragons of American identity. On average, too, African-Americans have been here longer than white Americans. The first 100 African "Americans" landed on the coast of South Carolina in 1546 with 500

Spaniards. Rebelling against their Spanish masters, the Africans freed themselves and stayed on while the Spaniards, reduced to less than a third their number, beat it back to Haiti.[3] If length of stay, or bloodline were a factor in becoming American, then African-Americans again have the superior claim.

At the same time, people who have been here much longer and who have supplied much of the labor (and for a time, capital, in the form of their own being) have never seriously been considered to represent the American character. Even today African-Americans are considered to stand outside the mainstream of America. We readily see young white Americans, barely in their third or fourth generation here, decrying the African-American presence and asking when black people will decide to become Americans, "just like us."

Why is it that even today the image of "American" freedom and character does not embody that of Africa along with Europe? Clearly it is not the fact that a people has labored in this country for centuries that makes it American in the popular image. Nor is it the fact of having genealogical ancestors who arrived on these shores early on. Nor is it the fact of sundering ties to one's older heritage, for no group has lost a greater portion of their heritage (had it forcibly removed, in actual fact). Nor is it the ability to understand the principles of American freedom, for history tells us it was only by forcefully articulating these principles that African-Americans made any progress at all in their treatment by white Americans. None of these things explain why one group has become "American" in the popular image and another has not, for if any of these explanations were true, African-Americans would be considered part of the true American image long ago, much as the English, Scots, French, and Irish were.

It is much easier to look at a world map to find who was allowed in. Beginning from England and moving outward into northwest Europe, then across central Europe and down into southern Europe we can trace the order of admission in terms of how far from England newly immigrated people originated. Those who got in first, historically speaking, were those who lived closest to England. Those living in the farther reaches of Europe to the east and south were the last to be admitted. Those outside Europe, even today, at best remain on the margins of both whiteness and Americanness as conceived in the popular image.

It was not so long ago, prior to the World War II, when most white Americans were not in the least way shy or embarrassed about proclaiming the superiority of the white man's culture, and the fact that the United States was a white man's country. Our recent shyness, historically speaking, about proclaiming whiteness is better than an open avowal of white supremacy, but it is nonetheless problematic. Rather than asking in a pained way why we can't all be "Americans," it might be more useful to figure out why we are not all Americans already. The answer, quite simply, is that our Founding Fathers left us saddled with a definition of American as white.

The true American culture was, and continues to be, a cultural process involving African-Americans, Native Americans and European-Americans, along with Latino/a-Americans and Asian-Americans all reacting to and acting upon one another. It was and continues to be a large-scale process, multiracial in character from the start. It is only by circumstance that European-Americans, i.e., white people, come to embody the image of "American." But the equation, American equals white, is there in our history and that history has shaped all of us, white and nonwhite alike. The image of American nowadays remains rooted in white culture, and even with the question of supremacy aside, the mainstream favors a cultural practice that is white in character.

Our Culture, in the American Context

If white Americans truly want for us all to be Americans, we will drop the pretense that we already own the American image. There is some irony. By holding exclusively to an "American" identity and not seeing ourselves as white, we block others from developing an identity as American that we all can share. This is because the American identity we value is based in white American culture. Americans who are white do not have to say they are white because the identity of American already contains whiteness as a built-in component, put there by the Founding Fathers we venerate.

Americans who are black, red, brown, or yellow might readily be expected to have second thoughts about taking on a new cultural identity whose foundation includes a devaluing of their own cultural experience in America. And many do. After all, their own American cultural experience is often older than the cultural experience and identity that white Americans maintain. They just have not had the luxury of being able to name it "American" and making everyone else teach it that way in our schools and institutions.

Since the term "American" was already taken by white American culture, Americans of color have had to use "hyphens" (African-American, Asian-American, etc.) simply to keep it straight whose culture was being discussed. The American is still there in the name and the identity, so it's not as if being American is unimportant to Americans of color. It's just that, having their own cultural experience in America, they are not so ready to buy into the delusion of many white Americans that our brand of "American" identity is the only legitimate one.

Certainly we white Americans could do a lot to clear up this confusion. For starters, we can acknowledge that white American culture is not all of American culture. There is something greater than our own cultural experience that comprises the totality of America. The specific cultural experience of white Americans has both shaped and been shaped by that greater process. Our own cultural experience exists as part of the greater American context.

When it comes to the process of developing an American identity that speaks for all Americans, some of the values of white American culture are important, like freedom and democracy. Other values, like the devaluing of people of color, are antagonistic and destructive to this greater American identity we seek. This devaluing, i.e., racism, keeps us from seeing that freedom and democracy are not uniquely white American inventions. Some American Indian cultures, for instance, displayed a level of democratic government and respect for individual rights that has never been matched by the European-American culture valued by white Americans.

Rather than camouflaging white American culture as simply "American," a more accurate description is as follows: White American culture is European in origin. As history tells us, it is predominantly English in origin, though it also has roots in Dutch, Spanish, German, and other European nationalities and cultures. It is also American. Some of the distinctive features of the culture evolved in the "New World." For Europeans, the newness of the American setting included the multiracial and multicultural character of the social environment, the geographic isolation from the "old world," and the availability of land and other resources for appropriation. White American culture is a large social and cultural formation which comprises a portion of the greater American culture, but which also contains many different subcultures. As with any large cultural formation, it has many boundaries with other cultures. These boundaries, which determine who is "white" and what being white means to those who achieve that status, change over time and according to other social factors such as class, gender, ethnic and national origin, and language. White American culture has proven to be highly assimilative of other cultures, incorporating people from other European cultures into its definition of "white" and appropriating elements of non-European cultures into its repertoire of white cultural practices. At the same time, white American culture has policed its boundaries and defined "blackness" as forever not white. This bipolar, good/bad, black/white, them/us way of thinking is itself an element of white American culture and the underpinning of the foundation on which the racial structure of American society has been erected. White American culture is the dominant culture in the United States, and as such, often refers to itself simply as "American."

The Dominant Subculture

Some people like to learn about different cultures. White Americans may also be fascinated by learning about our own culture. But aside from simple curiosity, another compelling reason to study white American culture is that it's the dominant subculture in the United States. By dominant subculture, I do not mean to say white culture always intentionally and actively dominates other cultural groups, though certainly that has been the case at many times and places. Dominance also refers to a "business as usual" assumption that things will be done according to how white Americans do them. It can be reflected in the very image of the typical "American" as white. It can be expressed by well-meaning people with no inkling of malicious intent who simply and unquestioningly believe that their way of life is the only way, and thus see no need to understand how other cultures and other groups might experience white American culture in a more negative, often damaging, and sometimes devastating way. It can mean "knowing the rules" because one is born to them as an insider, and not knowing that others must learn the rules as adults, provided they are fortunate enough to find appropriate and supportive teachers.

Cultural dominance refers to a systemic relationship. It is not the relationship of one individual to another, and it is not within the power of any single individual to change. Cultures tend to promote their own interests beyond the level of any individual action by its members. To say that white American culture is the dominant subculture in the United States, as I have done here, is simply to state a fact. It is not an indictment of individual white people, and it is not a claim that white people or white culture are superior (or inferior) in a moral or cultural sense. It does claim that white culture holds greater power to control resources, set rules, and influence events in comparison to other subcultures. But it does not make a statement about the correctness, the rightness or appropriateness for white culture to do so, nor does it offer a judgment on how this dominance was achieved.

Nonetheless, things such as the morality, history, and appropriateness of white culture as the dominant one have been discussed often. They are not moot issues and many people, including myself, have strong opinions on these issues. Because white American culture is the dominant culture, it bears much of the responsibility for race relations as they stand now, as they have happened in the past, and as they will be expressed in the future. On top of that, it is white Americans who bear a greater obligation for working on white American culture. Since white American culture is the dominant culture, we have less need, and thus less knowledge, of other cultures. This lack of knowledge extends to race relations and even renders our understanding of ourselves less clear.

If race relations are to change, then white American culture must change. And white American culture is best changed by those who have the power to change it, i.e., white Americans. This is all the more pressing as our world enters a new era. White American culture was created with a frontier mentality that encouraged a nearly ravenous exploitation and consumption of

111

newly appropriated natural resources, and a disregard of those defined as not white. In our contemporary world, these elements of white culture are clearly becoming dysfunctional. The other can no longer be pushed back, but rather lives among us. Resources are disappearing and there no longer are regions of the world so naive or unexplored that the hungry grab for more can continue unabated.

Some understanding of white American culture is needed to help address these concerns. Left unexamined and unfettered, white American culture has the potential to self-destruct. Race relations, always difficult at best, are not guaranteed to get better. The destruction of our environment, though lethal, is not unthinkable the way we are going.

Ultimately white American culture has a lot to do with who we are as a nation. This applies to both those who are part of the culture and those Americans who live outside it. Thus understanding and shaping the character of white American culture will have much to do with our nation's future. Not only must we work to ameliorate the damage of dysfunctional elements in the culture, we must also understand and appreciate the positive elements as well. All this needs to be done in a way that does not diminish the inclusion and empowerment of other American subcultures as we strive toward a fuller nationhood.

Characteristics of Contemporary White American Culture

Cultures may be described in many ways. One simple way to describe a culture is to list some of its characteristics. Perhaps the most comprehensive list, reproduced here in figure 6.1, was devised by educator and diversity consultant Judith H. Katz. The values and beliefs listed in figure 6.1 have an air of familiarity about them. When I've shown a copy of this same table to white Americans, many say "That's me." Other people take issue with some of the values and beliefs. One woman, for instance, did not like the component of "Wife is homemaker and subordinate to husband" listed under the heading of Family Structure. Though she considered herself white, she did not believe patriarchy should be part of her culture; it "wasn't her." However, the table does not discuss what should be, but rather what is. The woman in question, when apprised of this fact, readily agreed that patriarchy was something she had experienced all too often in white culture. In fact, it's pervasive, extending far beyond family structure alone.

Other people may legitimately point out that some components do not apply to them. Certainly Jewish Americans do not believe in Christianity. But many people, both non-Jewish Americans and Jewish Americans, consider Jewish Americans to be white. Some Jewish Americans believe themselves not to be white because of a past and present history of discrimination by

SOME ASPECTS AND ASSUMPTIONS OF WHITE CULTURE IN THE UNITED STATES

While different individuals might not practice or accept all of these traits, they are common characteristics of *most* U.S. white people *most* of the time.

Rugged Individualism
Self-reliance
Individual is primary unit
Independence and autonomy highly valued and
    rewarded
Individuals assumed to be in control of their
    environment—"You get what you deserve"

Competition
Be #1
Win at all costs
Winner-loser dichotomy

Action Orientation
Master and control nature
Must always "do something" about a situation
Aggressiveness and extroversion

Decision Making
Majority rules (when whites have power)
Hierarchical

Communication
"The King's English" rules
Written tradition
Avoid conflict, intimacy
Don't show emotion
Don't discuss personal life
Be polite

Holidays
Based on Christian religions
Based on white history and male leaders

History
Based on Northern European immigrants'
    experience in the United States
Heavy focus on the British Empire
Primacy of Western (Greek, Roman) and
    Judeo-Christian tradition

Justice
Based on English common law
Protect property and entitlements
Intent counts

Protestant Work Ethic
Hard work is the key to success
Work before play
"If you didn't meet your goals, you didn't work
    hard enough"

Emphasis on Scientific Method
Objective, rational linear thinking
Cause and effect relationships
Quantitative emphasis

Status, Power, and Authority
Wealth = worth
Heavy value on ownership of goods, space,
    property
Your job is who you are
Respect authority

Time
Adherence to rigid time schedules
Time viewed as a commodity

Future Orientation
Plan for future
Delayed gratification
Progress is always for the best
"Tomorrow will be better"

Family Structure
Nuclear family (father, mother, 2.3 children) is
    the ideal social unit
Husband is breadwinner and head of household
Wife is homemaker and subordinate to husband
Children should have own rooms, be independent

Aesthetics
Based on European culture
Woman's beauty based on blonde, thin—
    "Barbie"
Man's attractiveness based on economic status,
    power, intellect
Steak and potatoes—"Bland is best"

Religion
Christianity is the norm
Anything other than Judeo-Christian tradition
    is foreign
No tolerance for deviation from single god
    concept

Figure 6.1 Reprinted from Judith H. Katz, "White Culture and Racism: Working for Organizational Change in the United States," The WHITENESS PAPERS, no. 3, Roselle, NJ: Center for the Study of White American Culture, 1999, p. 5.

white supremacists that has specifically targeted Jews. It's not for this book to say who is what. Rather, it must be acknowledged that in describing a broad and evolving cultural group such as white Americans, not all people will fit every aspect of the description. Nonetheless, the list of values and beliefs in figure 6.1 aptly characterizes white American culture. The values and beliefs are not necessarily shared by other racial/cultural groups.

People of other racial/cultural groups who function within mainstream society know they need to understand and take into account the values and beliefs in figure 6.1. To various degrees they may hold similar values and beliefs. Even if not, they must demonstrate acculturation to white cultural values and beliefs in order to manage their affairs with white Americans. For many people of color, this means virtually their entire working day, plus many moments during nonworking hours, consist of acting in a way so as not to upset people who hold these values and beliefs dear to themselves. A white American who interacts with people of color who are sophisticated in their ability to manage their affairs in settings governed by white values and beliefs may come to believe that people of color also hold these values and beliefs as their own. In other words, to a white American, it will look as if all Americans hold the same values and beliefs. What the white American will fail to see is the difference when the person of color is in a setting where the values and beliefs of his or her own racial/cultural group are in effect.

Is it duplicitous or hypocritical for a person of color to "masquerade" as holding to one set of (white) beliefs while actually holding to another? It might seem so to many white Americans, but again, we need to look deeper. It's not uncommon for people of color in professional ranks to be rejected, rebuked, and even fired from positions if they dress, speak, or act "too ethnic." A person of color who openly insists on bringing his or her racial/cultural values into white settings is often considered too assertive, unwilling to fit in. In fact, fitting in is really about accepting the values and beliefs of the group. If the group is predominantly white, then fitting in means accepting white values and beliefs, or at least acting in a way that does not intrude on the sensibilities of those people who do accept these values and beliefs. People of color have long known this, and have developed cultural supports for adapting to the requirement that they be bicultural.

Figure 6.1 does not describe "American" culture in any generic sense. There may be some individual elements shared by some other racial/cultural groups. There may even be one or two elements shared by all racial/cultural groups. But the collection of values and beliefs taken as a whole describes white culture, which Katz defines as "the synthesis of ideas, values and beliefs coalesced from descendants of white European ethnic groups in the United States."[4] One can write an entire book discussing any one of the values and beliefs in figure 6.1. Indeed, many have.

Everyday Interaction

Imagine being a student in a class. After 16 weeks of sometimes emotionally charged discussions of race and culture, you come to the final class where the instructor proposes a classroom exercise. You and your fellow students are invited to share your impressions of the personal communication style of each and every fellow student. In this exercise, no student is to be excepted. All must participate, and hear what their fellow students have to say. But the decision, the instructor says, is up to the class. You must vote on whether to carry out this exercise. How would you vote?

A very similar situation actually took place in the classroom of Thomas Kochman, a professor of communication, who describes the event in a book titled *Black and White Styles in Conflict.* The class contained eight black students, all of whom preferred to speak their minds, along with two of the white students. The other fourteen students, all white, preferred to not hold the exercise. Says Kochman, "Their negotiation ultimately centered upon the issue of whether feelings or sensibilities should receive preemptive consideration: specifically, the rights of those students who had something to say and wanted to say it (whether others wanted to hear it or not) versus the rights of students not to hear what others might want to say about them, irrespective of how much others might want to tell them."[5]

Sensibility refers to the ability to receive sensation and to respond to the feelings of another. One's sensibilities might be offended when one is not prepared to receive the effects of another person's emotional expression. In white culture, people are expected to be "mindful of the feelings" (really sensibilities, says Kochman) of others. We do not act out our feelings spontaneously, but rather moderate them if we feel there is a chance others will be annoyed, that is to say, have their sensibilities violated. Loud spontaneous expressions of anger, sudden bursts of song, animated and heated discussions, and other activities of the sort take place only when bystanders are not present. Those who do not follow this rule are seen as "out of control" and other white people are likely to act aggressively in telling them so. Having broken the social rules, the offender loses his or her rights in the face of others, who then place more value on restoring the rule of social order than on trying not to offend the sensibilities of the offender.

When Does an Argument Become a Fight?

Communications professor Thomas Kochman believes black and white cultures in the United States have different rules governing the forceful expression of feelings. Black culture gives individuals room to express themselves forcefully. Though some regard is expected for others, the individual's right to expression is given paramount consideration. White culture gives individuals the right not to have their sensitivities violated. Though expression of feelings is considered important, the individual is expected to not intrude on the sensibilities of others.

People acting according to white norms are more likely to see a vocal argument as a fight than are people acting according to black norms. When the intensity of vocal expression becomes loud and regard for the feelings of others is not apparent, white norms hold that the situation is a fight. Participants are seen as out of control, and bystanders may fear that physical blows are forthcoming. In contrast, people acting according to black norms may see the same situation as still under control, with each person acting upon his or her right to expression. If one or another participant resorts to physical means, then the situation will be quickly interpreted as a real fight.

These differing definitions have a bearing on black/white interaction. In particular, white people in positions of authority may misinterpret strident vocal expression by black people as disrespectful when in fact, according to black norms, no disrespect is intended. Rather, in forcefully expressing one's views it is expected in turn that the other party will do the same. Respect is given in the belief the other party is capable of holding his or her own.[6]

To many white people this may seem only right and natural, but in fact it is simply a cultural rule in operation. Black culture observes a different rule. Feelings are given precedence over sensibilities. When a feeling comes upon a person, black culture says it is appropriate to express it. Those who might find the expression annoying are expected to defer their sensibilities. Consider the words of one social commentator, himself African-American:

> Why do black people tend to shout? Now there is a question for the ages. Black people tend to shout in churches, movie theaters, and anywhere else they feel the need to shout, because when joy, pain, anger, confusion and frustration, ego and thought, mix it up, the way they do inside black people, the uproar is too big to hold inside. The feeling must be aired.[7]

Certainly this does not mean all black people within hearing will appreciate the shouting. One might want nothing more than to quietly read a book. But black culture will be less tolerant of others interrupting the person expressing feelings. Rudeness, in this case, belongs not to the person "shouting" but to the people who would have this expression cut short for the benefit of their own sensibilities.

116

Some might say that black culture is not respectful of other's feelings, but this is a limited (and still white) view, for white culture itself is not respectful of feelings when they occur within a person and demand expression. Anger must be suppressed, not voiced. Joy must be reduced to quiet enjoyment, not effusive and animated performance. This containment often is not easy and is arguably unhealthy if strong feelings are chronically active and never given room for expression. White culture, then, works hard to keep the volume down, least we all go crazy from the demands we place on each other's capacity for self-control. Experience in the culture helps. We learn how not to step on toes, hurt other people's "feelings," to not make a scene, and all the other little social rules and practices of a lifetime. We rein it in, and trade spontaneity, flair, style, and rhythm, innovation, and maybe even some measure of ability to jump and dance, for an orderly demeanor and generally predictable and controlled everyday existence.

In black culture, the reins are loosened. Emotions come freely and the culture has a vibrancy that white culture lacks. But this is neither total freedom nor anarchy. Black cultural practices require one to develop skill in receiving emotional performances of others. Self-esteem, protected in white culture by the requirement that others restrain their feelings, is open to direct and forthright confrontation in black culture. One cannot opt out of the discussion, and faced with this, must learn how to preserve a sense of control and togetherness that does not count on the other person being emotionally restrained. Coolness under pressure and the ability to hold one's own betwixt and between others' forceful expressions of feelings are likewise learned from an early age. In return, one is able to express one's own feelings as they occur.

Moving from one cultural mode to another can be quite challenging. Having been at times immersed in settings where black cultural norms applied, I have personally felt at a loss. So many things are the same. People are people. The topics, sports, relationships, work, friends, politics, music, are really not that different in substance. Plus my experiences have often been good ones, with family and friends. Yet there is a pace, a tone, and practices that despite the sameness are somehow different. It has taken me years to become accustomed to the difference, and even though it is now more familiar and thus enjoyable, I doubt I have come close to mastering the stylistic requirements of this culture. Should my career, my public credibility, or the safety of my family or myself ever depend upon my ability to perform according to black cultural practices, I would be severely handicapped. I am generally a shy person and I do not have the expressive repertoire that black culture demands. Too many years in white culture, where my personal demeanor is more commonplace, make it hard for me to adjust my style to the spontaneous and energized expressiveness black culture values most highly.

117

Yet learning to perform according to the requirements of another culture is exactly what black people have to do when they enter career paths in the professional world. Even those not on track toward middle class status still have to contend with institutions, such as hospitals, schools, police agencies, and social welfare organizations that operate on white norms. Failure to get one's point across in these settings can indeed damage one's position in society, cause one's family to suffer deprivations, or even on occasion lead to fateful and perhaps fatal misunderstandings. The white cultural practice of suppressing emotional expression can be extremely demanding of those not accustomed to it. Whites on the other hand, view black expressions of emotion as overly assertive and threatening, when in black culture they would pass as nothing out of the ordinary. A heated discussion in black culture may, in the framework of white cultural norms, be interpreted as a fight. White participants may be led to act defensively to "tone it down," to the consternation of black participants who thought they were simply having a dialogue.

Black people who move in white circles learn how to adjust. Countless times I've gone with African-American friends and colleagues from private settings where we could be ourselves into public settings such as a business meeting where white norms apply. Privately we use a sort of pidgin set of cultural practices, partly black and partly white, as each feels comfortable. The language, the style of expression, and the perspectives that are expressed go back and forth. Generally my colleagues are much more facile in alternating between styles. My repertoire of black cultural practices is less developed than their corresponding command of white practices.

Once we enter the white setting, my colleagues act according to white practices. So accustomed are they to moving from one setting to another, they can accomplish the change almost naturally in the blink of an eye. Some might think this hypocritical or deceitful on the part of my colleagues, but in actuality this is what white culture demands of them. If my colleagues were to act according to a black cultural style they would suffer. At the very least they would invoke stereotypes about black people that white people hold. At worst, they would invite alienation, misunderstanding, condescension, and the loss of trust and opportunities that would be open to them when they operate according to white norms. When in Rome, as they say, do as the Romans do. In fact my colleagues sometimes take pride and pleasure in their command of white culture. Difference can be enjoyable.

But, white culture can be very trying for people accustomed to more freely expressing their feelings. This could be one reason, among many I'm sure, why black people experience high blood pressure and chronic stress in far greater numbers than white people. Every day literally millions of black people operate this way, unbeknownst to many white people who see their African-American colleagues as "just like one of us." Indeed, consider what is seen by a white person who has not had the opportunity to meet black people in settings where black norms apply. Suppose such a person believes color doesn't matter and we are all the same under the skin. Suppose, too, that same person is generally unaware there is such a thing as white culture. There would be nothing in his or her social setting to disrupt any of these beliefs. This figurative white person would experience white people and black people working side by side, acting in similar ways. The fact that most of their colleagues of color have mastered the skills of two cultures, are in fact bicultural, would simply be beyond the understanding of most white people in this position. This lack of understanding makes it easier for black people to pass within white culture without their alternative cultural experience being exposed. On the other hand, when that alternative cultural experience becomes an issue, white people fail to see the issue as cultural. Instead many simply interpret cultural differences as personal failings on the part of their colleague of color.

Believing Is Seeing (or Not Seeing)

The framework from within which white people interpret the actions of people of color is itself a product of our culture, claims Ruth Frankenberg, professor of American studies. Frankenberg interviewed thirty white women for several hours each, asking them about their lives and how they viewed race. She wanted to see if race had an impact on the lives of white women. Ultimately she concluded we are all part of a racially structured society, and the very ability of white women to conceptualize race, their own and that of others, is determined by that structure. Frankenberg is careful to limit the generality of her findings to white women, but it seems entirely plausible that the structure she describes applies to white men as well. Indeed, she often talks about white culture, which includes both men and women, as being the structure she investigated.[8]

According to Frankenberg, the way white women understand race could always be described as falling within one of three modes. First there was essentialist racism. This is the old-time racism that was in force for much of the history of the United States. Essentialist racism believes we are different under the skin and that biology has made us irreversibly so. Not only are we different, but some races are better than others and the white race, generally, is the best. Because of this, white people are entitled to exploit other racial groups.

The second mode Frankenberg described was colorblindness. Though colorblindness is discussed at length in Chapter 4, it is worthwhile to review Frankenberg's findings here since she analyzes colorblindness within and as part of the structural framework of white culture. Frankenberg prefers to name this mode of thinking "color- and power-evasiveness." Color- and power-evasiveness began to emerge in the 1920s and is now the prevailing mode of thinking in white culture. Racism is seen as consisting of individual, intentional acts. Outside of this, color- and power-evasiveness denies that race makes a difference in people's lives. White culture is seen as normative, correct, modern, universal, noncultural, and cultureless. That is to say, it's not seen at all, but rather understood to be the way everyone "naturally" is.

People using this mode of viewing race will oppose essentialist racism, but they also will oppose the third mode that Frankenberg calls race cognizance. This latter mode is believed to be dangerous, leading to a disuniting and disintegration of the central values of our society. In place of race, the color- and power-evasive mode prefers to use notions of ethnicity to name difference. It holds that we are all the same under the skin and our ethnic differences are converging. People of color, not white people, are seen as an object of study and while people of color are understood to face oppression, white people are not understood to have privileges. People of color are believed to be racial, but white people are not. Thus white people seldom name themselves in racial terms ("I am a white person") but rather use individualized descriptions ("I am a hard worker"). Though white culture is not seen, cultures of color are, and often they are valorized. To white people these cultures seem exciting, vibrant, ethnic, and authentic in a way the unnamed white culture is not.

Race cognizance emerged out of civil rights and later movements for cultural and economic empowerment of people of color from the post–World War II era to the present day. Like essentialist racism, race cognizance sees difference, but unlike essentialist racism, race cognizance does not believe difference is based in biology. Rather it reflects difference in cultures, and their attending values and standards. Inequality is not biologically determined. Rather, it is a product of our social structure, including our institutions. Whereas color- and power-evasiveness believes that seeing race is a racist act, race cognizance believes that not seeing how race structures our lives is a racist oversight.

These three modes of thought originated at differing times in our history, but all are present in white culture today. Frankenberg does not explore the extent to which other cultures employ the same modes of thinking. Conceivably they might, if only for the fact that white culture, and its underlying modes of thought, have such a profound impact on the affairs of other cultural groups. This impact can be measured in our legal processes, our educational system, our political bodies, and our media. But quite possibly cultures of color have other culturally determined modes of thinking through race not available to white culture.

These modes of thinking are antagonistic to one another. Each sees the other as wrong and dangerous. It's not hard to find people who are entirely bound up on one mode of thinking to the exclusion of the other two. But it's also equally possible, if not more so, to find people whose thoughts, beliefs, and feelings about race draw upon all three modes, forming a mixture depending on the issues and circumstances at hand.

Aside from looking at how white people conceptualize race, Frankenberg also points out that white culture has a certain way of thinking about culture itself. Culture is something that is "out there" in the cultures of other people. That which is different can be seen and named. This view of culture believes that culture can be separated from everyday life. Thus many white people hold that they have no culture, or if they do, they see their culture as rooted in a European ethnicity whose everyday impact on their lives is minimal. But in fact culture is something everyone has, whether they are aware of it or not. White culture is that which is left over after white people have ruled out all other cultures. It is that which is not black culture, not Latino culture, etc. Though not named itself by the people who practice it, white culture is nonetheless real. In Frankenberg's words, "Whites are the nondefined definers of other people. Or, to put it another way, whiteness comes to be an unmarked or neutral category, whereas other cultures are specifically marked 'cultural.'"[9]

The Positive Side

Often white people think of interracial contact as conflict-prone, stressful, and likely to dredge up negative feelings of fear, guilt, anger, and shame. But in a focus group I conducted among white people, several participants mentioned positive feelings resulting from interracial contact. The feelings included happiness, comfort, love, trust, and feeling accepted. Often these feelings occurred when individuals entered situations unfamiliar to them. One person attended a christening at a black church. Another person took part in an interracial sensitivity group. Yet another was involved as a volunteer at a community agency.

The positive feelings spoke to a deep and unrealized need for white people to experience our common humanity with people of color. The situations above all occurred in settings in which white culture was not dominant. When we find acceptance across racial lines, an event all too rare in the lives of many white people, we feel affirmed in a way that white culture alone cannot provide.

The culture may lack a readily identifiable character to those within it, but the cultural experience of white people is nonetheless marked by race. I found this for myself a few years ago by asking a focus group of white people if race affected them. Every person had a story to tell and these stories contained an impressive array of characters, settings, plots, roles, statuses, and activities. The stories voiced concerns, offered moral guidelines, and expressed feelings both negative and positive. Like Frankenberg, though coming from a different theoretical approach, I was able to show that white people very much are affected by race. One woman working as a volunteer felt flattered when a young Latino boy thought she was not white. A woman in the same group said she could not think of anything good about being white. A man described being in an African country and understanding how it felt to be different. Another man was frustrated with the government's attempts to have people identify their race.

The many stories these white people told had an air of familiarity to them. Seldom did anyone ask for clarification. The terms, the situations, the feelings, and the thoughts were all readily understandable to those in the room. But at the same time, they were feelings and thoughts that clearly belonged to white people.

It's doubtful that people from other racial groups would have had the same immediate understanding of the stories and the underlying experiences that informed them. For example, a woman told of working for an employment agency where discrimination was common practice. She felt trapped between her job and an interracial love affair. Here the details might be comprehensible to anyone. Surely African-Americans are not so naive as not to know that discrimination takes place behind closed doors in white-owned businesses like employment agencies. But can a person who has not been there really understand what it means when the system tells you directly you must discriminate, and, even if it violates your personal feelings you are expected to conform and respect the sensitivities of other white people in the office. In other words, keep your mouth shut or kiss your job good-bye. Yet every white person potentially faces a situation like that, and many have experienced it. Some go along and some walk. But all understand in a personal way the social forces at hand.

This is not to say that white people suffer as much from racism as people of color. But when you are part of a structure, as we all are in our racially structured society, then anyone challenging that structure will face repercussions, even if that challenge comes from a position of privilege. Everyone in the focus groups understood that implicitly. No words were spoken to interpret or explain the experience as I've done here. They were not needed. Though few of the people in these focus groups could name white culture or speak with any certainty of what it comprised, all were versed in the white cultural experience. It is our culture after all.

7

Inside the White Experience

Have you ever had something running through your head, unable to rid yourself of it? Something like a song, or maybe something less pleasant, like an upsetting conversation. Several years ago I had this happen, and "upsetting" describes the way I experienced it. It wasn't a song, and it wasn't a conversation. It was just a word. The N-word.

You know the word I'm talking about. It's the most powerful pejorative in white American culture. So much so that other people borrow it to tell how oppressed they are, or how despicable they find others to be. In its original usage it refers to black people, and that's generally how it remains understood today.

I don't mean to be overly cutesy using the term "N-word." Maybe I should just be forthright and spell it out in print. The shock value would make lively prose. But I'd just as soon not do that. It's not necessary to the discussion and unlike some people, both white and black I might add, I don't feel the need.

Whether or not I put the word in print, it was there in my head, popping up at the most inconvenient times. You see, I would often hear it when my family was present. It would be there in my mind when looking at my wife and my children. Not that I hated my family. Quite the opposite. They've always been my foundation and inspiration. We experience frictions, as does anyone in close quarters, but that pales before the bonds we have. We're a close family, and love for one another fills our lives.

They say if you have a song in your head, you can get rid of it by getting someone else to sing it. I've tried that and it works. But who was I going to tell about this particular word that kept bouncing around in the most disconcertingly disruptive way in my consciousness. Am I a racist? I wondered. Do I have some deep-seated hatred for my family? As much as I tried to repress this word and think positive things, it refused to go away. What was going on?

A lot. As it turned out, I was going through a psychological change. At the time I was close to forty years old, so I'd been through a few changes already. What was happening was painful, even distressing at times. Where it led was to a new perspective on myself as a person. To the outside world it probably wasn't apparent, and much of my character remains as it was before. My personality stayed intact, my conscious mind kept control of my life, and I found I was not irredeemably racist after all. In retrospect, I simply was putting together a lot of things I had ignored before, and learning something new about what it meant to be white.

White Racial Identity

Nearly all my life I knew what box to check on forms asking for my race. I knew the color of my neighbors. And I knew who were the slave holders and who were the slaves in American history. So when I say I was learning what it meant to be white, I'm talking about something deeper than knowing what census category I fit into. In psychological terms, I was moving into a new stage of white racial identity.

My wife, a sociologist, asks how it is that black people are viewed as psychologically maladjusted if they deny they are black, but white people deny that we are white all the time and this is seen as normal, even commendable. Indeed, the white person who publicly says he or she is white is seen as maladjusted. Another African-American woman, this time a psychologist, not only asked this question but developed some answers as well. Working in the early 1980s, Janet Helms began to explore how white people understand ourselves as racial beings.

In a society structured by race everyone has a racial identity. Having a racial identity is not the same as having a racial consciousness. Racial identity involves "the psychological implications of racial-group membership; that is, belief systems that evolve in reaction to perceived differential racial-group membership."[1] Racial identity refers to how one identifies with his or her own racial group. This is not the same for every person, even in the same racial group. Some white people, for instance, may not see themselves as white. Other white people do. Some white people may see racism as a problem for people of color. Other white people may see it as a "white problem."

Racial consciousness refers to whether people are aware that their racial group membership has an impact on their beliefs and perceptions. Some people have a racial identity that is repressed or subconscious. Other people clearly believe their racial membership structures their experience. The latter may be said to be racially conscious.

Though the particular expression of racial identity varies from one person to another, this is not a random occurrence. Rather, people develop and mature in their understanding of themselves as racial beings in a racialized society. This development moves through stages, and the stages can be described in terms of the beliefs, moral conflicts, and psychic defenses characteristic of each.

Helms was not the only psychologist to develop a model of white racial identity development. Working independently, Rita Hardiman, a white woman, developed a remarkably similar model.[2] In the past fifteen years other psychologists have expanded this line of inquiry and suggested additional variations. It's not possible to discuss all the variations here, so I'll focus on Helms's model for an in-depth discussion, adding some comments about other models from time to time. Psychologists have proposed models of racial identity development that apply to other racial groups as well. Because this is a book about white people, the discussion here focuses on models of white racial identity.

A Model of Black Racial Identity

Building on the work of other theorists, psychologist Janet E. Helms proposes a four-stage model of black racial identity development.

In the Preencounter stage, the person identifies with white culture, and denigrates black culture and people. Whites are felt to be deserving of the good things they have, and blacks must work harder to be like white people. Eventually the individual comes to realize he or she does not completely fit with the white group, and furthermore he or she does not fit with the black group either.

The Encounter-stage black person understands he or she will not be fully accepted in the white world and that some part of that world will view black people as inferior. This leads to bitterness, hurt, and anger. The person then struggles to obtain a "black" identity.

The Immersion/Emersion stage is characterized by rage and self-destructiveness at the outset, but may lead to a later impulsiveness and euphoria. Blackness is idealized and whiteness is denigrated. Black people and black cultural settings are sought out, and positive black images are incorporated into one's identity.

In the Internalization stage, the black person is calm, self-controlled, secure, and active in working against oppression. While retaining a black identity, the person is able to view white culture and white people for their good and bad points. The person will function within multiracial settings in a competent manner.[3]

More than once I have heard a befuddled white person describe how a black friend of their youth or early adulthood became angry and emphatic about his or her blackness (or the white person's whiteness) when previously it seemed race was not an issue in their relationship. Helms and other theorists suggest this is a necessary and intermediate stage of developing a healthy black racial identity.

Helms proposes that people move from one stage to another because they encounter moral dilemmas. Of course the biggest racial dilemma white people encounter is the "American dilemma," which simply asks, How can a country and people proud of freedom and democracy keep part of their populace in subjugation? Helms's theory looks at specific variations of this dilemma.

The first three stages of Helms's model are Contact, Disintegration, and Reintegration.[4] Basically a white person discovers there are black and white people in the United States. Thus begins the Contact stage. Not surprisingly, most white people make this discovery at some time early in their life. If you're reading this book and you're a white American, you've at least made it to the Contact stage. Contact people have an air of innocence and naivete about them. Simply learning to name difference does not mean they've learned the lessons behind that difference. They might believe race doesn't matter, and that being black or white is a style choice expressed in language and clothes, but nothing more. A Contact person realizes he or she is white, but fails to realize it makes a difference in any way. The white racial consciousness of a Contact person is low.

Depending on the circumstances the Contact person encounters in society, he or she may go through the teens and into adulthood in this stage. Some people may stay in this stage for a lifetime. For most white Americans, such is not the case. We live in a racially structured society, and this structure has rules for both white people and black people. Step outside the rules, and someone is going to put you in your place. If you're white, you get put in a white place, and it can be either a black or white person who puts you there. A Contact person, for instance, would see no harm in interracial dating, would believe discrimination never takes place, and would believe that all black people will like white people who try to act black. For most white people, this bubble pops. A young white child in racist surroundings may be told point-blank not to play with black children. A white teenager may witness black friends harassed by police when white youth are not. A young white woman at her first job may find her white co-workers resentful of people of color even though she can see no evidence or cause for the resentment. Or perhaps the white person dates a person of color, only to be ostracized by friends and family on either side of the relationship. Maybe an idealistic youth has volunteered in a black community and found his or her youthful idealism rejected and ridiculed by family and peers, or by members of the community where the youth performs volunteer services.

Welcome to the Disintegration stage. Aptly named, this stage speaks of disillusionment. Think back to the first time you realized you were white and it's quite possible you're thinking about the moment when you left the Contact stage. Seldom is it a pleasant experience. Possibly you realized white people have safety and comfort that people of color do not, and you found some relief knowing that. Regardless, youthful innocence is lost and the world looks more cruel, harsh, arbitrary, and unfair than you imagined. You were put in your place, and told how it is: You're white. They're not. It doesn't matter so much who tells you. Could be white people, could be black people. Either way, it's a painful lesson to learn, and all the more so since you have to abide by the rules or face rejection. If it's white people who burst your bubble, and it often is, there's a good chance you have to continue to live or work with the same folks. Could be your parents and siblings, your co-workers, or your peer group. Those closest to you often are the most direct enforcers of the rules that underlie our society's racial structure. What are you going to do?

Reintegrate yourself. That's the next stage. Few people can change their family, peer group, and work situation without great difficulty. It's easier to change your beliefs. Back in the Disintegration stage it became quite apparent to people that they were white. That was the very point being made to them. Now each person has to live with it. In a way, you make a deal with the devil. Race exists and it matters. You've been put in the white box, and someone's to blame for that. Being in the white box is not all bad, of course. Once a white person sees race as meaningful, it's also easy to see that whites have the better go of things. Big houses and good schools. Credit for all the good things in our country. The list goes on. Whose fault is it that you happen to end up on the good side of things? Black people's fault, it seems. They're lazy, stupid, and all the other things you heard before but denied. They deserve what they got. If "they" were the ones who made you realize you were white, then it simply serves them right. If it was your own people that told you so, well maybe they shared some hard truths with you, making you grow up a little.

The Reintegration stage is very stable. It's the point where a person first willingly steps behind the white veil and many, perhaps most, white people stay there. Realizing now one is white, though not feeling it as intensely as the Disintegration stage, a person can remain culturally encapsulated for the rest of his or her life. "What do people of color have to do with me?" the person might ask. "Nothing you need to know about," the answer will come. Safe within the confines of white culture, willing without question to accept its limits, a person in the Reintegration stage might be passively racist, or actively so. Either way, whether consciously or not, racist is what they are. Their world is white, and in their adult mind it seems only right that it is so.

The first three stages of Contact, Disintegration, and Reintegration comprise a process of "abandoning racism," Helms believes, though it appears to me as much a matter of creating whites who are satisfied to be racist. Describing the Reintegration stage as one in which conscience is diminished, Helms also notes that a person in this stage "considers White to be superior to all other racial groups....[and] denigrates, appropriates, and ignores the contributions to the society of groups other than Whites."[5]

Why some people move beyond this point is not clear. White culture offers ample reinforcement for people in the Reintegration stage, particularly if their views are of the more passive, less outspoken variety. But some white people begin to question that people of color are fully responsible for the circumstances they face. Racism exists, these white people begin to realize, and it oppresses people of color. In the fourth stage, the Pseudo-Independent stage, a white person is likely to be interested in helping people of color become like white people. One's own whiteness is not at issue and white consciousness at this stage is low. In this fourth stage, white people see people of color as needing help so that they might lift themselves up and "become like us."

Developing a nonracist white identity begins with the Pseudo Independent stage. Whites in this stage are less convinced that white culture is superior. Although there is a re-awakening to the moral dilemma posed by race, the re-awakening is largely intellectual. Kind of like a disinterested or even passionate look at racial disparities, but still from behind the white veil. It lacks a true investment in becoming part of a multiracial community.

This stage, which is characteristic of a "liberal" perspective according to Helms, can also be very stable and long lasting. Pseudo-Independent white people receive encouragement from people of color who often find white people in this stage preferable to those in the previous Reintegration stage. A person in the Pseudo-Independent stage may feel he or she has learned all he or she can to overcome the effects of racism upon one's self. They may feel they've come to the end of the road, racially speaking, and believe all they can do is live a colorblind life, hoping the rest of society will learn how to get along with one another. Somewhere, this person may feel, there are people who know more about race. Probably people of color and radical white people, but then again, maybe they are making a big fuss when they really need to forget the whole thing.

How do I know all this? Because I was there, for many years. I was there before I was married and after. I was there when our first child came along. I was there when I began working as a diversity consultant. I might still be there if it were not for an event that shook my worldview. Like an earthquake.

It wasn't a dramatic event. Nobody else knew what happened. I was working with my senior colleague at a diversity workshop. The client organization, a private foundation, had a staff of 30 people, about two-thirds of them white. Of the staff members of color, several were African-American. Some staff were openly gay or lesbian. Many had a history of involvement in liberal and radical causes.

Personally, I've never considered myself radical. Instead I've more or less identified with the mainstream, and I still do. But as a longtime liberal and at that time a Pseudo-Independent white person, I have a certain measure of respect for radicals. They often have been the moving force in social changes that have made our society more humane.

Finding such a group in a foundation surprised me. One staffer pointed out the foundation's funds came from politically conservative donors who individually would probably not agree with many positions held by various staff. But, he added, every calendar quarter the staff prepared their funding recommendations to the foundation board. They would go into the meeting and present their case, "and then a miracle happens." Their recommendations were funded and the poor and oppressed were given some small measure of financial relief.

To me it seemed these progressive people must be the ones who really knew about race. Weren't they diverse? Didn't people of color hold significant positions? Weren't they people with a history of struggling for social justice? They were indeed. And so it seemed to me they would be the ones to have it together, racially speaking. Our agenda that day covered many aspects of diversity—not just race but class, sexual orientation, gender, religion, and the many other things that diversity comprises. I don't remember the entire day so much as a single hour in which I spoke with the group and explored their racial attitudes, beliefs, and feelings. That friction existed between white people and people of color wasn't surprising of itself. But as the dialogue progressed, it seemed these people were talking just like other mixed-race groups I had experienced. White people lined up on one side of things and people of color on the other.

"Trust us," said the white people. "We are good people."

"You do not know yourselves," said the people of color. "You do us harm."

"We don't know what to do," said the white people. "Teach us," they said.

"I've taught and I've taught from the day I was born and I am weary of it," said the people of color. "It's time you taught yourselves."

And so it went.

I was struck by the way the white people, my people, were acting in this cross-racial dialogue. On every other issue they seemed very individualistic. I couldn't identify a racial character to their views. But suddenly here they were as a group all saying the same unoriginal things. It wasn't like they had formed a conscious decision to act in unison. But they did. They shared the same confusion and pain, voiced the same concerns, proclaimed the same innocence and denied the same responsibility and privilege I had seen white people do so often in other settings. In those other settings I had already heard voiced in return the very points made by staff members of color.

It surprised me the white staff members were hearing these things for the first time. Something surprised me even more in a way I can only explain as personal. I had spent many years married to a black woman and I felt a deep connection with our relationship. Our decision to be in an interracial marriage was simply a human one. Certainly we understood the racial context surrounding our marriage, but our relationship grows from our shared humanity. I also worked with people of color, where my role was significant, but not indispensable. They were running the firm before I got there, and would continue without me. Racially different, yes, but we shared some bonds. We had relationships that recognized both the difference and our underlying oneness.

Asian-American Identity Development

According to a model formulated by psychologist Larke Nahme Huang, the principle influences on Asian-American identity are a cultural value emphasizing a collective and situational sense of being, together with the presence of cultural groups and experiences outside one's own group. Expectations and behaviors differ between the ethnic identifications of one's own culture, and the non-ethnic identifications with people outside one's culture. Often the outside culture is white culture, but other outside cultures may be present.

The individual internalizes several identifications, both from inside and outside his or her culture, and learns how and when each identification can be expressed according to specific cultural surroundings. The same person can be an aggressive businesswoman at work in white culture, and an obedient wife and daughter at home in Chinese culture.

At the same time, society ascribes cultural roles to people. White culture may negatively value Chinese culture. Asian-Americans born in Asia may reject Asian-Americans born in the U.S. as too nontraditional. These group differences influence how the individual responds to his or her internalized set of identifications. Huang notes, "the interplay of ethnic and non-ethnic factors on the internal and external level, is particularly appropriate for Asian-Americans."[6]

From our dialogue with the foundation staff, it was clear many of the staff genuinely liked one another. I'm sure they would say their relationships across race were significant and meaningful. But when the topic turned to race itself, a barrier arose between white people and people of color, and their humanity was divided. They were unable to respond to one another on a fully human level. I grew increasingly distressed as I witnessed how the white people helped make this barrier. We weren't doing it in any willful way. I tried to make the white staff aware of their shared responses and how these responses reinforced the racial barrier that weighed so heavily on the group. If I had, I'm sure they would have done anything in their power to make the barrier dissipate. But they couldn't see it. Until that moment, neither could I. Thus I failed, and it shook me.

A barrier like that, unseen by ourselves, but fully present, could only mean one thing. It was a thing so powerful it led every white person, whether gay or straight, woman or man, secretary or boss, Christian or Jew, to act in concert, even without prior discussion or agreement. It joined white people—who had no individual wish to be joined that way—in a common experience It held such power that it could withhold from us the basic human link we believed we shared with everyone, leaving people of color estranged and angry on the other side. I knew there was only one thing that could do that to us white people. It was our culture.

I know now, I can't make you see it. But I saw clearly that as white people we share a culture. It shapes our outlook and our experience in real and powerful ways. I had the strange sensation of being one with my people, and simultaneously standing outside of their immediate experience. Like the literary man without a country, temporary exile gave me new eyes to see my culture clearly.

As a trainer, however, I wasn't having an easy time of it. You might say I lost my place. I kept probing to see if the white staff members could move past this barrier and, in effect, break through the white veil. The staff members of color were not particularly helpful. Most simply interpreted my actions as if I shared the same consciousness as the white staff. There's no reason why I should have expected otherwise. It was only in that moment I saw there was "something else" to being white myself.

It was then, too, I first understood my people needed help. Ultimately, that realization changed my frame of reference. The insight I had was not common. But it's not unknown, either. I was entering the fifth stage, which Helms called Immersion/Emersion. This stage, she says, is

> characterized by an effort to understand the unsanitized version of White history in the United States. It involves an active exploration of racism, White culture, and assimilation and acculturation of White people. During this stage, the person assumes personal responsibility for racism and develops a realistic awareness of the assets and deficits of being White. The moral re-education of other White people becomes a central theme of this stage.[7]

I did all that. Seeing white culture in operation made me realize it had always been present in my life, operating as an invisible force. Few things can be more disconcerting, particularly since one of my cultural values is that the individual shapes his or her own destiny. What was this thing that made us white people act alike, and how did it function as part of the racial structure of our society? Suddenly these questions became very pressing.

There was another element to the sense of urgency I felt. For years I believed that much goodwill and earnest desire by white people to create a multiracial society had been squandered. Racism was still present in our society, despite the best efforts of many good white people to eliminate it. A piece of the puzzle seemed to be missing. It wasn't as simple, I knew, as a bunch of bad-hearted white folk wanting to abuse people of color. But goodwill and good intentions never seemed to be enough. There had to be something else going on. Maybe, I thought, this is the piece I hadn't been seeing. Maybe, I believed, this is what my people need to see if we're to make some progress.

There's a certain undoing that accompanies the Immersion/Emersion stage. For me it was akin to a "eureka" experience, where a new discovery opens up a vision of the world formerly withheld. Everything invites reinterpretation. Gradually this begins to wane. The sheer intensity of questioning everything draws a lot of energy and the new insights begin to age and become part of one's life. In the wake of the workshop experience, I researched many topics and found other white people had experienced the same things I had. Still, it seemed to be a little known story. Virtually every white person discovered these things on his or her own. Go to any bookstore and you're likely to see a section on African-American culture. There are probably sections for American Indian culture, for Hispanic culture and for Asian-American culture. Look for the European-American (white) culture section and you'll be disappointed. I've yet to see one.

The experience I had was real and the interpretation not one likely to be reversed. In time, however, I've settled down to a less energized and more integrated questioning of my cultural surroundings and how white people fit within a racially structured society. The sixth and final stage in Helms's model is Autonomy. In this stage a person retains insights from before, and makes adjustments he or she needs to live with newly gained knowledge. During the Immersion/Emersion stage a person is acutely conscious of whiteness. In the Autonomy stage the acuteness fades to a moderate level of white consciousness. A willingness to unmask the racial structure of society emerges. Often a person will surround himself or herself with friends from many racial backgrounds. Living behind the white veil no longer is a real or comfortable option. People in the Autonomy stage are likely to work to change the racial structure of our society and undo the effects of racism. For me it took the form of co-founding the Center for the Study of White American Culture, Inc.

Helms claims her model has limits. Not all white people reach the Autonomy stage by any means. Most remain at earlier stages. Of those people, most function quite well, though this is made possible because they function within white culture. Even those people who do reach the Autonomy stage are only changed in their racial identity. Other values, beliefs, and personality characteristics are likely to remain the same. A habitually optimistic person in one stage will probably be optimistic in the next. Grouches will continue to be grouchy. Backsliding from one stage to another occurs, and a person may even be at differing stages of racial identity in different situations, such as work, family, romance, and politics.

After the workshop with the foundation, the N-word, which I had found so intrusive on my consciousness in the weeks before, faded to a minor annoyance. Occasionally, even today, it resurrects itself. I take it as an unwelcome part of my past "on the playground," so to speak. A part of my cultural history that has marked me, it remains part of my present but does not define who I am.

Innocence and Guilt

Recently I was talking to an African-American reporter from a major metropolitan daily newspaper. He was trying to figure out how to convince his editors there was a story to be found in the incipient white awareness movement. In a moment of candor about his profession, he told me his editors believed that people such as I were guilt-ridden. The terms "liberals," "do gooders," and "idealists" also come to mind. But "guilt-ridden" strikes to the heart of the matter. Let's not mince words. Many white people believe guilt is the issue.

I was unable to come up with the magic reply that would convince his editors their opinion was inaccurate. Certainly "guilt-ridden" is a caricature of people who put themselves on the line to create a multiracial society. I might just as readily characterize the editors as "pleading innocence," for much of what passes among white people as a supposedly detached and rational view of race is simply feigned ignorance and denial of the racial structure of our society.

Feelings about racial guilt and innocence lurk within the mind of every white American. Essayists as different as James Baldwin, Shelby Steele, and Andrew Hacker have written about white guilt, noting its pervasiveness as a seemingly near universal component of the white American psyche.[8] Declarations of innocence also seem to be a universal element of the white racial experience, though perhaps they stem from a shallower portion of the individual white person's being. These feelings echo from the past as well. Historian James Oakes studied the lifestyle of slave owners and remarked on "their startlingly frequent declarations that when they died they would go to hell."[9]

What is guilt? It can be a political fact and assignment of blame by an external entity. Thus courts determine the guilt or innocence of defendants brought before them. Guilt can also be a personal feeling, as when we blame ourselves for doing wrong. Either way, guilt involves a judgment that one's actions have violated a moral code of behavior. The code may be external, such as the law, or it may be a person's internalized standards. Guilt is also a social emotion whose effect is to bind us to a community. When we violate standards of behavior, whether externally or internally defined, it is always in reference to some larger social entity. A society in which no one is capable of feeling guilt risks falling apart in the hedonistic pursuit of self-interest. Guilt demands confession and may require acts of penance, punishment, retribution, and restoration which limit the freedom and consume the resources of the guilty party. A person judged guilty may be separated from the community, shamed, physically and socially isolated, and no longer trusted. It's little wonder that no one wants to feel guilty. If guilt felt good, it wouldn't do its job.

Like any emotion, guilt can be either healthy or neurotic. When we act contrary to our values, a healthy sense of guilt will signal this and lead us to make amends. But all too often we deny any connection with wrongdoing. Our jails are filled with people, most who presumably have committed crimes, who nonetheless proclaim their innocence and name some other party as the cause of their misbehavior. Psychopaths kill without a hint of remorse. Simple denial of guilt is no sure measure of blamelessness. Nor is acceptance of blame always a measure of culpability. Some people are so overcome by their private demons they surrender all moral authority and confess to every moral judgment placed upon them by others. Neither blind denial nor masochistic self-flagellation is healthy.

Which Way Would You Go?

Haresh B. Sabnani and fellow researchers at Fordham University proposed a model of white racial identity development based on their experiences training white students as psychological counselors in multiracial settings.

In their model, white people begin not knowing much about ourselves as racial beings. Interaction with people of color leads to a breakdown of one's previous notions about racial difference and whiteness. Once this breakdown occurs, the individual tries to make sense of his or her world again. We choose one of two ways, either by becoming pro-minority and denigrating white culture, or by rejecting interracial contact and retreating back into white culture. Ultimately one must strive to assimilate newly learned information about whiteness with an integrated view of one's own worth.

The "one way or the other" nature of this model aptly describes how white people may react to exposure to information about racial difference that strains prior white cultural conceptualizations based on limited contact with people of color. Interracial contact, alone, is not enough to guarantee more flexible attitudes among white people in cross-cultural training situations. Care must also be given to how trainees resolve the new experiences they encounter.[11]

If guilt stems from a failure to live up to a moral standard, it's easy to see where white Americans might succumb to guilt feelings. The American dilemma—freedom and equality for all versus racism and exploitation of people of color by white Americans—has already been noted here and in numerous other writings for well over two centuries. The very fact our society is racially structured conflicts with our other moral values as white Americans. To the extent that white Americans feel ourselves responsible for creating our culture and our institutions, we must admit to bringing forth a social structure that seriously questions and contradicts our noblest aspirations. Nor is this simply a matter of past behavior. History is carried within us, says James Baldwin, and we are "unconsciously controlled by it in many ways....It could scarcely be otherwise, since it is to history that we owe our frames of reference, our identities, and our aspirations."[10] When you get right down to it, people of color did not create America's race problem. White people did.

Neurotic guilt might have us dwell in past problems, inflicting new wounds by fighting old battles. Neurotic guilt, or more accurately a neurotic reaction to guilt, might also have us dwell among idealistic visions of future solutions we foolishly believe are already present. This colorblind form of denial assuages guilt prematurely, creates a false sense of innocence, and leaves us unwilling to change. White innocence is a myth. Our innocence was lost long ago, and like the deflowered virgin, we can only pretend to its restoration. Realists must admit the only path to the future is through redemption that comes from dismantling the racial structure of our society as it exists and creating a society that is centered on multiracial values. Any pretense to innocence is a narcissistic ploy that simply delays the hard work before us. The issue before white Americans is not one of creating innocence, but rather managing a component of genuine guilt that pervades our psyche. This guilt is both collective and individual. It can lead us to denial, to self-flagellation, or to making genuine amends.

It's worth a closer look at some ways in which white guilt shapes our responses to the task of creating a multiracial society. White people seem endlessly preoccupied in the production and proof of our own innocence. Somewhere in our psyche every white American feels accused of racism, but several years ago I reflected upon this feeling in myself and realized these feelings did not match my reality There simply were not a lot of people of color actually accusing me of doing racist deeds. Certainly national leaders and public events have raised the issue, but these events did not warrant the immediate defensiveness that white people, myself included, have about race. In fact, we seem overly sensitive and if anything, I've often noticed a tendency for people of color to tiptoe around the subject, if only not to have to deal with white people flying off the handle. If that were all there were to it, perhaps it would be a minor problem, but in the service of proving our innocence we have purged our history books of things that make us look bad, and we continue to define events as equal when white people often have the advantage. The political, cultural, and social philosophy of colorblindness serves this purpose. Being the dominant culture, we invariably use our power to set the standards and control the rules of dialogue.

If we can't prove our innocence, we spread the guilt around, finding ways to blame people of color for the racial structure of our society. Countless theories of dysfunctional cultures and reverse discrimination have had this one point in mind. Worse, we harbor a not-so-secret fear that people of color will do to us as we have done to them.

Some white people simply cannot handle the possibility they have any guilt to bear. Since the assignment of guilt is often done according to a community standard, they take the expedient of limiting their community to other like-minded and morally fragile white people. This leads to an encapsulated life deep behind the white veil, permanently walled off from people of color. Still other white people become so overwhelmed by the heinous crimes of white people that they are no longer able to function as independent agents. Some totally reject the white culture that has placed them in such moral distress and gravitate toward cultures of color where they (mistakenly) see only purity of purpose. Others remain within white culture, but find themselves conceding to demands of people of color in a way that does not create multiracial community, but rather simply seeks appeasement of anger and hostility in the most expedient way possible. These are all things we do as white people from time to time, and none of them are particularly helpful. The best we can do is admit our feelings as white people are going to be tempered by some measure of guilt because we are not living up to our own expectations of what our society should be. From there we need to work together with people of color on restructuring our society in a multiracial way.

Shame, Shame, Shame

Guilt-centered explanations do not give us insight into the character of the initial acts that shape our psychology as white people. In her recent book, *Learning to Be White,* scholar, theologian, and researcher Thandeka convincingly demonstrates that shame plays the central role.[12] It is, of all our white experiences, the core theme. Not guilt, not anger, not fear, not inflated feelings of superiority. Shame is where it begins.

Thandeka, a black woman, asked hundreds of white people to recall when they first realized they were white. Being white, remember, is not based in biology. It is something we learn from our cultural surroundings. Thandeka found people often recalled painful experiences. A white woman whose family was living for a year in Mexico at age five was told not to play with the Mexican children. A white college fraternity man who admitted an African-American man to membership in the 1950s was forced by the national chapter to rescind the membership he had granted. A sixteen year old white girl was told by her mother never to let her best friend come visit again. The friend, of course, was black.

Not all the stories told of blatant rejection. Often it was more subtle. Another five year old boy at his own birthday party among relatives, invited his black neighbors over and noticed how uncomfortable his family became. He had done something wrong. A college student who had never encountered black people found himself unable to join the black table in the cafeteria, despite his interest, because he feared he would not be able to return to the white table. A four-year-old boy was taken on a driving tour of the black section of town, receiving this exposure so as not to embarrass the family by staring at black people when going to New York City on a later vacation. According to Thandeka, this young boy learned "there are black people and 'they' live/belong over there—beyond the pale. It was as if everyone already knew this. [He] simply had to catch up." She continues to say "after listening to several hundred Euro-Americans recount their early recollections of experiences that not only made them think of themselves as white but also taught them to act in ways that would keep them within this racial pale, I learned to doubt the validity of other Euro-Americans' initial claims that there were no such childhood incidents in their own lives."[13]

Often, Thandeka found, people would recall memories that had been repressed for years, if not decades. When these memories came to light, they were accompanied by feelings of shame. We experience shame not because we are born as racist, but rather precisely because we are not. Everyone has a core self. It is that part of ourselves we might call the child within. It is the part that is innocent and the part that wishes to relate to others in an equally innocent way. It is the part of us that, racially speaking, gets us in trouble with the caretakers within our own white culture.

Particularly when we are young, our caretakers control our fate. To the young child, the loss of a parent's love is not simply painful, it can be fatal. To be cut off from one's parents, one's family, one's community is the worst fate that can befall a child. When the child, the adolescent, or even the young adult first explores relationships across racial lines, he or she is led by that core self that seeks relationship with others. However, white culture is not accepting of cross-racial relationships. The child explorer is punished and the punishment often threatens the loss of parental love and acceptance, and the loss of one's place in the white community. These threats are not against knowingly wrong actions the child performs. In other words, they do not call out guilt as a response. Rather, the threats condemn feelings that come from within the core self. Part of one's own core self is viewed by one's caretakers as impermissible, unacceptable, and condemned. It is this essential unworthiness of one's own being that constitutes shame. To avoid loss of one's caretakers, one must cut off the part of the self from which the feelings arise. In the act of doing that, the child begins to develop a racial identity as white.

We are literally victimized by our culture, frequently by those who love us most.

> The Euro-American child…is a racial victim of its own white community of parents, caretakers, and peers, who attack it because it does not yet have a white racial identity. Rather than continue to suffer such attacks, the Euro-American child defends itself by creating a white racial identity for itself. It begins to think and act like its community's ideal of a white self. When the adult recalls the feelings and ideas it had to set aside in order to mount this defense, it feels shame. More precisely, white shame.[14]

Forcing the child to deny a portion of its core self, Thandeka points out, is a form of child abuse. At best, it's a form of "tough love" where the child is hardened against its better nature. It learns safety comes from staying with one's own, lest they turn on you. Once learned, this lesson is quickly repressed "because the process that creates this racial identity entails attacks upon one's core sense of self by those who ostensibly love it the most: its caretakers, legal defenders and protectors. Such an awareness is too much for most persons to retain in conscious memory."[15]

The Race Game

Do you feel a sense of shame about your whiteness? The African-American theologian Thandeka claims that shame is the central emotional experience shared by white people. She suggests white people play a little game in order to see her point. Called the Race Game, it has one rule: "For a week, the player, in all white settings, must use the word *white* whenever he or she mentions the name of a Euro-American."

It seems simple enough. Give it a try.

Despite its simplicity, though, the Race Game proved nearly impossible to play for most white people. One brave soul reported "Every time I decided to play the game with someone new, I felt that I was about to be rejected, that the person would turn away, and that I would be shunned."

According to Thandeka, the game violates a norm among non-supremacist white Americans that we name others by their race but do not name ourselves as white. The game player makes the category of "white" relevant, conscious, and apparent. This threatens to raise awareness of shaming by past caretakers who told us that to be white, we must reject our connections to people of color, and thus humanity at large.[16]

It is not only seeking relationship with racial outsiders that is a source of shame to the young Euro-American child. Equally potent is the demand that the child conform to the white Anglo-Saxon Protestant ideal of white culture. The child must contend with "a Euro-American pecking order among ethnic groups." White people who depart from the WASP ideal, whether as children or adults, are given the message that they are deficient. Either they disown the "ethnic" portion of their self and take on the demeanor and cultural practices of WASPs, or they find themselves correspondingly lowered in the status hierarchy of whiteness. One ends up feeling one is never quite white enough.

White Pride

Okay, it's a shock headline. A while ago I saw the term emblazoned on a Web site, "Aryan"-style. We associate white pride with white supremacists, but our association is based on a superficial acceptance of a distorted and unhealthy notion of pride. Listen to Lillian Roybal Rose, an educator and healer, explaining the real thing to us white folk.

> Collective pride, which is a form of nourishing, group self-love, is an emotional experience that many white people find elusive. I want to be clear about what I mean by *pride*—for, even as I write, there is an increase in various forms of supremacy, or separatist or nationalist groups using the idea of "pride" as a framework for their philosophy based on hate. When I talk about pride, I am using the word in its purest sense, like love in its purest sense. The paradox, that we can only love someone else to the extent that we love ourselves, applies to "pride" as well. I am not talking about false pride, the pride that says, "I am something and you are nothing." I am talking about the pride that says, "To the extent that I love and appreciate myself, I can love and appreciate you." In collective pride we say, "To the extent that I can love and appreciate my group's difference, I can love and appreciate yours."[17]

It's not easy to talk about white pride in this way. As a race we have very little experience doing it. And our legacy of white pride as a supremacist tool embodies, for us, the worst the white race has to offer. Where do we find this pride? Rose, a Latina, tells white people to

> think of their ancestors, in isolation from anything that is wrong with society. I urge them to remember the essence of their grandparents—their hard work, their wisdom, their kindness, their survival, their family devotion.[18]

Any time I begin to get comfortable with my feelings of pride about being white, or European-American if you will, I am distracted by the idea that I might become mindlessly so, or that my pride might be read as a supremacist one in even the slightest way by both white people and people of color. So I need to be clear, and beg your indulgence, and make it clear that after honoring a multiracial stance in the rest of this book, where I keep both the positives and the negatives of white culture in view, I need some space to talk in an unconstrained way about what makes me proud of being white.

I am proud that neither I nor any white person was born inherently "white." Our basic human character has been severely abused, but it carries our potential. I have pride in my family, simple and deep. I am proud of the political institutions that arose under the direction of European-Americans. I am proud of cultural traditions in food, art, music, and a hundred different items. I am proud of our intellectual and material empowerment. I am proud of our individualism. And I am proud of a cultural flowering that has remade the world. I am proud of the many white heroes who, from the start in early Virginia until today, have resisted the caustic and deadly effects of our culture on a multiracial world. I am proud of many white individuals who are as kind, selfless, giving, hardworking, and deserving as can be found among all peoples.

Does it matter? Yes, it does. Elaine Pinderhughes, professor of social work and an African-American, has trained hundreds of social workers, many white...

> Few Whites are able to say honestly that being White is an identity that brings them a sense of pride. Although some may feel that being White means being powerful, lucky, comfortable and secure, it can also mean confusion, entrapment, and threatened self-esteem, hardly attributes that would promote helpfulness to people of color....Changing the meaning of White to a more positive one thus becomes an important step in preparation for [clinical and therapeutic] effectiveness.[19]

Rose echoes Pinderhughes:

> The white person who understands collective pride on a deep personal level is usually our best ally....I say in my workshops, "If you don't know pride, in your gut, then our pride will always threaten you. It will always feel as though People of Color are something because you are nothing, that we are colorful because you are bland, and that anything we gain is at your expense."[20]

Clearly this sort of white pride is something we need to develop. Getting there means some hard work. No pain, no gain. True self-esteem is based on accomplishment; we have to work for it. We can start by taking a good look at where we are.

Two Sides of the Same Coin

The contemporary racial structure of our society places white people in a position of dominance, advantage, and privilege while people of color are placed in a position of subordination, disadvantage, and oppression. This structure requires that individuals hold a certain view of one another. The dominant culture develops a collection of images about the people it oppresses and these images serve its purposes. White culture views people of color in stereotypical terms as ignorant, lazy, stupid, incompetent, over-sexed, irrational, criminal, dangerous, and subhuman. Chapter 5 illustrated how white culture developed some of this imagery (of black people as sub-human) following the Revolutionary War. The dominant group also main-tains images of itself as noble, worthy, industrious, deserving, intelligent, capable, entitled, innocent, and good.

These images are portrayed in our media and reproduced in our everyday interactions. The nature of the images has changed over time and nowadays many of the blatant stereotypes of the past have been muted. But they remain and still creep into our consciousness. The assignment of social resources, the official explanations of social issues, and the development of policy for social actions all weigh heavily in favor of the imagery of the dominant group. Members of oppressed groups must be ever vigilant of these images since failure to act according to the image may lead to sanc-tions from the dominant group.

If you're saying to yourself this sounds like plain old racism, it is. There's nothing new in the notion that white people have stereotypes and these stereotypes are used to oppress and demean people of color. It becomes a little more interesting when we ask what these images do when people inter-nalize them. Since the 1960s a small number of people of color have stud-ied what happens when people of color absorb the negative and racist imagery of the dominant culture. This process of absorption is somewhat inevitable, given the incessant barrage of images we encounter through radio, television, and everyday interaction. Avoiding this imagery is not a possibility, particularly since it is interwoven within the institutions, the social programs, and the social community of the dominant culture.

The process whereby people of color absorb this imagery has been called internal colonization, internalized racism, or more commonly internalized oppression. At some level, often a subconscious one, people of color begin to live up to the image. It can lead people of color to engage in self-destructive activities, turning on one another and disrupting the bonds of their communities from within. The symptoms are violence toward one's own people, self-hatred, and sabotage of positive efforts toward empowerment of oneself and others. Internalized oppression limits the ability of people of color to resist the dominant group. In a perverse way, it makes people of color complicit in enforcing their own oppression.

The work on internalized oppression within communities of color is a significant and crucial task. Often this work is done in workshops open only to people of color. It requires people to confront deeply painful issues within themselves. Yet those who do this work with others point out that internalized oppression is not a matter of individual self-esteem and self-hatred. Rather, it is part of the racial structure of our society that imposes itself on the individual psyche of each person of color. It's not so much a matter of who you are as what society says about you. Like the proverbial ancient water torture where one is chained under a slow and unceasingly steady drop of water, the imagery of our society confronts us relentlessly from cradle to grave. Even individuals with high self-esteem and a positive self-concept, if they are people of color, must deal with internalized oppression as part of their psychological environment and inner experience.

The internal experience of white people is also affected by this imagery. This, too, has received study under names such as internalized racism, unconscious racism, and prejudice. Most of this research, while very useful, has been done independent of the work on internalized oppression. That is, some people have studied how the racialized images produced within the dominant society affect people of color. Different people have also studied how the racialized images of the dominant society affect members of the dominant society itself.

Few people have looked at how the experience of both white people and people of color are jointly embedded within the overall racial structure of American culture. One person who has is Maureen Walker, a psychologist at Harvard. Walker coined the term "internalized dominance" as a companion concept to internalized oppression, though obviously internalized dominance refers to the experience of white people. According to Walker, who is African-American,

> I thought about the idea of internalized dominance while I was sitting with a young white female client some years ago during my clinical internship. We had gotten to a point in our relationship where she felt free to express her original misgivings about having me as her therapist and surprise at finding out I could "speak English." In spite of all the trappings of the external situation that weighed in my favor (differences in institutional power, professional credentials, the fact that she needed my help, etc.) our racial

difference in her mind shifted the balance in her favor. She could-
n't imagine that I had any capabilities she could respect. In addition
to some really productive work, that situation led to protracted
introspection on my part as I grappled with my own internalized
oppression, the linkages between that as a working, active force
and what seemed to me to be a defining reciprocal, internalized
dominance.[21]

Walker defines internalized dominance as "a self belief system grounded
in miseducation and in the politics of social inequality. This belief system is
the result of an advantaged relationship to privilege, power, and cultural
affirmation. The premise of white superiority undergirds the various attitu-
dinal and behavioral expressions of internalized dominance."[22]

Internalized Dominance in the Workplace

White people let an internalized sense of dominance shape our behaviors
toward people of color in the workplace. Psychologist Maureen Walker has identified several ways we might do this.

With the Center Stage Syndrome we view people of color as "minorities"
regardless of their numbers, and identify them as "diverse" while making ourselves the standard. Missionary white people work against racism and expect
people of color to be grateful the white person is using his or her power. "I'm not
like other Whites who are racist," the missionary says. The "White Is Right"
Mentality believes white is superior. Ideas are not recognized until a white person
speaks them. Also regarded as superior are white standards of beauty, artistic
expression, and cultural norms. Whites who believe in The Inferior "Other" will
question the competence of people of color, express surprise when competence
is found, and require more proof of competence from people of color than from
white people. Negative Attributions are made about race when applied to people
of color, but about individuals when applied to white people. "He did that because
he is black," but never, "She did that because she is white."[23]

Internalized dominance is something that we white people need to
know about. It's about us. We are victims of it, just as people of color are
victims of internalized oppression. I'm not trying to say white people are
socially disadvantaged. We hold the power and privilege in our racialized
structure, but this structure is not benign. It shapes and warps us just as
it shapes and warps people of color. I recall a few years ago seeing the
photo of a man of color in the newspaper who had just been appointed
to a high-level position in the New Jersey state government. Though I
knew nothing of this man, it flashed through my mind that he was not
competent. Immediately I held a little conversation with myself to suppress this thought. I experienced the thought as racist, and believing
myself to be racist was painful to me. Yet I still recall the moment

because shortly afterward I realized it was an example of my internalized dominance.

Internalized dominance and internalized oppression share much in common. Taken together they comprise a psychological underpinning to racial inequality. They are the psychological means by which the social and political structures of our country acquire their racial character. Having thought about elements these two psychological orientations have in common, I have identified the following:

Imposed by an outside structure. No one asks to take on internalized dominance or internalized oppression. We are born into it. It is out there, in the racial structure of our society and there is little that we, as individuals, can do to change it.

Internalized. The ready-made imagery of our society is so prevalent and interwoven with everything else that it becomes part of our inner psychological makeup. We incorporate this imagery even before we can think clearly. By the time we are adults, it has become part of our psychological framework. While we might become aware of it, and thus work to reduce its effect upon us, we can never completely remove or expunge its effects from our conscious and, more importantly, subconscious minds.

Culturally supported. The imagery in question is culturally based. We learn it as we learn our culture, and in the same way. The learning is by example, by witnessing others, by viewing media. Seldom are we told directly we are learning imagery that supports our dominance or oppression. But we learn, nonetheless. Because it is cultural, the learning and the imagery itself are widespread. They run through every sector of our society. They are universally learned. Each person, regardless of where he or she was raised, has some common access to this imagery. And unless one has been exposed to alternative images, they will appear to be the natural order of things.

Painful to hold in consciousness. Internalized dominance and internalized oppression describe beliefs and thoughts that we hold. In my earlier example, I had an image flash in my mind that an African-American man was incompetent. Because I knew nothing about the man, I realized this image came from some racist indoctrination I had internalized. It was at that moment I experienced the thought as painful. Had I known the person and judged him incompetent based on personal knowledge, the pain would not have been there. But it is painful for white people when we realize we have incorporated racist imagery into our own psychological being. Few white people want to be racist. We've discredited that view, even among ourselves. But the imagery persists, and the fact we have it within ourselves forces us to confront that we are flawed, indeed psychologically damaged. I've sometimes heard people of color wonder why white people are so hurt by being called "racist." The reason is that it points to our internalized dominance.

If white people pick on the internalized oppression of a person of color, it is painful to the person of color as well. A woman of color told me of having a spat with her lover, who was white. As things happen, the argument turned heated, and in that heat her partner called her "stupid." It pushed her button in a way that even she found surprising. She reacted with violence and then stormed out of the room, and eventually the relationship. Surprised as she was, it was clear to her that being called "stupid" tapped a very painful part of her self-image.

My friend is no more stupid than I am racist, but we each experience pain and insecurity over these issues. If someone were to call me stupid, I'd laugh it off and in a similar way my friend would probably take little offense at being called racist. In a similar vein, if a white person were to call me racist, it wouldn't have the same impact. I imagine had my friend's lover not been white, my friend would not have experienced the same intensity of reaction. It's the cross-racial character of these accusations that wound us most deeply. Even if my friend had nothing of her character that was stupid, the implicit message is "That's what every white person thinks you are." Likewise, even if I were thoroughly and completely devoid of racism, being called racist puts me in a place vis-à-vis people of color that I cannot escape.

Because of the pain that arises when we are confronted with our internalized racial imagery and beliefs, it's no wonder that workshops on internalized oppression are limited to people of color. In a similar way, when white people confront our own incorporation of racist imagery we sometimes need the safety of working among our own kind if we are truly to get to the heart of it.

Self-awareness is suppressed by psychological defenses. No one wants to go around thinking of themselves as damaged goods and being consciously aware of images that violate one's own sense of being a good and complete person. Because of this, we use psychological defenses to suppress conscious awareness of our internalized dominance or our internalized oppression.

They damage mental and spiritual health. Internalized dominance and internalized oppression set up inner conflicts within ourselves. They tell us that something is out of kilter between who we want to be and who we think we are.

They impede formation of interracial relationships. The images we incorporate and defend from our consciousness still do their work. They make it hard to see people for what they are. Because much of the pain of this imagery is activated by people of a different race, people of color and white people face numerous psychological barriers to forming relationships. We must overcome stereotypes we hold of racial others, defend ourselves against painful feelings the racial other might call up within ourselves, overcome stereotypes about ourselves held by others, be sensitive enough not to step on the sensitive and vulnerable points of the other person, and be ready to acknowledge and address real material differences in wealth and power. All this simply from the presence of internalized dominance and internalized oppression, which are socially and culturally based after all. Little wonder it becomes hard to find the true inner nature and individual character of a person across racial lines.

They require the presence of a psychological "other." Some white people are raised in completely monoracial neighborhoods. It's possible to be born, to live, and to die within an all-white environment. People of color invariably encounter white people at some portion of their lives, even if only as police and other service personnel within their own neighborhoods. But personal contact and knowledge can be quite limited. Under such limited personal contact across racial lines, people still develop internalized dominance and internalized oppression. The images come through the media and from interactions among one's own. A person of color might just as easily develop a sense of internalized oppression from other people of color as from white people. White people, of course, have been producing images of internalized dominance among ourselves throughout our history, and people of color, at our insistence, have reflected these images back to us.

While actual contact and lived experience with the "other" is not necessary, both internalized dominance and internalized oppression refer to a "psychological other." Dominance and oppression are in relation to one another. To be dominant is to stand over someone else, and to be oppressed is to be oppressed by someone. Even within our isolated communities, we come to sense that we know that "other." This happens though we may never have the face-to-face contact truly required to know another person, another culture, another people.

They filter and often misunication from the psychological other, often in aid of psychological defenses. Internalized dominance and internalized oppression act as "filters." As a white person, if I am not aware of how my internalized dominance shapes my impressions of people of color, I will find myself misinter-preting their actions and their communication. I may sense hostility when none was intended. Or, I might think I am being accepted when my presence is merely being tolerated. These sorts of filters occur in other situations, of course. Our individual character and experience give us a whole set of ways to interpret others who communicate with us. Internalized dominance operates along with these other filters. This is true when we are communicating across racial lines. It is also true when race is an issue as we communicate among people of our own race.

While hidden from the self, their effects are quite evident to the other. My own racism is not evident to me. In my life I have worked hard to eliminate what racist tendencies I have learned. Still, it crops up, and sometimes I find to my embarrassment that it has been glar-ingly obvious to people of color all along. That which we hide from ourselves, our personal blind spots, are sometimes those very things that are seen most clearly by other people. Internalized dominance is one of those things. In a similar way, I sometimes experience quite clearly a sense of internalized oppression on the part of people of color.

On a cultural scale, white people frequently attack commu-nities of color on their weak points. These weak points, many times, reflect symptoms of internalized oppression. Thus we talk about dysfunctional cultures that breed violence, drug use, and disrupted families, all of which seem glaringly obvious to us as problems. At the same time, we fail to see the racism that exists within our own communities and how it feeds back upon com-munities of color.

White people and people of color, each as a group, have become quite skillful in pointing out the internalized attitudes of our counter-parts, while avoiding our own internal processes. This creates a con-stant friction, with each side insisting the other work on its obvious flaws, while failing to see the work we need to do within our own com-munities.

By now it should be clear that internalized dominance and internalized oppression are two aspects of a larger system of psychology and internal-ized imagery that comes from, and perpetuates, the racial structure of United States society. Each of us, white people and people of color alike, has work to do understanding and overcoming our internalized experience. Since the focus of this book is on white people, some additional focus on internalized dominance is appropriate.

There are many ways in which internalized dominance enters into our thinking, either affecting us directly and shaping our experience or by causing us to set up psychological defenses. Within the scope of this introductory section it is not possible to discuss each and every one of these effects, but a brief listing should at least help point out some of the ways in which we as white people are affected by internalized dominance.[24]

Internalized dominance influences our relationship with **ourselves,** leading us to:

- Shame
- Guilt
- Self-righteousness
- Refusing to see or degrading all but a narrow range of human possibilities
- Restricting trust, love, and openness to others
- Rigidity and repression
- Disconnecting from one's body and nature
- Using defenses such as:
    Denial
    Projection
    False justification
    Disassociation
    Transference of blame
- Remaining mentally underdeveloped, even infantile
- Becoming isolated from our own humanity and that of others
- Failing to understand what we need to do to make our ideals of fairness and equality truly work

Internalized dominance influences our relationship to **other white people.** Often we try to set ourselves apart from other white people and pretend we are not affected like others are. Yet we do things such as:

- Name other white people as "guilt ridden"
- Assume other white people are racist
- Assume one has a unique relationship to people of color compared to other white people
- Feel angry at being misled by our culture
- Avoid white identity and claim we are oppressed in other ways due to our gender, our ethnicity, or class, etc. *and thus are not white*
- See whites as either good or bad, racist or nonracist rather than recognizing we each have elements of both
- Reject other whites as less racially aware
- Compete with other whites to be the "best ally" and "least racist" among people of color

- Fear expressing positive feelings for people of color when around other white people
- Fear naming ourselves as white and seeing ourselves collectively as a racial group

Clearly internalized dominance affects our relationships with **people of color.** It leads us to:

- Fear people of color in general
- Fear retribution from people of color (if they did to us what we did to them)
- Feel superior to people of color
- Discount and disbelieve people of color
- Become psychologically disoriented in nonwhite settings
- Need approval, affirmation, and exemption from guilt by people of color
- Fear saying the wrong thing and feel excessively self-conscious among people of color
- Fear being seen as prejudiced or racist
- Misjudge the intent and abilities of people of color
- Take on roles such as "missionary" and "savior" of people of color
- Live physically and psychologically isolated from people of color
- Sometimes unknowingly place people of color at risk of psychological or physical harm
- Appear to people of color as[25]
    - Arrogant
    - Childish
    - Crazy
    - Dangerous
    - Hypocritical
    - Ignorant
    - Insensitive
    - Out of control
    - Selfish
    - Spoiled

Through our internalized dominance we also view ourselves in a certain way in relation to **the racial structure of United States culture,** by:
- Marginalizing talk and feelings about racial structure
- Seeing ourselves as "normal" and people of color as not "normal"
- Denying our identity as part of the dominant culture
- Experiencing uncertainty or paralysis in mixed-race settings

- Remaining ignorant and unaware of racism
- Feeling dull, plain, and feeling one has no culture
- Feeling inadequate about effecting change
- Accepting our mis-education on matters of race without question
- Not realizing that race structures where we live, travel, work, play, and with whom we socialize, love, and marry
- Being unable to perceive common social, community, and economic interests with people of color
- Opening ourselves to manipulation and economic exploitation by cynical leaders using race as a wedge

The psychology of whiteness is still a little studied area. Yet it impacts us all the same. Our internalized dominance affects us every bit as much as internalized oppression affects people of color. Is a position of privilege and relative material wealth worth the psychological price? In a world where we aspire to be one with our fellow citizens of all colors, the answer is "No."

The Academy Awakens

Asking the Right Question

Thirty years ago historian Sig Synnestvedt argued that white professors should eschew teaching in the new field of black studies and turn their attention to educating whites about the historical and present reality of race relations in the United States. His was not an original thought by any means. Gunnar Myrdal, in his epic World War II–era study, *An American Dilemma,* framed the plight of black Americans as "a white man's problem."[1] Finding that "in their basic human traits the Negroes are inherently not much different from other people," Myrdal, a Swedish sociologist, went on to say that black Americans faced unusually trying circumstances in a social environment created by white Americans.

Long before Myrdal, black Americans had been discussing white Americans, both as a necessary tool of survival and as part of the historic effort to rid themselves of the problem white people presented. A recent anthology by David Roediger attests to this history of examining whiteness. Roediger, nominally a white person himself, cites the work of many black intellectuals and activists in the introduction to his book, *Black on White.* The anthology offers selections dating back to the mid-19th century.[2] Black people, it seems, have been on record studying whiteness for a long long time.

By the 20th century, some white people were listening. "It keeps coming to me that this is more a white man's problem than it is a Negro problem," wrote noted journalist Ray Stannard Baker in 1908.[3] As mentioned, Myrdal in 1942 and Synnestvedt in 1970 echoed this insight. Doubtless occasional other white people felt the same along the way.[4] Yet in the hallowed halls of "the academy" (as folk in higher education like to call themselves), these echoes rang empty and unanswered. White academicians, and there were few others in historically white colleges and universities before 1970, continued to focus on black people and other minorities as a point of scholarly interest. Thus it was that Professor Synnestvedt's wry observations passed unnoticed. Regardless, he was the first to suggest a new area of scholarly attention in the title of his article, "White Faces and White Studies."[5]

Leap ahead to April 7, 1997, when a 70-word blurb ran in *USA Today* announcing a conference on "The Making and Unmaking of Whiteness" at the University of California at Berkeley. White supremacists at Berkeley. What a story! The national news media reacted. Over 30 reporters called the conference organizers who, rather than being avowed white supremacists, were simply graduate students in the Berkeley Ethnic Studies Department. Their modest aim had been to invite several scholars together to discuss a newly emerging field of white studies.

Expecting a turnout of 50 people, the organizers were unprepared when nearly every invited scholar accepted their invitation. Some unknown confluence of interests created what was, in retrospect, a debutante ball for whiteness studies.[6] It didn't stop with the scholars. From across the country and beyond, a thousand people flocked to Berkeley where, between April 11 and 13, they witnessed more than 30 presentations with titles like "Whiteness Redux: Banality, Contradiction, and the Rise of Whiteness Studies," "'You're Stealing My Soul': Preserving Whiteness as Quality in Public High School," and "White Racial Projects: A Comparative Perspective." Many were activists who, expecting more in the way of dialogue and action, expressed frustration with the scholarly demeanor of the events.

Prior to the conference, recognition slowly had grown within the academy of a common thread emerging among scholars, including "sociologists, historians, anthropologists, as well as practitioners of ethnic, legal, cultural and literary studies."[7] This recognition was partial at best. In 1995, when a sociologist and close friend of mine mentioned to a fellow sociologist in her department that she was studying whiteness, her surprised colleague replied, in all sincerity, "Oh, you can't do that!" There was no such thing as white culture, he claimed. But scholars were indeed studying whiteness, even if their colleagues looked askance and questioned the appropriateness of their work. Later that year the *Chronicle of Higher Education,* a major trade journal of the academic world, printed an article naming fifteen scholars from around the country engaged in research on whiteness. Many had published, or would soon publish, books on the topic. Reportedly, the scholars sought "to understand what it means to be white, and how white identity came into being."[8]

The *Chronicle* report helped legitimize the study of whiteness among academicians. A year later *Lingua Franca*, another journal devoted to identifying academic trends, ran a lengthy report on "the rise of whiteness studies." Cautiously saying, "It may not be premature to speak of a new humanities subfield," the *Lingua Franca* article mapped the recent evolution of thought taking place.[9] Whiteness studies had become "the in thing."

Word was getting out within the exclusive realm of the academy, but one still had to be an insider to stumble upon this new academic phenomenon. The public, including even educated observers of cultural trends, were still by and large unaware of this emerging body of scholarship. The Berkeley conference changed all that. Reports of the conference appeared in several newspapers and magazines, including the front page of the *Wall Street Journal,* and reporters started asking about this new thing called "white studies."[10] Before the Berkeley conference, occasional articles and book reviews discussed the work of individual scholars studying whiteness in isolation. Afterwards, the media began to report on "white studies" as a field. So it was, for example, that later the same year in a *New York Times Magazine* article on the topic, Margaret Talbot characterized white studies as "a new, very hot academic field," that was "the academic trend de jour."[11]

Since the Berkeley conference, several other academic conferences on whiteness have taken place, including at least one in Australia. Although the United States seems to be the acknowledged leader in the field, scholars in Canada, Great Britain, South Africa, Australia, New Zealand, the Netherlands, and Germany are exploring the topic. Within the United States, whiteness studies has become, to quote an invited presenter at the Berkeley conference, "an academic industry."[12]

It is a common observation among people working in race relations that white people will not believe something if a person of color says it, but the same white people will accord the same message credibility if they hear it from another white person. This is a dynamic of the privileged. Much the same happens between men and women. Many hold this dynamic to be racist, or sexist as the case may be, and indeed it is. There is an element of this phenomenon in the growth of white studies. People of color have been studying whiteness for a long time, but it has only become a featured topic in the academy now that white people are talking about it too.

Yet if anything is to become a topic of mainstream interest, even if that stream is an elite rivulet within the academic world, it necessarily must involve white people. We form a numerical majority and we hold power and resources in even greater proportion than our number. So it is inevitable that, as white studies moves toward the center of academic activity, white people will be increasingly involved in the undertaking.

The involvement of white people in popularizing white studies is thus problematic, reflecting a long-standing trend. Like Elvis appropriating the style of black rock and rollers and then cracking the white mass market, the academic market has been wedged open by white scholars responding to earlier calls from people of color. Indeed, given the racial structure of our society, which is after all a racist one, it could not be otherwise. Had white studies remained an enterprise exclusively among people of color, it would continue to be as marginal as the position of people of color in that racial structure.

Why White Studies?

Why study "whiteness?" Is it a ploy to bring white supremacist views into colleges and universities? The academic world supports the expectation that anything is worthy of study. Thus explaining one's purpose for studying something is sometimes viewed as superfluous, if not an outright sign of loss of objectivity. Occasionally, though, some explanations are given. The organizers of the 1997 Berkeley conference on the "Making and Unmaking of Whiteness," for instance, wrote that their purpose was to be "critical of whiteness in a society which has traditionally valued 'white folks' above all others."[13] Mike Hill, a prolific contributor to the field, has said of white studies, "The explicit goal of this work...is to move whiteness from the center."[14] Looked at another way, the problem under study is white people and our central role in the racial structure of our society. The aim of this study is to modify our role in that structure in a way that fosters a society centered on multiracial values.

Yet those white people who began to popularize the notion that whiteness needs to be studied not only answered a call from people of color. They also inflected their work with their personal experience, which was itself white. If the task at hand was, and is, to act upon the role of white people in our society, then it necessarily involves speaking to and changing white experience. People of color, as outsiders, have often displayed penetrating insight into the white psyche. But those who are white themselves speak with an authority and experience of their own.[15]

How did it all come about? How did the notion of whiteness, originally raised as a topic by people of color and lingering on the margin of white academic thought for nearly a century, finally become an academic industry? While academic phenomena, just as any other, involve people and places, it is the history of published works that provides the greatest definition to a scholarly enterprise. So it is worthwhile to review some of the earlier published works, beginning around about the time some white scholars began to answer the call of people of color and look at their own whiteness in earnest.

Laying the Foundations

In a 1970 book titled *White Racism: A Psychohistory,* Joel Kovel used psychoanalytic theory to explore the psyche of white people .[16] Unlike previous studies, Kovel departed from examining the psychologically disturbed bigot and turned his attention to the average white person. And

154

he did not confine his analysis strictly to the individual mind. Rather, he believed history and culture contributed to the psychological makeup of white Americans. Much of that history and culture had racist origins and continued to have racist undertones in the present, Kovel argued. In fact, racism remained a constant in America, though its expression had continued to change over time. Psychohistory was, according to Kovel, "the study of the changing meaning of things" (p. 96). Racism had changed from a hot and personal form he named "dominative racism" to a cold and removed form he called "aversive racism." Rapidly developing on the horizon was "metaracism" which expressed itself in institutional forms. All three forms continued to exist, although the latter two forms were less commonly understood by white people to constitute racism. Kovel's book took the important steps of locating racism outside of individual bigots, identifying its changing nature, and pointing to the structural aspects of white culture and its institutions as a source of the continuing "white problem."

In the same year, 1970, Robert W. Terry explored the social and political implications of white consciousness.[17] Repeating the theme that racism is a "white problem," Terry affirmed that many whites felt "threatened, bewildered, upset and angry" (p. 15) after receiving contradictory messages from outspoken black people about what to do regarding racism. White people should not only listen to black people, said Terry, but also begin to develop our own agenda. Many white activists took on a colorblind perspective, yet "Protestations to deny whiteness eliminate neither the fact nor the problem of white privilege" (p. 18). Other activists overidentified with blackness, but the sticky problem of privilege remained. "To understand whites as the basic problem, is to change consciousness radically" (p. 25). Something new was needed, something which Terry named a "new white consciousness."

Racial consciousness, the bugaboo of colorblindness, was not the problem. It was what you did with it. New whites, those antiracist white people conscious of whiteness, needed to recognize that white people could change, develop ethical clarity, recognize racism, create strategies for change, plan tactics, and live personal lifestyles affirming new values. For those who might misunderstand his notion of new white consciousness, Terry cautioned that no group has the "one best way" to end racism. Though whites are the problem, we are not the exclusive solution. Solving the white problem requires people of all races working in coalition. Also, white people are at different stages in understanding whiteness and racism, and approaches need to be tailored differently for each stage. Finally, action, not changed feelings, ultimately measures new whites.

155

Terry's book remarkably anticipates themes of our new century, including those guiding and motivating much of white studies. Continuing and reinforcing the conceptualization of racism as a white problem, he identified white privilege as an issue that whites can deny but cannot avoid, and called for an explicit examination of whiteness as a point of theorizing and action. He even anticipated stage theories of white racial identity. Terry also raised the point that "Being anti-racist is not enough. Defining what we are *against* moves into clarifying what we are *for*" (p. 1). Even today the question "What are we for?" begs an answer. The scholars are preoccupied finding the dimensions of the problem.

"Racism is a white problem," Judith H. Katz and Allen Ivey forthrightly state in the first line of their 1977 article, "White Awareness: The Frontier of Racism Awareness Training."[18] Noting that racism made white people in the helping profession less effective, Katz and Ivey argued that white culture encapsulates white people, leaving us unable to see that we, and not simply people of color, are affected by racism. *"White people do not see themselves as white"* (p. 486), they observed, and this is a way of denying personal involvement in the "white problem."

Katz and Ivey critiqued existing antiracism training programs stressing communication and helping people of color for ignoring the fact that white people "need more help than those whom they are tying to help" (p. 485). Citing several formulations of counseling that describe the goal of treatment as resolving incongruities between attitudes, self-concept, and actions and behavior, the authors observed that white culture implicates white people in racism. We deny this, and in doing so distort reality and build a false identity. White people experience a split between attitudes and behavior, the "American dilemma" posed by Gunnar Myrdal. "Whites must identify with the culture and their whiteness, not as a luxury but as an integral part of who they are. To deny or reject any part of our being hinders us from becoming a fully developed and whole person" (p. 486).

Placing people of color in the position of teaching white people about racism exploited the teachers, explained Katz and Ivey, both white themselves. The learning benefits accrued to white people, and thus other whites should take responsibility for designing programs and learning experiences. People of color should not be required to do all the work. Thus the authors called for white-on-white training programs, suggesting and detailing one model in their article.

Pointedly writing to an audience of helping professionals, Katz and Ivey underscored that denying whiteness made white professionals less helpful. Their article contains an early and powerful argument that racism affects white people and since we are affected, we need to take the responsibility for changing our culture.[19]

A Structure Deeper Than Words

Writing also in 1977, sociologist David T. Wellman criticized his profession for viewing racism simply in terms of hatred and misinformation held by individuals.[20] According to Wellman, "Most white Americans experience some sort of privilege at the expense of black people....Thus in varying ways, all white Americans have formulated strategies for justifying their privileged position" (p. 43).

Middle class academicians made poor whites the scapegoats for racism. But if the racial structure of society is to be undone, Wellman argued, then all white people will have to share power and resources. When, where, how, and to whom that happened was key to analyzing racism. Integrating working class neighborhoods and schools is one thing, but forcing open positions for faculty of color in historically white colleges and universities is quite another. Or maybe, as Wellman said, only the language is different. The issues changed from "black" and "white" to "quality" and "merit," but the effect was the same and that was the point. By whatever means necessary, white people of whatever social class, from poor, to middle, to upper, all acted to keep the racial structure of our society in place, and in doing so, preserved their privileged and advantaged position as white people.

Racism is more than prejudice. Middle class white people are trained to be tolerant and consequently they feel constrained to uphold egalitarian ideals. Yet they act to maintain their privilege. Thus the "concrete problem facing white people is how to come to grips with the demands made by blacks while at the same time *avoiding* the possibility of institutional change and reorganization that might affect them. Put another way, they must be able to explain racial inequality *without* implicating themselves" (p. 42). Explanations are found. Generally the onus is put back on black people and "white racial privilege is maintained" (p. 42).

Wellman based his ideas on a series of interviews with white people. Their concerns rested not so much on rejecting black people as they did upon fears that their own white American norms, institutions, standards, and priorities would change. In traditional terms, these people were not prejudiced though, from a standpoint of dismantling the racial structure of our society, they might as well be. Racism was not hatred and bigotry, but rather defending a system of white racial privilege and advantage. Consequently, the "racist nature of their thinking is not minimized by the fact that white people are often unaware of the extent to which their advantaged position is based on race. The consequence is the same as if they were conscious of it" (p. 235).

Social scientists Benjamin P. Bowser and Raymond G. Hunt found that "Of the hundreds of writers who have produced thousands of books and articles on race in the last three decades, few of them had ever directly confronted the question: What effects does racism have on Whites?" (p. 245). So in 1981 they edited a book titled *Impacts of Racism on White Americans.*[21] Repeating an increasingly expressed perspective, they, too, took the starting point that racism is a "white problem."

Before compiling their book, the editors made an extensive search for information, going as far as securing a grant from the National Institute of Mental Health and holding a conference of interested researchers. Bowser and Hunt found "after thinking about the task we were proposing for them, several…prominent students of racism either declined to accept it, or, after a first cut at it, abandoned it, or else never were able to get beyond talking about non-Whites as objects of the effects of racism" (p. 245). Writing about white people was not easy, partly due to the fact that one's own culture is hard to see. According to Bowser and Hunt, that is "why white America has had to depend so heavily on non-Whites, as in this book, to tell it about itself" (p. 255).

Impacts contains twelve chapters by sixteen authors discussing topics of socialization, attitude change, mental health, white values, poverty policies, economics, U.S. foreign relations, capitalism, and interracial coalitions. It was a forward-looking book and the first reader in white studies (though not acknowledged as such either then or now). Editing and publishing such a book took more than scholarly persistence and acumen. It took courage to swim against white subconsciousness that disdained those who chose to examine it. One of the editors, in retrospect, believes the controversial nature of the book had a negative impact on his career.

Troubled Visions Among Feminists

Social and cultural critic and black feminist bell hooks devoted a chapter of her 1981 book, *Ain't I a Woman: Black Women and Feminism,* to dissecting the underlying whiteness (and middle- and upper-classness) of the post-1960s feminist movement.[22] Sexism was a worldwide problem, hooks agreed, but racism was the organizing concept behind American society. White men did not exclude white women as they had men and women of color. Though white women often blamed America's racism on white men, saying in effect they were innocent and the guys did it, hooks points out that white women benefited from the arrangement. Furthermore she carefully documented the history of feminism in the United States going back to the first half of the 19th century, during which time white women frequently excluded women of color from their ranks.

Modern white feminists showed a distressing tendency to write as if white women represented all women:

> The force that allows white feminist authors to make no reference to racial identity in their books about "women" that are in actuality about white women is the same one that would compel any author writing exclusively on black women to refer explicitly to their racial identity. That force is racism. In a racially imperialistic nation such as ours, it is the dominant race that reserves for itself the luxury of dismissing racial identity while the oppressed race is made daily aware of their racial identity. It is the dominant race that can make it seem that their experience is representative (p. 138).

Even more problematic was their frequent comparison of the circumstances of "women and blacks" as if the women were only white, and blacks had no gender:

> It was not in the opportunistic interests of white middle and upper class participants in the women's movement to draw attention to the plight of poor women, or the specific plight of black women. A white woman professor who wants the public to see her as victimized and oppressed because she is denied tenure is not about to evoke images of poor women working as domestics receiving less than the minimum wage struggling to raise a family single-handed. Instead it is far more likely she will receive attention and sympathy if she says, "I'm a nigger in the eyes of my white colleagues" (p. 142–143).

Patriarchy, hooks acknowledged, was significant and the moving force behind racism, and unity among women was critical for progress. She was not a separatist, yet she was voicing a sense of realism. Feminism was based on promoting the entrance of middle- and upper-class white women into the white male power structure, without otherwise changing that structure to make it multiracial and responsive to working class and poor people. According to hooks, "it seemed incredible to black women that they were being asked to support a movement whose majority participants were eager to maintain race and class hierarchies between women" (p. 149).

Two years later, in 1983, Marilyn Frye published a collection of nine essays in feminist theory. Among them was one titled, "On Being White: Toward a Feminist Understanding of Race and Race Supremacy."[23] Having listened to the running critique of feminism by women of color, Frye felt obliged to examine her status as white and ponder the implications of whiteness in general. Finding herself personally criticized by women of color for either acting or not acting, Frye experienced the frustrating feeling that no matter what one did, one was wrong because it was done from a position of race privilege. Noting that her thoughts were preliminary and should be read as such, Frye asked "What is this 'being white' that gets me into so much trouble, after so many years of seeming to me to be so benign? What is this privilege of race? What is race?" (p. 113).

Race is Gendered

Feminists have pointed out that the racial structure of our society is intertwined with a gender structure as well. White women, for instance, have historically been used by white men as an excuse to police black men. However, historical facts suggest that white women had little desire for such protection, and that white men had little concern for the general welfare of white women. Under the guise of defending white womanhood, white men were able to economically exploit black people. Respectability, a property ascribed by white men to white women, has never been granted by white men to women of color. Womanhood was only sacred when white. In the meantime, some white men acted as sexual predators toward women of color, and white men as a class failed to condemn their actions. Rape was only condemned when the offender was black or the victim white. Not only are race and gender intertwined, so too are class, sexual orientation, and other forms of social difference. Privilege and oppression interact in sometimes complex ways. One cannot lose sight of these interlocking structures.

Replying to her own question, Frye noted that whiteness is socially constructed. And among other things, white people claimed the right to supervise its construction. On one occasion we might exclude people of color because they do not have the "pure" white heritage that whiteness historically has required. At other times, we might insist that a light-skinned person of multiracial heritage who has white cultural communication skills is in fact white. This might be done over the protestations of the person involved. Either way, it is white people deciding who is white, and that is one example of where privilege lies.

Though Frye's essay is disjointed, given its exploratory nature, she raises several ideas. White people, or white women—for Frye was focusing on a gendered experience as well—need to educate themselves, studying not only about others of whom one is ignorant, but also why one is ignorant to begin with. This effort might be obscured if one aspires to the social and political rewards of whiteness, and thereby nearly white maleness, itself.

According to Frye, white men need white women to support our own white supremacy and to reproduce ourselves and our system. Tying this to the concerns of women of color, Frye asks with whom are white women seeking equality. She wryly points out "we can hardly expect to be heard as saying we want social and economic status equal to that of, say, Chicanos" (p. 125). Yet equality with white men means being equally complicit with white men in racial dominance. Thus Frye contends pursuit of white women's liberation from white men and our attending need for racial dominance is "disloyal to Whiteness" and recommends "that we make this disloyalty an explicit part of our politics and embrace it, publicly" (p. 126). What the social constructedness of whiteness "can mean to white people is that we are not white by nature but by political classification, and hence it is in principle possible to disaffiliate" (p. 118).[24]

If people have heard or read anything about white privilege at all, it is likely to have been Peggy McIntosh's 1988 paper *White Privilege and Male Privilege: A Personal Account of Coming to See Correspondences through Work in Women's Studies*.[25] Working from her experience that men often failed to see male privilege, McIntosh considered that she might be equally unaware of her privilege as a white person. Thus alerted, she began to make personal observations about how white privilege acted in her life. Eventually she developed a list of 46 specific situations in which white privilege granted her an advantage that her African-American female colleagues did not have.

Oppressions and privileges are acknowledged and highlighted by McIntosh as interlocking with some generalized aspects, yet with other characteristics that are particular to the type of privilege and oppression under consideration. She makes several observations about the operation of white privilege, including that she was taught to "remain oblivious" to its existence. Taboos exist in white culture silencing discussion of white privilege by either white people or people of color. Our schooling fails to teach us about oppression, advantage, and the effects of all this on white people, let alone people of color. Our schools, the media, even "the economic system, [and] the general look of people in the streets" (p. 11) teach us that white people count and people of color don't.

McIntosh kept forgetting the points on her list of privileges until she wrote them down. The pressures on white people for denial are great because the stakes are so high. "Describing white privilege makes one newly accountable" (p. 2), she wrote, adding,

> If these things are true, this is not such a free country; one's life is not what one makes it; many doors open for certain people through no virtues of their own. These perceptions mean also that my moral condition is not what I had been led to believe. The appearance of being a good citizen rather than a troublemaker comes in large part from having all sorts of doors open automatically because of my color (p. 9).

Individual awareness of privilege, McIntosh warns, is not enough. A massive redesign of social systems is needed. But awareness is a first step, for,

> to redesign social systems we need first to acknowledge their colossal unseen dimensions. The silences and denials surrounding privilege are the key political tool here. They keep the thinking about equality or equity incomplete, protecting unearned advantage and conferred dominance by making these taboo subjects (p. 18).

This article, among all the articles written on white privilege, has probably done the most to bring the notion of white privilege before the white public in a way that is immediately understandable. The list of 46 items is particularly powerful, leading white people to recognize, "aha" fashion, a formerly unacknowledged part of their lives. Used repeatedly in workshops, classrooms, and other settings, McIntosh's article has paved the way for additional work with the interested and concerned white public.

Representation of What?

Using the succinct title, "White," Richard Dyer opened up whiteness as an area of investigation in film in 1988.[26] Representations of other, non-dominant, groups such as "women, working class, ethnic and other minorities" (p. 44) had been studied but the norm itself, whiteness, remained unexplored. Not that such examination was easy. Dyer began by saying,

> this is an article about a subject that, much of the time as I've been writing it, seems not to be there as a subject at all. Trying to think about the representation of whiteness as an ethnic category in mainstream film is difficult, partly because white power secures its dominance by seeming not to be anything in particular, but also because, when whiteness *qua* whiteness does come into focus, it is often revealed as emptiness, absence, denial or even a kind of death (p. 44).

Whiteness had a power to be everything and nothing, following a contemporary social form in which power "passes itself off as embodied in the normal as opposed to the superior" (p. 45). Hence whiteness is often invisible and seen as an "historical accident" (p. 46) rather than the product of a specific history that includes domination of people of color. The invisibility of whiteness—the "colourless multi-colouredness," as Dyed named it—preserves white power by making whiteness hard to analyze. Thus:

> The subject seems to fall apart in your hands as soon as you begin. Any instance of white representation is always immediately something more specific—*Brief Encounter* is not about white people, it is about

English middle-class people; *The Godfather* is not about white people, it is about Italian-American people; but *The Color Purple* is about black people, before it is about poor, Southern U.S. people (p. 46).

Yet difficult as the task may have been, Dyer analyzed representations of whiteness in three popular films: *Jezebel* (1938), *Simba* (1955), and *Night of the Living Dead* (1969). Noting first the similarities among them, Dyer found they associated whiteness "with order, rationality, [and] rigidity," (p. 47–48) and a "dependency of white on black in a context of continued power and privilege that throws the legitimacy of white domination into question" (p. 48).

In the *Night of the Living Dead* the dead were white, and even the living white people characterized in death-like poses, sometimes inseparable from the zombies they sought to destroy. Interestingly enough, the zombies could be vanquished by destroying their heads, or by burning. The former method invokes images of white hyper-rationality (cold rationality and logic) and the latter the prevalent association by whites in 1969 of fire with black protest ("Burn, baby, burn," as heard in the white imagination). The fact that eventually all three of the *Living Dead* films had a black man in the lead role was significant "because it makes it possible to see that whites are the living dead" (p. 59). Ultimately, the whites, both living and dead, lose control of their bodies, expressing another deeply seated white cultural fear.

In 1989 Toni Morrison discussed the process of incorporating African-American writing into the "canon," a term used by academicians that corresponds roughly with the notion of "great works of literature."[27] Within the scope of a much longer article, she argued that literary critics (such as professors of English, literary studies, and related fields) have missed something.

> I am made melancholy when I consider that the act of defending the Eurocentric Western posture in literature as not only "universal" but also "race-free" may have resulted in lobotomizing the literature, and in diminishing both the art and the artist (p. 13).

Literary criticism looks behind the surface of a written work to discover its deeper social, psychological, and cultural meanings. Racial conditions influence and inform each of these levels of meaning, but are often ignored by both the writer and critic. Morrison offered as an example that around 1850 when racial strife was tearing the nation apart, American writers turned to romance as a theme. Kind of like Nero fiddling while Rome burned. Somewhere, Morrison argues, the smoke and flames must have found their way into the literature of that time. Ferreting out the unconscious and hidden presence of race is a task suitable to the critic.

American "Madmen," Fictitious and Real

Captain Ahab, of *Moby Dick* fame, is a classic example of a character so seized by an obsession that he forsakes all other social concerns and single-handedly pursues his impossible scheme, ultimately to his own destruction. Not only was he dragged down to his doom, but those who were unwittingly caught in his plan shared a similar fate. Toni Morrison has brought fresh insight to the *Moby Dick* tale by suggesting the great white whale was in fact whiteness itself. As she points out, in the mid-19th century, any white man tackling whiteness would indeed seem crazed.[28] Though Morrison did not draw the comparison, it's note-worthy that by the end of the same decade in which *Moby Dick* appeared, a real white man took on whiteness in the real world of politics and racial dominance. History accords John Brown and his deeds the same character of heroic and trag-ically doomed madness as his fictional white counterpart, captain Ahab. And like Ahab's ship and doomed crew, the nation itself was dragged into a violent fate—the Civil War.

Using the quintessential *Moby Dick* to make her point, Morrison took issue with the traditional interpretation that the white whale stood for brutish nature challenged by the madman captain Ahab. It wasn't so much that the creature was a whale as it was that the whale was white. Melville himself titled a famous chapter "The Whiteness of the Whale" and wrote of this whiteness, "I almost despair of putting it in a comprehensive form. It was the whiteness of the whale that above all things appalled me. But how can I hope to explain myself here; and yet in some dim, random way, explain myself I must, *else all these chapters might be naught*."[29] Morrison italicized the last portion of this passage quoted in her article to demonstrate the impor-tance Melville placed on his metaphor. She pointedly said she did not believe Melville was "satanizing white people." Rather, "he was overwhelmed by the philosophical and metaphysical inconsistencies of an extraordinary and unprecedented idea that had its fullest manifestation in his own time in his own country, and that idea was the successful assertion of whiteness as ide-ology" (p. 16). In other words "Melville is not exploring white people, but whiteness idealized" (p. 17).

Set against a multiracial crew, Ahab, the captain, is a madman. Not mad because he opposes slavery, or capitalism, or the savagery of nature as previous critics had suggested. He is mad because he opposes the very notion of whiteness itself. In the end he is destroyed and the whale goes on. Morrison added that not only Melville, but also Poe, Hawthorne, Twain, Cather, Hemingway, Fitzgerald, and Faulkner "will sustain such a reading" (p. 18).

Twenty Years in the Making

The foregoing articles and books appeared over a twenty year period, from 1970 to 1989. Other important works included the white racial identity theory of Janet Helms and a line of research on white racism identified with psychologists John F. Dovidio and Samuel L. Gaertner.[30] Altogether about a dozen significant articles and books appeared. Significant because they identified whiteness and developed an analysis of white privilege and white racism as part of the racial structure of our society. They characterized the negative impact of whiteness on democratic values and expressed a desire for transforming whiteness. Finally, they were well-known among those people who might make some effort to find them, as reflected in multiple printings, second editions, and frequent citations in later works.

During this same period other works were authored, but today are not as well-known or easily obtained. Examples are doctoral dissertations, unpublished papers, and reports given limited circulation. Some appear in the reference sections of works already cited. Others can be found by the dedicated researcher. The early 1970s seems to have been an important time and might even be characterized as a first wave in whiteness studies, but the work died prematurely.

Still other works appeared not directly discussing whiteness in name, but laying the foundation for future efforts. One example is *American Slavery, American Freedom,* by Edmund S. Morgan, identified by *Lingua Franca* as a significant predecessor to the line of historical research on whiteness appearing in the early 1990s.[31] Other books discussed whiteness under a larger perspective on race and ethnicity and/or in comparative terms. Examples are *Black and White Styles in Conflict,* by Thomas Kochman (see Chapter 6) and *Understanding Race, Ethnicity, & Power,* by Elaine Pinderhughes (see Chapter 7).[32]

Looking at the body of work up to 1990, contributors consisted of feminists, psychologists, sociologists, and other occasional scholars. They were scattered, isolated, out of the mainstream of scholarly interest, and marginalized, even in their own fields. I believe it is important to acknowledge their contributions. Indeed, even more importantly, we must recognize their intellectual courage and moral fortitude, for it could not have been easy. They stand as pioneers, blazing a path in an uncharted wilderness. Yet the wilderness remained vast. In any given month between 1970 and 1989, among all the scholars in the academy, hundreds of books and thousands of articles were published. Looking over that twenty-year period, the totality of work on whiteness, counting even the hard-to-find reports and dissertations, measured less than a single day's total output from the academic knowledge factory.

Putting Whiteness on the Map

Whether it was the efforts of the forerunners already discussed or whether it was something whose time had simply come, in the 1990s something different happened. Over the four year period from 1990 through 1993 the output of significant work on whiteness equaled that of the preceding twenty years. Though certainly opinion may vary, a list might include: 1990 — *Ethnic Identity: The Transformation of White America,* by Richard Alba; "Representing Whiteness: Seeing Wings of Desire," in *Yearning,* by bell hooks; *Rise and Fall of the White Republic,* by Alexander Saxton; *Black and White Racial Identity: Theory, Research and Practice,* by Janet Helms; 1991 — *The Wages of Whiteness: Race and the Making of the American Working Class,* by David Roediger; 1992 — "Representing Whiteness in the Black Imagination," by bell hooks; *Playing in the Dark: Whiteness and the Literary Imagination,* by Toni Morrison; *Beyond the Pale: White Women, Racism and History,* by Vron Ware; 1993 — "Whiteness as Property," by Cheryl Harris; *White Women, Race Matters: The Social Construction of Whiteness,* by Ruth Frankenberg; *Love and Theft: Black Face Minstrelsy and the American Working Class,* by Eric Lott.

It was becoming increasingly clear that the old comparative approach, in which people of color are regarded as different and white people as normal, was being challenged. These new works went beyond pointing to Eurocentric bias and calling for other views to appear. Rather it was whiteness itself that was being studied as a perspective. Scholars had moved from saying the universal normative perspective is white. Using that as a starting point, they asked instead, "What are the particulars of the white perspective, and how do they allow whiteness to make itself out as universal?"[33]

In the two years of 1994 and 1995 as many, if not more, books and articles were published as in the previous four years. The study of whiteness was developing a critical mass, growing exponentially with each new year. By 1996 it became a full-blown area of academic involvement. Whether measured in courses offered,[34] research undertaken, doctoral dissertations written, articles and books published, curriculums revised, dedicated issues of journals released, or conference panels and symposia organized, white studies had worked itself into the heart of the academic world. The name "white studies" itself began to emerge around this time as scholars realized their individual efforts were embedded in an enterprise that had acquired a life beyond their individual acts of creation.[35] By the time the Berkeley conference came about in the Spring of 1997, white studies had become a clearly recognized feature on the terrain of the academy.

White Studies — A Tourist's View

It's one thing to understand white studies has arrived and quite another to understand what it is being studied. The most common observation among people doing white studies is that whiteness is hard to see and describe. So what exactly do scholars look at when they do white studies? In 1997 a prominent scholar said of white studies, "it is impossible to analyze this large body of work in any great detail." Bearing that in mind, let's take a quick walk through some of the topics scholars have scrutinized.[36]

In the field of **American studies,** George Lipsitz described how whiteness has been given government support throughout United States history, including the 20th century, yet white people, who believe in a liberal individualism, fail to see this structural support for their material, social, and economic conditions. Instead, they use cultural explanations to describe white privilege and black disadvantage. Shelley Fisher Fishkin reviewed over 100 books and articles that together convincingly demonstrate that American culture, held by many to be so obviously white that it hardly deserves comment, is anything but so. Whiteness, American-style, is influenced by, and in turn influences, other racial and cultural traditions. Maria Deguzman examined the way one of these traditions, the imagery and symbols of Spain, shaped the Anglo-American identity formed after the Revolutionary War, and Mia Elisabeth Bay looked at images of white Americans expressed by black Americans in the 19th and 20th centuries.

Anthropologist Karen Brodkin Sacks described the 1920s as a time when scientific and popular opinion held that Jews and other groups of eastern and southern European heritage formed distinct and inferior races, yet in the 1950s suburb of her childhood these groups had become "white." She showed how massive government outlays from the GI bill coupled with explicit bans on funding of mixed-race neighborhoods by the FHA helped accomplish this amazing transformation. John Hartigan Jr. looked at white people who did not move to the suburbs, discussing his findings from working and living among poor whites in Detroit.

Business and marketing expert John P. Fernandez described how whites, and particularly white men, in corporations are affected by racism. David V. Day and Christina A. Douglas assessed the racial consciousness of white managers in an exploratory study intended to incorporate whiteness as a component of models of organizational functioning. Sharon L. Howell demonstrated how a contemporary management theory of "the learning organization" implicitly embeds whiteness at its core.

Cultural studies has taken a comparatively broad look at whiteness. Leslie G. Roman analyzed a tendency for whites to believe that simple knowledge of people of color, and an assumed position of love and concern for their condition, change the material and structural conditions of oppression. Thus multicultural programs that do little more than incorporate images of "the other" into texts may simply sustain white privilege. bell hooks, standing outside of whiteness as an African-American woman, described how whiteness seems foreign, invasive, and terrorizing to people of color. Relatively early, in 1990, she called for white producers and consumers of culture to be aware of how their own race figured in their experience. France Winndance Twine has explored the formation of white identities among young, suburban, multiracial women of African (along with Asian or white) descent raised in white middle-class suburbs, and their subsequent diverging experiences from monoracial white women in a shared college setting. Fred Pfeil has taken a long (book length) look at "white guys," analyzing everything from action films to rock and roll artists and the men's movement. Educator Peter McLaren has considered different ways white people might transform their current monocultural and privileged identities. Rejecting schemes that position whites as inherently exploitative or suggest that becoming black is a solution, he calls for a hybrid multicultural identity connected to a global, as opposed to a nationalistic and white, frame of reference.

Educators like McLaren, though still not reflecting the central ideology of their field, have positioned education in the vanguard of the service professions when it comes to examining the impact of whiteness on their practice. Christine E. Sleeter has described her classroom methods designed to encourage white in-service teaching students to examine perspectives other than that of their own culture. Alice McIntyre looked at the way white female student teachers constructed their racial identity and how this impacted their role as teachers. Pearl M. Rosenberg talks of the difficulties of looking at race with preservice teachers in a virtually all-white (literally 99%) university setting in New Hampshire. Classroom discussions faltered and teaching strategies were not institutionally supported, but covert discussions between teacher and students during off hours revealed an assortment of racial concerns. Linda Valli described the issues and resolutions white preservice teachers confronted in their student teaching practice among students of color in urban settings.

Henry A. Giroux, taking the lead from other scholars of whiteness studies, asked how a pedagogy might be developed to encourage students to reformulate their identity in support of social reform directed toward a racially just society. Discussing the popular film, *Dangerous Minds,* he suggested analysis of its images of whiteness affords one such technique. Maryann Dickar reviewed several autobiographical accounts by white teachers of their experiences teaching in urban schools with student bodies predominantly of color. She identified deflecting, evasive, and individualizing strategies used by the teachers to avoid confronting their own whiteness and the racial structure of the setting. Gary R. Howard considered the role of whites in multicultural education and called for a redefinition of white identity that eschews dominance by critically looking at past and present practices. Dario J. Almarza looked at how the Eurocentric history curriculum being taught to Mexican-American adolescents ignored the experiences and culture of the students and produced a generally negative and alienating experience of history.

Charting the Growth of White Studies

In the mid-1990s the Center for the Study of White American Culture performed a computer keyword search for articles in psychology, sociology, education, and social work that discussed whiteness and white identity. Altogether 85 articles were identified as having been published in the 28 years prior to 1994. From 1965 to 1979 the number of articles increased during each five-year period, with 18 articles published in the last five years of the 1970s. The decade of the 1980s saw a clear drop, with an average of 10 articles published in each half of the decade. In the first four years of the 1990s, however, a record number of articles, 32 in total, appeared. This four-year total exceeded the entire output of the 1980s by a factor of 50%, and even eclipsed the more prolific 1970s. A similar study of dissertations in 1998, again by the Center for the Study of White American Culture, confirmed this pattern. Publications rose in the 1970s, dropped in the 1980s, then exploded in the 1990s. Forty-eight dissertations, more than half of all dissertations published since 1970, appeared during the three- year period of 1995 through 1997. The data clearly show an initial interest in white studies took place through the 1970s, only to wither during the 1980s. Now the second and greater wave of interest is upon us, with no signs of diminishing.

Ethnic studies scholar and lead organizer of the Berkeley conference, Matt Wray, recounted being steeped in visions of the Apocalypse common to the "white trash" religious surrounds of his boyhood. From an explicitly Afrocentric stance, Marimba Ani authored a comprehensive critique of European (and European-American) culture from the time of Plato to the present, arguing that an unchecked drive to dominate corrupts its essential core. Among the many **film and television studies** scholars have produced on whiteness, Eric Lott looked at *film noir,* a genre of 1940s and 1950s movies in which people of color in minor roles often foreshadow, accompany, and set the stage as white characters descend into the murky and troubled depths of moral disintegration. Ann duCille recalled her frustrated attempts as a black girl to live up to the film image of Shirley Temple. The image, she demonstrated, enhanced its whiteness through contrasts with supporting and submissive black characters. Corrine Squire found contemporary television talk shows follow the mainstream practice of not naming whiteness, but highlight both a "white trash" whiteness and then complicate it with unremarked images of miscegenation. Daniel Leonard Bernardi explored the television and film series, *Star Trek,* locating ways it was influenced by political imagery from white culture.

Historian David Roediger wrote an early and influential history of the formation of the white working class in the United States during the first half of the 19th century. At times comparing themselves to slaves and in other moments emphasizing their status as free white labor, the white working class solidified their whiteness and made race the most meaningful division among the laboring classes. Theodore W. Allen mapped the process of racialization developed by the English in both Ireland and the United States, and the different course and resulting outcomes it produced in each setting. Noel Ignatiev looked at Irish immigrants in the Philadelphia area. Originally living and working side by side with black people, and considered by native white Americans to be black, the Irish took great pains, including mob violence, to force blacks out of the trades and from their neighborhoods. Grace Elizabeth Hale mapped the transition of the post–Civil War South to a consumer economy in which segregation marked the boundaries of whiteness.

Law professor Cheryl I. Harris demonstrated the law has treated whiteness as property, with rights of use and enjoyment, transfer, and exclusion of others. Consistently upholding the property interests of whiteness, the courts have been unreceptive to counterclaims based on rights of inclusion. Ian F. Haney López looked at the series of cases determining who was white. The very physical appearance of our population and nation has been determined by these cases, he pointed out convincingly. Barbara J. Flagg identified "transparency," the inability of law to see race as a component in white people's lives (only people of color have a race) as a major source of bias in the law and recommended several procedures to correct the skewed reasoning transparency produces.

Putting on a **literary studies** hat, Toni Morrison arguably wrote the most influential work in white studies and the humanities when she elaborated on the ideas of her 1989 *Michigan Quarterly Review* article in her 1992 book, *Playing in the Dark: Whiteness and the Literary Imagination.* Among several dissertations following this line of inquiry, Stephanie Athey looked at how white women writers used black women's bodies as a topic to demarcate white women's position in society, while black women writers simultaneously sought to undermine images of white womanhood. Maria Joy Bergstrom interpreted novels and film to show writers used the American West and racialized others to explore white American masculinity. Exploring another regional version of white masculinity, James Hull Watkins found that

Southern white autobiography emphasized community honor over the individualism valued in other regions such as New England. Martha Groves Perry found that Southern turn-of-the-century white supremacists used an Anglo-Saxon ideal to further their political beliefs and notion of nationhood. According to Marcia Klotz, German women achieved a privileged status in society to the extent that they supported colonial aspirations of the white German nation. Their position declined following World War I when women were scapegoated during a crisis of masculinity. Giavanna Jo Munfaro has shown how contemporary women novelists have explored social constructions of womanhood, both black and white, through interactive conflict, in the process exposing the hidden white patriarchal and supremacist practices of our society.

Gayle Wald takes whiteness as a topic in **music studies**, uncovering Janis Joplin's use of black women blues singers to develop her style and stance toward the 1960s' socially constraining images of white womanhood. Jeffrey Melnick raised the question of doo wop, a singing style performed by African-Americans that cut across racial lines, incorporated white imagery and styles, including Shakespeare (*West Side Story*), and did not present itself as racial, making the point that appropriation and cross-experimentation with racial styles are not limited to something white people do to black people. Robert Kenneth McMichael discussed integrationist cultures found among jazz audiences and communities from the 1920s to the present, looking at ways in which white members interpreted the character of African-American performers.

Psychologist Janet Helms further elaborated her stage theory of white racial identity (see Chapter 7) in a 1990 book, providing a scale to assess the stages of development among white people. Ann Phoenix surveyed 248 youth in London and found white Londoners, in comparison to black and mixed-race London youth, were less pleased and by far less proud of their racial identity. Espousing an egalitarian philosophy, they nonetheless experienced life in racialized terms. White people in the United States may not be anti-black in their attitudes but still are pro-white according to Samuel L. Gaertner, John F. Dovidio, and five additional researchers reporting on a line of investigation begun in the 1980s. Pro-whiteness does not fit the typical profile of hatred and bigotry, but has far-reaching legal and social policy implications.

Sociologists Joe R. Feagin and Hernán Vera produced a book-length study of white racism in 1990s mainstream society, documenting the costs to both people of color and white people. Notably their book includes discussion of whiteness, white consciousness, and white privilege. White America has been transformed according to Richard Alba, who surveyed white people in the late 1980s and found virtually all had lost their ethnic roots and blended into a nondescript mainstream version of whiteness.

171

Their children, according to Charles Gallagher, have become explicitly aware of being white due to media reporting on race, identity politics by people of color, the decline of ethnicity found by Alba, and a redefinition by the new right of whiteness as a positive, although besieged, identity. Howard Winant identified the visibility and vulnerability of whiteness to critique by people of color as a major change in the politics of the post–civil rights era, and mapped the impact of this change on five political "projects" ranging from the far right to the far left. Ashley W. Doane Jr. has critiqued sociology itself for its failure to examine dominant group identity and allowing whiteness to remain hidden, concentrating instead on "social problems" between minorities and the mainstream.

In the area of **speech communication,** Deborah Lynn Marty found white speakers on antiracism commonly opposed injustice for people of color but failed to take white privilege into account. Writing of her **theater** experience with a New York theater collective featuring feminist and lesbian works, Kate Davy explored how performance pieces critiquing an assumed norm of respectability for women in fact were white in character. Counter hegemonic performances by women of color accorded respectability a different function. She concludes whiteness itself must be marked in performance as social critique. **Theologian** James Willard Perkinson took on the task of developing "a white North American theology which is capable of challenging white racism."

In **women's studies** and other fields, scholars versed in **feminist theory** have been prolific in their examination of whiteness, in particular as it intersects with social roles of gender and class. Feminist interpretations and analysis have informed many of the works cited in this brief survey. Ruth Frankenberg's study, mentioned previously in Chapter 6, proved to be one of the more influential early works on whiteness of the 1990s. Becky Thompson also published an early autobiographical account of white identity development.

And we haven't even looked at **architecture, poetry, photography and art exhibits, performance art, economics, political science,** and **social work,** all of which have examples I might have included in the list. Doubtless other examples exist in other fields as well. Complete citations for the works covered in this tour are available in the Appendix.

Is It a Good Thing?

White studies, as a field, has received a mixed reception. The public at large finds it a curiosity, though recently some have come to view it as another attack on white men and are raising the reactionary hue and cry we've heard so often this past 20 years. Others simply see it as so much silliness being perpetrated on an otherwise centered public by a group of guilt-ridden white liberals, aided perhaps by a perpetually complaining cohort of people of color. Doubtless there is something of this going on, but no more so than in any other aspect of the "culture wars" that have pitted multiculturalism and conservatism against one another.

Perhaps the best indicator that white studies is a new paradigm, is that among those of a more liberal persuasion, this incipient "subfield of the humanities" has been viewed suspiciously. Some claim it is simply a "me too" response from white people who are jealous of the attention given other racial and cultural groups, each of whom has its own named programs of study. Though late in the game, white people supposedly are trying to catch up. Again, there is a ring of truth here, but as conservative critics have pointed out, white studies has displayed a different character from other programs of ethnic and cultural studies. While these other programs focus on celebratory perspectives and the uncovering and recovery of lost cultural experiences, white studies presently dedicates itself to dissecting white supremacy and domination, hardly something to celebrate except in its hoped-for passing.

Does White Studies Demonize White People?

The public has generally received white studies with curiosity and amusement. The obvious contrast with images of white supremacy often attracts attention. But once assured that white studies is not a white supremacist plot, most people chalk it up to simply another weird but not really important thing being produced by ivory tower eggheads. Some people see it as an attempt to portray white people in the worst possible light. Indeed, for those inclined to fear multiculturalism, there is some substance to their concern. White studies is not simply a clone of other ethnic studies programs that uncover and celebrate positive and unacknowledged aspects of cultural heritage. Instead, it focuses on how whiteness has led to racial domination and hegemony, two favored words in the white studies lexicon. Although many academicians admit there are positive aspects to white culture, little scholarly work has been done to describe them.

On the other hand, our secondary and elementary school systems continue to valorize white American culture, often simply calling it "American." And past scholarly practice has had a strong bias toward describing white American culture as the primary and positive force shaping our nation. White studies is a reaction to this unrealistically glowing treatment of white culture. Viewed in isolation it appears largely negative. But in the larger picture, it seeks to restore balance by presenting the side of whiteness left out of high school text books, mainstream public celebrations of "American" heritage, and media portrayals of our society in which color, especially whiteness, is described as unimportant.

Other critics have accepted that white studies may have a valid focus, but dismiss practitioners of white studies for having their heads in the clouds. It won't lead to real social change, they believe. Instead, it's simply a momentary trend, a fad. For those who are even more cynical, the claim is made that white studies is a good angle for a white person seeking a job in the highly competitive and chronically glutted labor market for faculty positions in higher education. But as this chapter describes, white studies has seen several decades of groundwork. Its recent blossoming in the 1990s may have the aspect of a fad, but if so, it was a long time in the making. Nor is the topic a superficial one. We are talking about the racial structure of the United States. Few topics have greater import.

A criticism of greater concern, at least to those who desire that we undo that racial structure, rests in the belief that white studies is not a fad, but a growing behemoth that will co-opt many of the resources now given to ethnic and cultural studies programs of other racial/cultural groups. After many long years of struggle to establish what even today is a tenuous foothold in the academy, proponents of these programs feel that white people, once again, will grab the goodies for ourselves. This might happen, it's true. But this fear is based on the assumption that a limited number of dollars is available for cultural and ethnic studies, when in fact society will increase or decrease the amount of funds depending on how important the topic appears to decision makers. White studies might just as easily be a force to expand the size of the entire pie in a way that all ethnic and cultural studies programs benefit. Other people, such as the New Abolitionists (see Chapter 9), fear that white studies diverts revolutionary energies into studying whiteness, when we really should be destroying it.

Finally, several critics claim white studies is simply a way of "centering" whiteness once again. According to this concern, whiteness has been on the run and multiculturalism has been making headway. Now white people have found a way to bring whiteness back into the center of attention. As with other criticisms, there may be something to this, but only in a limited way. In the wider landscape of our nation, outside the liberal confines of the academy, whiteness and white culture still remain very much central. It is this very centered whiteness that looks askance at white studies as an idle curiosity or a demonizing threat.

Coming Soon to a University Near You

Whether white studies will have a long term impact on the racial structure of United States society, I can't say. Certainly it will take many years, if not decades, to accomplish such a thing. On a shorter time scale, I expect white studies will continue to grow. Already the hectic pace of the early and mid-1990s seems to have slowed, but this appears to be a simple maturing of the field. In place of new and boldly challenging books and conferences dedicated to the topic, the study of whiteness is settling into the less dramatic work needed to establish a long-term presence.[37] Within each of the disciplines where white studies has established a presence, it is becoming incorporated into the existing process of publishing, conferences, and so forth. No longer is it new, or even remarkable, to have a symposium, a panel, or a series of articles on whiteness. This work, once dramatic simply in its presence, is now becoming an accepted area of inquiry. Courses are being offered, curriculums are being revised, and most importantly, a rising cohort of graduate students and junior faculty has emerged.

It will still take many years for white studies to establish itself. To my knowledge, no college or university has yet created a program of white studies, much less a department. But it's not hard to imagine that such a program might emerge over the next few years. More important, white studies has begun to be felt in the applied professions. Education is one clear example. The law is another. Even in these fields the presence is minimal, but it is there and growing.

The promise of white studies is that by making whiteness and white culture a visible area of study, we will learn how white people fit into a larger, multiracial society. Still in its early stages, white studies is preoccupied with white supremacy and domination, so much so that some practitioners believe there is nothing else to whiteness. But most seem to feel that whiteness is based in the cultural experience of European-Americans. In the past that culture has mistakenly been named "American" as if it were the only aspect of the American culture worthy of our attention. Now correctly characterized as white American culture, it can be studied for what it is. In time white studies will hopefully branch into some of the non-supremacist aspects of the culture as well. And in time, too, this inquiry promises to free the space needed for us to see what the greater American culture might be.

9

Grass Roots—Old, Deep, and Spreading

The First Conference on Whiteness

Five months before the Berkeley conference, in November 1996, the first conference on whiteness in recent times took place in Burlington, New Jersey.[1] There 54 people from 17 states assembled for a two-day process of workshops, presentations, and ongoing dialogue. Unlike Berkeley, the conference at Burlington was not sponsored by a prestigious institution of higher education. And unlike the Berkeley conference, it did not attract an avalanche of press interest or waves of attendees. But the people at the first National Conference on Whiteness and White American Culture, as it was called, felt they were making history. I know. I was one of them. In fact, I organized the event.

Those of us who were there felt we were treading on a significant social taboo, and we were. Go try to talk with your white neighbor about whiteness and you'll see what I mean. Even today the topic is not easily raised. And here we were doing a conference. The site I chose required that I obtain insurance for the event, but the controversial nature made this difficult. Ultimately I found an enlightened and hardworking broker who arranged coverage at six times the going rate, the best he could do.

The people who came, though nearly all middle-class, were diverse by other measures. A fourth of the participants were black, and the remainder white. Women outnumbered men slightly more than two to one. We had representatives from colleges and universities, business, social service organizations, religious organizations, and even the U.S. military. In age the participants ranged from late teens to elderly. The mix included students, professors, administrators, private consultants, managers, counselors, trainers, and activists.

176

All of us were focused on changing the racial structure of our society and each of us felt whiteness was a key focus in that change process. The conference was very different from most in content, context, and process. For once whiteness was explicitly named and it was not presumed to be everyone's experience. Participants considered what it meant to be white, and asked how matters of privilege and identity acted upon white people and influenced our approaches to antiracism. Collectively there was an awareness that an assemblage such as this had never happened. We each worked hard, taking the risks necessary to make the experience meaningful.

The conference was not without its pretenses. White participants invariably used the term "people of color" as a collective reference to any non-white people. One African-American participant remarked late in the conference that this had become exasperating, and if the conversation was about African-Americans, for instance, this should be said explicitly. No one felt the conference had yielded solutions to the pressing problems of racial conflict and inequality in America. But in many ways the experience was more real than the everyday life participants encountered "outside." For once we could say many things on our minds, and have them heard, in a give-and-take atmosphere that allowed us to clarify, modify, affirm, and sometimes even change our point of view. When the conference was over, it was more than the November winds that made the prospect of returning to the outside world a cold one.

What stands out about the conference in Burlington, aside from the pride we took in being the first, is the commitment to activism on the part of the participants. Even though many participants had connections to the academic world, their participation at Burlington reflected a personal commitment to social change. We were not there to calmly, objectively, and rationally contemplate the possibility of a multiracial society. We were there to make it happen in the face of whatever ridicule, resistance, and taboos that might oppose us. Our modest group of fifty-four people in Burlington reflected a much larger, grassroots awareness—some would even call it a movement—to raise consciousness about whiteness and the role it plays in the racial structure of our nation. The following year, with greater resources, national pre-conference press coverage, prominent institutional sponsorship, and a scholarly demeanor, the Berkeley conference tapped this grassroots awareness, exposing it to the nation.

Is there a pattern in our society? Is white consciousness on the rise, or is it still hidden behind a veneer of colorblindness? Does awareness of whiteness simply exist among scholars, and as part of the marginalized experience of people of color, or is there something brewing that's expressing itself in broader arenas, maybe even coming soon to a neighborhood near you? Some sociologists believe a fundamental change has taken place in the United States. The very question of what it means to be white has become problematic, especially among youth. Sociologist Charles Gallagher has taken a look at how white youth at an urban university in the Northeast view themselves racially. Race, it seems, is a prominent component of their identity, far more so than ethnicity. Unlike their elders, who felt a sense of being Irish, Italian, or you name it, white youth today simply see themselves as white. Gallagher's findings are ironic since much of white studies puts forth the notion that white people do not think of ourselves as white. Gallagher's work suggests it's a generational thing.[2]

White youth today do not recall the civil rights era of the 1960s. They see other racial groups asserting racial pride and identity, yet if white youth respond in kind, their elders fear a resurgence of an explicit white supremacy and act to suppress any collective public recognition of white identity. Thus black, Latino/a and Asian clubs, and cultural groups are common on college campuses and even in high school settings. But white youth understand clearly that similar efforts on their part will be repressed by those in control of the institution. And as Gallagher points out, it's not as if an Irish-American or Italian-American club can fill the void. Such an organization would need to call on the very ethnic identity that has become irrelevant in the lives of many white youth.

European-American Heritage Month

According to a September 1998 report in the *San Jose Mercury News,* the California state legislature passed a resolution declaring October of that year as European-American Heritage Month. Is this a good idea? Opinion varies on the matter. The *Mercury News* report implied that those people lobbying for the bill had connections to white supremacist groups.[3] Many people with whom I have raised this issue fear that a celebration of European-American culture will play into the hands of white people who want nothing more than to restore white culture as the undisputed and openly acknowledged center of power in the United States.

Yet white youth, faced with a plethora of events targeted to youth of other racial and cultural groups, commonly ask why there is no white history month. Some people reply that every month is white history month, meaning our educational system is Eurocentric. But why not designate a month to study European-American heritage and change the year-round Eurocentric curriculum to reflect the true multiracial character of American heritage? Furthermore, a European-American Heritage Month gives educators the opportunity to talk explicitly about whiteness and white culture. This need not be the exclusive tool of white supremacists. Such dialogue, as this book hopes to exemplify, can be done in the service of creating a multiracial society. Presently little such dialogue exists, and white youth are given little encouragement to explore, and perhaps work to change, the meaning of their heritage as white. Given this state of affairs, an European-American heritage Month might be worth considering.

Instead, white youth now experience the fact of whiteness as the major component shaping their lives. Political demagogues have reinforced their feelings of racial identity by characterizing white identity as a source of victimization. Since the late 1960s politically conservative groups have reformulated notions of colorblindness, merit, and privilege. Now claiming that affirmative action makes people of color the privileged groups, these political opinion-shapers have created a group of disaffected white people, not simply youth, who see themselves as innocent, their values besieged, their material prosperity threatened, and the very meaning of their lives as Americans at risk. This perspective wins votes, as the 1994 congressional elections demonstrated, but it creates a strange sort of equality in which everyone, no matter what their racial group, comes to feel equally screwed.

There never was a sense of racial safety for various Americans of color in the United States. In the post civil rights era white people have now entered a similar zone of insecurity. Sociologist Howard Winant describes this as a dual consciousness, a term first used by W. E. B. DuBois to describe how it felt to be black in America around 1900. One has the feeling of being both oneself, and seeing reflected back an image of oneself from others. Our self-image and the image reflected back are at odds with one another, yet each persists and each is insistent on the correctness of its representation. To white people, this is a very new experience. All of which is to say, the notion of what it means to be white is very much contested today.

Several years after our conference in Burlington I still remain in contact with many of the people I met there. Since that time we've staged three additional conferences and as of this writing are planning a fifth. Each of us is working toward a multiracial society in which white people have a role side by side and together with people of color. Ours is not a vision of separate racial states, each contending for its own interest. Nor is it a vision of white people under attack and losing out at the hands of undeserving people of color. Rather, we believe that white people and people of color are able to live together respectfully, in a society that takes everyone's interests into account. We also believe everyone, white people included, has some work to do with his or her own group to make this vision happen. Awareness of whiteness, as I've argued, is a necessary and needed step to bringing this vision about.

But other activists view things differently. To some, awareness of whiteness means advocating for the political interests of white people and defending them from incursions by people of color. To still others, whiteness is superior. This is the old-time white supremacy that today is sometimes peddled by white men in three-piece suits with briefcases and quasi-academic credentials. So, the picture is a complicated and muddled one. In the midst of all this agitation, mainstream white America remains by and large committed to its colorblind vision of a universal society based on individualistic, and historically white, values.

Who is to prevail, I cannot say. White supremacists have been around since Jefferson's time (see Chapter 5). Despite the best hopes of the vast majority of white Americans today, they still exist among us, sometimes in our very families, or side by side with us at work, in our neighborhoods, or elsewhere. Giving the rest of us white folk a perpetual bad name, white supremacists still purvey their distorted vision of racial superiority. Then there are others who, using thinly veiled allusions, try to convince the white voter her or his best interest lies in supporting their position. Colorizing poverty as black and using code words like "pimps" and "poverty queens" they hide from us white folk the fact that most blacks are not poor, and more importantly, most poor people are not black. They're white people, like us. Colorblindness allows these demagogues to carry out their masquerade, and I admit there are probably sincere leaders among them who truly wish a multiracial society might emerge centered upon their (unnamed as white cultural) values. Others are simply looking to protect their historical privilege and advantage. Still others admit that race has disadvantaged people of color in the United States. While not ready to admit that white people enjoy privilege, these people nonetheless believe it's important to seek racial equality and to heal the racial division our society suffers. Yet they lack a willingness to examine the role of white people, as white people, within the very society they hope to heal.

These positions, and a multitude of others in between, have been around for at least decades, and some have existed for centuries. Many articles and books have been written about white hate groups and the reemergence of an explicitly articulated white supremacy. Many, if not more, articles and books have been devoted to analyzing how the political left, the political right, the Democrats, the Republicans, the this and that and whatever, have incorporated a racialized view of society into their perspectives, from Willie Horton to "playing the race card." But what of groups, perspectives, and positions that do not espouse a white supremacist agenda, and yet take an explicit look at white people and how we fit into a multiracial society? Far less has been written about this latter category of activity, yet some things can be found. It's worthwhile to take a look at how this rise in white consciousness is being expressed in various sectors of our society.

Government

In 1968 the National Advisory Commission on Civil Disorders, informally known as the Kerner Commission, issued a report on the civil uprisings and rebellions that took place among African-Americans and other people in the urban centers of the United States from 1965 through 1968.

The report pointed the finger at white Americans, saying, "What white Americans have never fully understood—but what the Negro can never forget—is that white society is deeply implicated in the ghetto. White institutions created it, white institutions maintain it, and white society condones it." The report added, "It is time to make good the promises of American democracy to all citizens—urban and rural, white and black, Spanish-surname, American Indian and every minority group."[4]

All the more remarkable was the composition of the commission, which included, among others, a former state governor, a former police chief of Atlanta, the president of the United Steelworkers, a CEO of a Fortune 500 company, and both Democratic and Republican congressmen and senators. In total the committee comprised eight white men, one white woman, and two black men, with the latter themselves being identified with moderate stances toward race relations. Hence the report painted "a picture that derives its most devastating validity from the fact that it was drawn by representatives of the moderate and 'responsible' Establishment—not by black radicals, militant youth or even academic leftists. From it rises not merely a cry of outrage; it is also an expression of shocked intelligence and violated faith."[5]

Finally white America had admitted its involvement in the "white problem." With this admission the report predicted dire consequences for the United States if nothing was done to treat minorities more equitably. Though the bulk of the report consisted of documentation and description of conditions of the uprisings, it was the far more brief portion implicating white America that had the greatest impact. Released a few weeks before the assassination of Dr. Martin Luther King Jr., together these two events signaled the end of the civil rights era. Government activism had made great strides toward positive racial change through legislation, executive orders, and jurisprudence. Since that time, however, the government has done little, and what little has been done has often been at the hands of conservatives seeking to dismantle government activities from policing against discriminatory practices.

Over the years the Kerner commission frequently was cited by newspaper editors and social activists to point to the crisis of race in the United States, yet recently Stephen and Abigail Thernstrom revisited the predictions of the report in their book, *America in Black and White: One Nation, Indivisible,* and concluded that none had come to pass.[6] The Thernstroms concede that not all is perfect, but they document that racial conditions have substantially improved. Residential segregation, for example, has loosened considerably since the 1960s. This is certainly good news. One might wonder if the Kerner report had something to do with that. Dire predictions are made not in the hope they will occur, but rather to rally a citizenship against a problem they have not yet faced. The Kerner report provided a baseline to race relations in the United States. As white folk, we could hide or deny the problem only so far. A blue-ribbon panel of our own people appointed by our highest authorities told us with unmistakable clarity it was our problem to handle. If conditions have improved—and I personally agree with the Thernstroms that they have—then it has come as the result of hard work, incessant struggle, and sincere commitment from many people of color and a goodly number white people alike.

The struggle continues. In our contemporary age we no longer look to government to lead us in our quest for a multiracial society. Rather, if the society becomes multiracial, the government will accordingly reflect that. Not that government cannot be a player. As the institution commanding the most wealth and greatest coercive power in the nation, it surely can effect change. Simply enforcing civil rights laws already on the books can do much to improve things. But everyone has a right to mobilize the government to their own ends, and in recent times the conservative backlash has stalemated the former leadership role government held.

Yet the government can at least document current conditions, by collecting statistics and monitoring compliance to existing anti-discrimination laws and regulations. And recently under the aegis of President Clinton, another presidentially commissioned group made another report. The Advisory Board to the President's Initiative on Race was itself a picture of progress, being far more multiracial than the Kerner commission exactly 30 years prior. Of the seven members, three were white, two were black, one Latina, and one Asian. Three of the seven were women, indicating progress in gender representation as well. Ironically, this multiracial commission's report was far more optimistic.[7] "One of the Board's most gratifying discoveries was the vast number of existing efforts to improve race relations in communities throughout the country" (p. 29), they wrote. Assessing the climate of the nation, they found "common themes and concerns emerged throughout the year that reinforced our view that we are indeed more united as a country than divided" (p. 15). Still, deep-rooted racial problems persist. Looking at civil rights enforcement, education, poverty, welfare, economic inequality, housing, the criminal justice system, health, immigration, and stereotypes, the Advisory Board documented a multitude of pressing concerns.

Being careful in an exemplar fashion to consider all perspectives, the board took a look at the role of white people in our racially structured nation and found that "To understand fully the legacy of race and color with which we are grappling, we as a Nation need to understand that whites tend to benefit, either unknowingly or consciously, from this country's history of white privilege" (p. 47). That's hard work for most of us white folk. Giving us some credit, the board found "Research revealed steadily improving racial attitudes, especially among whites, over the past four decades. It is fair to say that there is a deep-rooted national consensus on the ideals of racial equality and integration, even if that consensus falters on the best means to achieve those ideals" (p. 48). Yet we need to look at the racial structure of our society a little more critically, for this same board documented clear evidence "that many whites, in general, are unaware of how color is a disadvantage to most members of other groups" (p. 46). In other words, white America can be thankful, and even a little self-congratulatory, that it averted the national catastrophe the Kerner commission predicted thirty years ago, but if we truly want to achieve our ideals, we need to stop kidding ourselves that our country's race problem is solved. Americans of all races, as a nation, have much to do. We white Americans need to look a little closer at our own continuing role in this process. We have to set a new baseline and rise to a new challenge. Or so say our nation's leaders once again.

Business

Everyone's heard of diversity. A *Wall Street Journal* reporter confided he receives countless books trumpeting the topic. *New York Times* columnist Russell Baker bemoaned the fact he could not get through the day, any day, without encountering the term. Even the Republican party put on a multiracial front at its 2000 convention in Philadelphia. And that was not even new. Four years prior a critic of "diversity management" complained the Republicans staged a "contrived celebration of ethnic diversity at the 1996 Republican National Convention."[8] But suppose you drew up a list of the 50 best workplaces for people of color among major corporations. How do you think their bottom-line corporate performance would look? Would they be a good investment, or would their CEOs be candidates for replacement by someone more hard-nosed and profit-oriented? Put your money on diversity says *Fortune Magazine,* who actually drew up the list in question. Companies with good workplace climates for people of color outperformed the S&P 500 stock index over a five-year period at the end of the 1990s, and the top company, diversity-wise, saw its stock appreciate 34% annually during that time.[9]

Notably, the topic of the *Fortune* study was racial diversity. Many other types of difference come under the diversity banner. Gender, age, sexual orientation, ableness, religion, family configuration, personality type, you name it. Most of these are significant concerns, though the list can be extended into trivialities. But from the standpoint of addressing the racial structure of our society, the emphasis on diversity is a mixed blessing. On the one hand it introduces notions of culture, systemic disadvantage, and change into the business setting, softening up an historically rigid monoracial, monocultural environment. On the other hand, so many different types of difference come under the diversity banner that the really hard work of addressing racial difference frequently has been shuffled to the wayside. Thus consultant Lou Schoen revealed, at "a 1993 conference at the Minneapolis Convention Center I heard trainers, experienced in preparing corporations for a more diverse workforce, assert that they never spoke the word 'racism.' That, of course, could offend their mostly white audiences and the human resource chiefs and CEOs who paid their fees."[10]

In one way at least, whiteness and white culture have been the central focus of diversity proponents. The traditional business culture of the United States has been characterized, rightly, as white and male, or more precisely, white male. During the early 1990s many diversity practitioners, some operating internally in large corporations and others as consultants, wrote of the need for white men to open up the workplace, acknowledge our advantages, and champion agendas for change. AT&T, among others, held workshops for white men. Statistics told of the absurd concentration of white men at the top among CEOs and members of governing boards. Changing only slowly, even today the numbers are overwhelmingly white.[11]

What's a Whitetologist?

Among the many people promoting a consciousness of whiteness, Lowell Thompson, with his trademarked "WHITEFOLKS" publications, is unique. Thompson is the author of two books, his first in 1996 titled *"WHITEFOLKS": Seeing America through Black Eyes,* and recently, his *"WHITEFOLKS" Funny? Book.* A freelance advertising consultant and recipient of industry awards who went independent after exposing racism in the advertising business, Thompson brings to his writing both humor and flair for commonsense treatment of complex ideas.

Describing himself as the world's first whitetologist, Thompson concluded several years ago that the reason America still had a race problem was because we were studying the wrong race. His self-published series of books set out to correct this oversight. Ever the entrepreneur, in his spare time he claims to be studying the people who are studying whiteness.[12]

White men heard the message, and reacted in many different ways. Some learned new skills. Some championed change. Some reacted, building defensive walls. Companies themselves reflected these different reactions. Some made *Fortune*'s list. Others, like Texaco, "got religion" after being whacked on their white male heads with multimillion dollar settlements. Still others remain in denial. When the President's Initiative on Race held a forum for corporations in St. Louis in July 1998, according to a *Post-Dispatch* report, heads of the major St. Louis corporations failed to show.[13] Worse, instances of unchecked racism still occur in many companies.

Sometimes lost in the picture, even among enlightened (and financially strengthened) corporations, is the fact that the problem is not white men, per se, but rather white culture. By focusing so intently on white males, diversity-inspired change efforts do not name the great unnamed. This point is not lost among the top diversity practitioners. "I want to name it," says Elsie Y. Cross of Elsie Y. Cross Associates. "The problem is the system of white supremacy. Every company contains norms that were built into its culture long ago. It is those systemic norms that create an environment in which a white person doesn't invite a person of color to the golf course—the white man doesn't even think about it."[14] According to Judith Katz of the Kaleel Jamison Consulting Group "the dominant culture in many organizations is white culture. It is crucial for white change agents to recognize this and dissect exactly what kind of values, beliefs, and behaviors underlie white culture in our organizations and in ourselves."[15]

For any number of reasons, getting the point across is difficult. Even though it seems virtually every white male in the country, myself included, has gotten the message that white women and men and women of color are tired of us holding all the goodies, the point is often lost that white culture has led to and continues to support white male advantage. A recent study of black and white male managers found the white managers had little sense that their race had an effect upon their career. They seldom thought about it in that context, and assumed that their organizations were race-neutral in their treatment of people of color.[16]

Yet white culture in the corporate battle place is not neutral to white men. Sometimes it's not even friendly. Though it gives advantage, it also exacts costs. White culture as experienced among white men can be competitive, harsh, cold, and alienating, demanding that one forsake family for career and profit. It can mean ulcers, heart attacks, and family disintegration. It can impose a moral code that dehumanizes others and locks one's own humanity into a small and distant part of one's soul beyond reach within one's lifetime. The corporate world, however slowly, is beginning to realize it's in everyone's interest to change this.

Church Groups—Spiritual Approaches

With representatives of all major faiths and many minor ones as well, the United States has been characterized as very religious compared to Europe and other parts of the world. Among these many faith groups are several who work for racial justice, harmony, and equality as part of their spiritual testimony. Recently, for example, Jewish and African-American groups have joined together in programs of racial healing. And the Christian men's group Promise Keepers has made racial reconciliation number six of its seven Promises. To acknowledge these and the many other worthy efforts would take a book in and of itself. At odds with the faith-based work for racial reconciliation and healing are smaller groups, such as the Christian Identity movement, that espouse an explicit dogma of white supremacy based on an idiosyncratic reading of the Bible. Together these two phenomena—efforts toward racial healing and efforts justifying white supremacy—characterize two roles the church has played in our history.

Within that history, as Marian Groot of the Women's Theological Center in Boston points out, there was

> something in European culture that allowed whiteness to flourish. It is not, therefore, unrelated to Europeanness, in particular Christian Europeanness, and even more particularly Protestant Christian Europeanness. Though Catholics and Jews were eventually allowed under the umbrella of whiteness, the term first applied to Protestants, more particularly WASPs as they have come to be known.[17]

Mark Twain aptly explained how it worked:

> As I have said, we lived in a slave-holding community; indeed, when slavery perished my mother had been in daily touch with it for sixty years. Yet, kind-hearted and compassionate as she was, I think she was not conscious that slavery was a bald, grotesque, and unwarrantable usurpation. She had never heard it assailed in any pulpit, but had heard it defended and sanctified in a thousand; her ears were familiar with Bible texts that approved it, but if there were any that disapproved it they had not been quoted by her pastors; as far as her experience went, the wise and the good and the holy were unanimous in the conviction that slavery was right, righteous, sacred, the peculiar pet of the Deity, and a condition which the slave himself ought to be daily and nightly thankful for.[18]

Not so long ago I had the opportunity to speak with a white minister and share some materials and experiences illustrating how white American culture operates at a level most white Americans cannot see. Though it was not my plan, he became quite enthused about the insights he gained and decided to bring them before a local council of ministers of suburban congregations who were considering their agenda for the coming year. Two weeks later I again met the same minister. His colleagues, he revealed, had laughed at him and mocked his purpose. Upon learning I was married to an African-American woman, his partners in the cloth seized on this, saying white culture was my issue, not theirs. As he told me this, the minister's shoulders sagged and he looked defeated, whipped, apologetic, and beaten. He could only do so much, he said, and he had to go along with his colleagues who decided they would emphasize spiritual needs. "That's our issue!" they claimed.

The proposition that white people might question the racial structure of our country proved as unpopular in my 20th century suburban New Jersey as it did in Mark Twain's 19th century Missouri slave country. I felt no ill will toward the minister who tried to raise the issue. Indeed, I admired his well-intended, if reckless, attempt. If he had any failing, it was underestimating the power of whiteness to bestow a veil of normalcy upon the racial structure that white culture created in the past and supports in our present times. Not all members of the white Protestant clergy run from the issue of whiteness. In March 1994, the Episcopal House of Bishops issued a pastoral letter on the sin of racism, stating in part,

> Institutionalized preference, primarily for white persons, is deeply ingrained in the American way of life in areas such as employment, the availability of insurance and credit ratings, in education, law enforcement, courts of law and the military.

They added,

> In the United States our primary experience is one of white privilege, even in places where whites may be a minority in the surrounding population. This comes as a surprise to many white people, because they do not think of themselves as racist. They may even see themselves as victims of various violent reactions against the dominant culture. Yet there are many in our society at all levels who seem to find a certain security in racially restricted communities, schools, clubs, fraternities, sororities and other institutions.[19]

Irony aside, the clergy in my story above were themselves Episcopalians living in the racially restricted (though they would likely not admit it), affluent white suburbs of northern New Jersey. The razzing of their colleague took place a year after the pastoral letter was issued by their leadership. Statements have their limits. Recently other denominations, notably including the Southern Baptists, have owned up to their whiteness, but a true commitment to change requires a sustained effort.

Working at Home

In the first half of 1966, black activist Stokley Carmichael was elected chairperson of the Southern Nonviolent Coordinating Committee in a move that turned white leaders out of the organization. The following year white activists heard a disturbing message. "Whitey," they were told, "go home and free your own people!"

Some were confused and daunted by the task. One activist recalled speaking to some displaced staffers who admitted *"that middle-class, Northern, college-educated whites* [such as themselves] could best organize *back home,* among middle-class, Northern, college-educated whites." Characterized by Carmichael as "incapable of confronting white society with its racism where it really does exist," they understood the point, adding "but frankly we're just not ready to face it yet."[20]

Now more than three decades later this redirection of effort has come to fruition. Some, like Joseph Barndt of Crossroads Ministry, responded to the challenge and began working in the white community. Perhaps after many long years their efforts are bearing fruit. There seems to be a rising awareness in the white community that racism exists, and whereas we have been part of the problem in the past, we need to become part of the solution for the future.

One such effort has unfolded over the last four decades through the ministry of Joseph Barndt. An early participant in the civil rights movement, in 1967 Reverend Barndt found himself the verbal target of Stokley Carmichael, the same black activist who brought the phrase "Black Power" into usage. Carmichael told Barndt, and many other white people as well, to "go home and free your own people." Taking it to heart, Barndt began a ministry to white people to free us from racism. In 1986 he founded Crossroads Ministry, which today trains people and organizations in antiracism. Some major church groups have lined up with Crossroads, including the Unitarian Universalist Association, the Mennonite Central Committee, the Christian Church Disciples in Christ, the Minnesota Council of Churches, the Greater Dallas Community of Churches, and the Evangelical Lutheran Church in America. All these groups have pledged to become antiracist, multicultural institutions. Crossroads Ministry works with other, non-church, institutions as well.

White consciousness is an explicit part of Reverend Barndt's approach. Together with Charles Reuhle, also of Crossroads, he explains,

> As anti-racism educators and trainers, we have struggled with identity issues. We feel that those of us who are white but who oppose white racism must pose the question of how to achieve a redeemed and transformed racial cultural identity in whose being and action we can have pride.[21]

In the Introduction to his book, *Dismantling Racism: The Continuing Challenge to White America,* he says,

> This book on racism is addressed primarily to a white audience. It is written for white people and about white people, and it is written by a white person. It is about our white racial problems....about us, the "majority people," and about the problems of our whiteness, especially the problem of our white racism.[22]

Other faith-based groups have produced articles, books and additional resources supporting a ministry aimed at helping white people become conscious of our whiteness and understand how to use that consciousness to fight racism and foster a multiracial society. Jody Miller Shearer of the Mennonite Central Committee has written a book titled *Enter the River: Healing Steps from White Privilege Toward Racial Reconciliation,* and produced a video, *Free Indeed,* about "White privileges and how we play the game."[23] Sojourners, a publisher in Washington, DC, describes itself as "a progressive Christian voice with an alternative vision for both the church and society…[that] includes Evangelicals, Catholics, Pentecostals, and Protestants; liberals and conservatives; blacks, whites, Latinos and Asians; women and men; young and old." While their magazine, also named *Sojourners,* covers many issues, they are not shy about discussing whiteness. Over the past two years they have published at least five articles examining whiteness, white culture, and white identity. Sojourners also publishes study guides, two of which focus on racism and highlight whiteness as a point of explicit discussion.[24]

Working from a broader foundation of spirituality than Protestant, or even Christian, faiths alone, the Women's Theological Center (WTC) of Boston has been active in an antiracist witness and practice that includes explicit recognition of whiteness and the role white people have in creating a multiracial society. Founded in 1982, WTC has been working against racism since 1987 through activities such as trainings, workshops, and publishing. Among their publications is *The Brown Papers,* a monthly series launched in 1994 which includes several papers discussing whiteness and the role of white people in antiracism.

One paper, "Wanting to Be Indian," by Myke Johnson, explores the damage done when white people attempt to adopt Indian religious practices for our own ends. White people, Johnson emphasizes, need to do our own spiritual work and if we find a spiritual void in our lives, it behooves us to fix our own culture and not borrow from, and thereby bring harm to, Native Americans. Another paper, "The Heart Cannot Express Its Goodness," by Marian Meck Groot, I've already mentioned. It's one of my all-time favorite articles on white people. WTC is a perennial co-sponsor of the National Conference on Whiteness that began in Burlington, NJ. A multiracial group, WTC believes white people and people of color have different tasks in confronting racism. Thus they offer "programs for white women who are conscious of their whiteness" and "a place where white women can come together to explore the meaning whiteness has in our lives."[25]

The News Media

In 1988 *Mother Jones,* a magazine devoted to leftist causes, published a humor article titled "The Unbearable Being of Whiteness."[26] Although this piece represented one of the earliest discussions of whiteness in any form in a publication with a large white audience, it was odd and disconcerting that a magazine championing social justice took such a cavalier attitude toward a serious and pressing topic. True, we need to be able to laugh at ourselves. But when humor is the only response, and no serious discussion takes place in an otherwise serious medium, then one is not taking a serious matter seriously. The article was, in my opinion, moderately humorous in the immediate context, but in the larger scheme of things, a blatant and unapologetic exercise of white privilege. *Mother Jones* was not alone. Earlier, in 1985 and 1986, comedians Martin Mull and Allen Rucker produced two somewhat successful books and accompanying video productions on the "History of White People." Being comedians, of course, the context of their work was different, and their selection of topic prescient. But in 1991 another serious mainstream publication, *Newsweek,* published a humor piece about "BMCWM" (boring, middleclass white men), the gist being that white men were just trying to get by, minding our own business in a world changing beyond our control. Humorous, yes, but in a "let them eat cake" way. Such was the tenor of the times.[27]

Moving into the 1990s, things began to get serious. Newsrooms, not inconsequentially the province of white men, began to grind out stories of white male victimization. *Newsweek* dropped the humor and ran a cover story on "White Male Paranoia" in early 1993 and one month later *U.S. News & World Report* ran a column on "the demonizing of white men." Early in 1994 *Business Week* headlined a cover story, "White, Male & Worried." Not surprisingly, this was the same year we saw the Republican "Contract with America" strategy that led to a Republican electoral landslide that many characterized as driven by white male backlash against a growing movement of multiculturalism and diversity.[28]

Appearing at the same time, other stories began to feature whiteness itself. The New Orleans *Times Picayune* ran a series on race relations, including a feature piece looking at how "Both elusive and exclusive, whiteness sets itself apart." In the same year, 1993, the New York *Village Voice* ran a cover story, "White Like Who?" with eight additional articles and lengthy sidebars. Less than three months later the *Washington Post* ran a story describing a white staffer's reflections on his own whiteness at the National Association of Black Journalists. The title, "White Like Me," though surely by coincidence, appeared to answer the question raised by the *Village Voice.*[29]

Following the Berkeley conference on whiteness, the media began to take a look at this thing called "white studies" (see Chapter 8), and presently numerous articles have been written on the topic. My organization alone, the Center for the Study of White American Culture, has received mention in two dozen stories. The news media, of course, are not supposed to make the news. Rather, their role is to report on it. So one might not hold them accountable for raising white consciousness, but rather see them as indicators of that consciousness as it arises among other sectors of society.

Public Interest Groups

Alexis de Tocqueville, the 19th century observer of United States society, noted that Americans love to form associations. This is no less true in matters of race than in other sectors of society. White supremacist associations, of course, have a long history in the United States. Some have softened their approach and upgraded their image, but their basic message is that white people are better, more deserving, and morally, culturally and, according to some, biologically superior to people of color.

However, a far smaller number of groups take the position that an awareness of whiteness is important to a multiracial society. Aside from this one basic position these groups vary considerably in the details of their approaches. One group, the European American Issues Forum (E/AIF), describes itself as "the only civil-rights organization dedicated to the civil rights of European Americans." Founded in 1997 in the northern California bay area, E/AIF does not claim that European-Americans (they do not use the term "white") are superior to other racial/ethnic groups. E/AIF also favors multiculturalism, and seeks a seat at the table whenever policy-making multicultural groups assemble. But at the same time, they are emphatically opposed to affirmative action.

E/AIF clearly does not understand racism as a white problem, unless one frames whites as victims of racism. And at least one member of the city Board of Supervisors feels E/AIF members "generally do not indicate an understanding of a diverse city or an appreciation of multiculturalism." Still, some of E/AIF's concerns have merit. Summaries of hate crime statistics, for instance, usually hide the fact that European-Americans are often victims. Press reports stereotype whites as perpetrators, naming our race when we commit hate crimes and hiding our race when we are victims. The FBI itself counts Hispanics as "Hispanic" when victims, but as "white" when perpetrators.[30]

At the other end of the spectrum are the New Abolitionists. In 1992 John Garvey and Noel Ignatiev founded a journal named *Race Traitor*. Using the tag line "Treason to whiteness is loyalty to humanity," *Race Traitor* aspires to be "an intellectual center for those seeking to abolish the white race," which, according to *Race Traitor*, is nothing more than a political entity consisting of white skin privilege. By the fall of 2001 *Race Traitor* had published fifteen issues. Contributors are a multiracial assortment of academics and activists, generally of a leftist or radical perspective, and their contributions range from scholarly articles to poetry and creative prose. Over the past few years

Race Traitor has gained public notice due to the novelty and stridency of their approach. Noel Ignatiev and, to a lesser extent, John Garvey have been featured on numerous panels, radio programs, and in newspaper and magazine articles.[31]

In May 1997 *Race Traitor* held a conference in New York City, forming the New Abolitionist Society. Unlike *Race Traitor,* simply a journal, the New Abolitionist Society is a membership organization with chapters in Boston, Chicago, Los Angeles, New York, Phoenix, Tulsa, and Washington, DC. Both *Race Traitor* and the New Abolitionist Society disdain "whiteness studies," despite the lineup of professors appearing in their midst. They aim not to study whiteness, but to destroy it. And they criticize antiracism activists for being linguistically incorrect (since race is a fiction) and complicit with "official society" (which needs to be destroyed). Noel Ignatiev has gone so far as to state, "I operate from a sense of class. My aim is not racial harmony. My aim is class war." Whether other New Abolitionists are equally geared for battle is not clear, though certainly race, the white race in particular, has effectively prevented organizing among working class and poor people since it was founded for that very purpose (see Chapter 5).[32]

In their public posture the New Abolitionists make a point of being ideologically clear and confident. They call for those people who are nominally white and enjoy white skin privilege to act in ways to disrupt the institutions that support whiteness. "We know what to do," they claim. It's simply a matter of finding the will to do it (i.e. destroy the white race). At the same time, action-based tactics seem hard to come by, or maybe it's simply that the will to challenge the system has not yet emerged even within their ranks. One program, Copwatch, shows promise. Originally reported in *Race Traitor* by AntiRacist Action (another independent group) of Milwaukee, Copwatch has been used by the Phoenix chapter of the New Abolitionist Society. It consists, basically, of hanging out on the streets in disenfranchised neighborhoods and videotaping police when they detain individuals.[33] New Abolitionists take as their heroes John Brown and Malcolm X, echoing the latter's remark in another tag line, "Abolish the white race—by any means necessary."

Because they view whiteness as simply a political construct, New Abolitionists believe white culture does not exist. Exactly what cultural experience they believe does exist for white people they don't specify, though some claim the ethnic heritage of their European origins serve this purpose. Seeking a sense of pride, developing an antiracist white identity, or reaching the autonomy stage of white racial identity development (see Chapter 7) represent false paths to change for New Abolitionism advocates. I disagree, of course. Yet I admire their determination and find value in their analysis. They pose a forthright challenge to white privilege, at least verbally, and demand action on pressing issues of police brutality, economic injustice, and educational disparities. How their program unfolds in the future should be interesting to follow.

In between the E/AIF approach that denies white privilege and the New Abolitionist approach that denies white culture, there are several organizations that recognize both white privilege and white culture. Generally these organizations promote antiracism and define racism as "prejudice plus power." Coupled with this definition is recognition that in North America, those with the power, racially speaking, are white people.

One unique program, the Recovering Racists Network (RRN) was founded in 1995 by John McKenzie of Pleasant Hill, California. McKenzie began simply by wearing a badge displaying the words "recovering racist." Now he has expanded his program, selling badges, offering workshops, and recruiting members to RRN. Highly individualistic in his approach, McKenzie does not presume to tell any specific person that he or she is a racist, but he makes it clear he believes white people benefit from white privilege, saying, "I have come to understand that I am living in a racist culture and have learned to be a racist, and I want to work diligently to end racism in myself and be an example to others." His badge has led to many interesting conversations, including generally favorable reactions from people of color.[34]

Had Enough of Left Overs?

Horace Seldon, the white male founder of Community Change, Inc. of Boston, has been an antiracist activist since 1967 when the Kerner Commission report identified racism as a "white problem." Twenty years later a critic called him a "left over from the sixties." Never one to be daunted in his hunger for racial justice, Seldon took pride in this description, explaining people like him were still needed because there was a lot of racism left over from the 1960s too. Not only that, there was racism left over from the 1860s, the 1760s, and the 1660s as well.

A tireless opponent of racism, Seldon emphasizes that developing awareness is not enough. People need to act on their awareness by working against racism and joining in "building multi-racial coalitions to build a new future." He disputes those who would tell white people that opposing racism is in their own self-interest. While there may be truth to that, he believes an appeal to one's sense of justice is the stronger argument for change. Since white people benefit from racism, he points out, the "self-interest" argument can wear thin and become suspect. But an appeal to justice has a universal and uplifting character that can move people beyond their self-interest, whatever it may be.[35]

A still older organization grew from the People's Institute for Survival and Beyond of New Orleans, itself a much respected multiracial and antiracist practice of activists led by people of color. In 1986 at the urging of Institute leadership, white members organized a white antiracist collective to "actively look at, analyze, change and help other whites to change the ways we as whites participate in racism personally, culturally, and institutionally." Recognizing their heritage, they call themselves both European *Descent,* and more commonly, European *Dissent.* Over the years European Dissent has been active locally, working against the political campaigns of David Duke and protesting incidents of racism, and nationally at workshops, conferences, and other events.

European Dissent stresses the need for white people to be accountable to people of color. Though not always clear in practice, accountability emphasizes at a minimum that white people thinking up "good ideas" on our own, without having some input, reality check, analysis, critique, or other access to the perspectives of people of color, is neither wise nor helpful, and often counterproductive if not outrightly racist. In their own practice, European Dissent maintains close ties and accountability to the People's Institute. Notably, the Crossroads Ministry of Joseph Barndt described above acknowledges and maintains a relationship of accountability with the People's Institute as well.[36]

In 1968 Community Change, Inc., was organized in Massachusetts to "address racist views and policies held by white people and white controlled institutions." Moved to action by the Kerner Commission report, founding member Horace Seldon served as executive director for nearly 30 years. Community Change, Inc., though still a small organization presently located in Boston, has compiled an impressive record. In 1970 they provided antiracism intervention, consultation, and training to the National YWCA, helping that organization develop its antiracist mission. Since then, Community Change, Inc., has followed a strategy of networking, catalyzing, and resourcing that has launched many new organizations and provided crucial support for existing ones.

One good example is support they provided the National Conference on Whiteness. After the initial conference in Burlington, the organizer (really me at that point) needed a place and logistical support for the next conference. Community Change, Inc., provided that support. Their interest and reputation were the catalyst attracting a broader group of participants from the Boston area who joined the process. The resulting conference in November 1997 attracted 300 people and raised the visibility of antiracist action around issues of whiteness to a new height. Community Change, Inc., continues to be a perennial sponsor of the conference series.[37]

Several other organizations with missions revolving around antiracism and social justice have developed workshops that emphasize an awareness of whiteness and how it fits within the racial structure of our society. The Challenging White Supremacy Workshop (CWS) of San Francisco is a project of the Tides Center. Its principal organizer, Sharon Martinas, acknowledges her indebtedness to the People's Institute for Survival and Beyond as a source of inspiration. CWS has been offered not only in the traditional workshop format of people gathering together in a room, but also online as a year-long process conducted via the Internet. Recently CWS has released an 800-page reader called *Creating an Anti-Racist Agenda* that tells how white antiracist activists can challenge white privilege.

The Los Angeles chapter of the National Conference for Community and Justice has operated the White Racial Awareness Process (WRAP) workshop series since 1992. Modeled on the white awareness work of Judith Katz and other forerunners, the WRAP workshop series, and the program itself, to my knowledge, is the oldest continuing program in the country. Over 300 people have gone through the program to date. In Philadelphia, the organization Training for Change offers a three-part workshop titled "White People Working on Racism." In the Washington, DC, area Judith Katz now facilitates a weekend workshop, "What White People Can Do about Racism," that takes place twice annually. Similar workshops have cropped up on organizational agendas and at several conferences in the late 1990s.[38]

White-on-white discussion groups have also arisen. One example from the Boston area, White Women Challenging Racism, has been described in detail in the book, *Off White: Readings on Race, Power, and Society.* I have heard from many other groups, some for white men, some for white women, and some of mixed gender. Though these groups are often informal and may not remain active for more than a few months or years, I know of examples in San Francisco, Philadelphia, Tennessee, and Minnesota. Hard to find since their activities don't make headlines, they nonetheless represent a widespread and growing phenomenon of white people taking an interest in our own culture, trying to understand our role in a racially structured society.[39]

Center for the Study of White American Culture, Inc.

Of course I have to mention my own organization, and with no small amount of pride I will. Dr. Charley Flint, who is my life partner, and I founded the Center for the Study of White American Culture, Inc. in April 1995. It came as an outgrowth to experiences I've described in this book. Being married to an Afro-American feminist sociologist and, for a time, part of a minority-owned social work practice that trained people in diversity-related issues, I often found myself the only white person either at home or at work. Is it any wonder that I might question how race and gender influenced my life? The questions occurred, but when I sought answers, I found little to describe my experience. There were some works on maleness and masculinity. But whiteness and white identity were harder to grasp. Amidst the many dozens, if not hundreds, of books available to me describing the experience of other racial groups, there were none to describe my own.

Eventually I found other people had written about whiteness but in 1995, and even today, these works were hard to find. This, coupled with my experience with white people during a workshop in Washington, DC (see Chapter 7), proved to me that we white people needed to understand our own culture. To do that, I realized we had to begin talking and learning about it. And we had to begin bringing to a wider audience the wisdom of those pioneers who had already made this journey. With that in mind, together my partner and I co-founded the Center.[40]

The Center is a 501(c)3 corporation. We are a multiracial organization whose mission is to define and examine white United States culture and to address its role in, and impact upon, the greater American culture. Some people mistakenly believe we are an advocacy group for white people. We are not. I personally believe that white people will be far better off by learning how to live in a multiracial society. Furthermore, I believe many white people want that to happen, but are lacking in the understanding and means to bring this vision about. But we are advocates first for a multiracial society, one no longer structured by race. Other people believe we are a white-hating group of people of color. We are not. Again, I believe all people, white people included, benefit by undoing the racial structure of our society. I personally aspire to improve the position of white people. It is a struggle to regain our humanity.

Still other people believe in our views but are afraid of our directness. They suggest we change our name to avoid confusion with white supremacist groups. Early in our formation our board of directors tackled this issue. We are in fact an organization, i.e. a center, that studies white American culture. It couldn't be clearer. True, there is a model in the larger society that says the only people talking about whiteness and white culture are white supremacists. But it is that very model we are trying to discredit, and talking about whiteness is the very thing we believe needs to happen among white people who aspire to dismantle our society's racial structure. Our name, as we understand it, is part of our work. By putting it forth, we declare an alternative to the models of white supremacy and colorblindness so prevalent today.

This simple stance has power. As I write this, a newspaper reporter from a major metropolitan daily has asked me to help locate people in her coverage area who are willing to talk about whiteness. She has found sources on her own, but they are afraid to go on record. Imagine that! Among the millions of white people in her metropolitan area, she cannot find even a few with the courage and understanding needed to discuss whiteness in public in an antiracist context. The social taboos are very strong, particularly among white people. White people need models and leaders to begin this crucial dialogue. The Center intentionally stands up to meet this need.

Our willingness to discuss these issues with media representatives is an important part of our work. Sometimes we become part of the story. Other times we quietly answer inquiries and direct people to other sources more appropriate to their interests. We see this as a means of raising issues before the public. But we also provide other services, generally of an educational nature. This includes offering workshops and seminars on white culture, publishing a thought-provoking series of papers, operating a popular Web site at **www.euroamerican.org,** and providing information and networking services to our membership through a newsletter and email list.

The National Conference on Whiteness, which we founded in 1996, has met four times, and promises to continue. We are a small organization and our capabilities are limited. But I believe the issues we raise are growing in the public consciousness, and that rise in consciousness has fed back to us in growing public recognition and membership. There is much, much more to be done and I hope in time we will continue to develop and promote an understanding of the role that is needed for white people living in a multiracial society.

The Public

Over the past few years many people have expressed feelings and thoughts about the issues the Center raises. Most are responding to our Web site, which contains a range of materials concerning our positions. Collectively these people mirror opinions among the public at large. Often they ask if we hear from white supremacists. Yes, we do. One writer identified himself as white and proud to be racist. He wondered if we wanted to discuss "the real issues" and asked if we were "cowards, or just stupid?" Neither, actually, and in no need to prove our masculinity. Another writer accused us of being "nigger lovers" with "sick dreams." Others write of feeling insulted by our Web site, claiming we are bashing whites, accusing us of being guilt-ridden, and asserting they are proud of their white, or European (it varies depending on the writer) heritage. It's not so easy to categorize these people. Some, granted, are probably self-identified racists filled with hate. But others impress me as troubled souls.

Pride in one's heritage is important and developing a nonracist sense of pride in being white is very difficult nowadays. A man wrote to tell me white people "formed and developed this country" and out of the goodness of our white hearts gave minorities rights neither "earned nor deserved." Later this man wrote me again saying he was not a white supremacist but simply expressing pride in his heritage. I believe he believes that, but his ignorance of what it took—the valiant struggles and the many deaths of people of color and some white people through the centuries—to gain those rights is appalling. Another white man was pleased by our site. He thought (incorrectly in my experience) that many blacks would consider it racist. He saw it as a reminder "of the worth of whites" and applauded us for our courage. Another man in his early twenties said he was "very proud to be white." He found our site "excellent" and he favored "UNITY" among all racial groups.

Is It Worth It?

White men are often accused of benefiting from white culture, which itself is hierarchical, patriarchal, and historically antagonistic to people of color. Yet in the competitive and driven world of white men, even white men suffer from its effects. Psychologist Anthony J. Ipsaro has studied thousands of white men in the workplace and found many living lives, as Thoreau said, of quiet desperation. Taught not to complain, and to measure our worth in terms of our material productivity, modern day white men are socially isolated, ignorant of our inner needs, and suffering from confusion and insecurity in our work roles. This stressed-out lifestyle is reflected in health and divorce statistics.

According to Ipsaro, "With all the economic gains of the twentieth century...the paradox is that we have less rather than more time for reflection and depth, friendship and intimacy, beauty and sensitivity, even common decency. These values seem incidental in the quest for more productivity, more material things, more wealth, more notoriety, more titles and prestige." To meet the requirements of the 21st century, white men need to learn more of the relational world of women, and women need to learn more about the world of productivity of men, Ipsaro recommends. Ironically, this more balanced lifestyle parallels gender roles in traditional cultures. It may be the way humans are truly meant to be.[41]

White people sometimes ask me what people of color think of the Center. Generally, I reply, they are encouraging. An Asian-American woman wrote of the difficulties she experienced with her white friends who fail to understand their own whiteness. Failing such, they unwittingly tried to place the writer in a box that didn't fit and were unable to recognize and value her Asianness. A Latino man wrote describing how many Latinos aspired to whiteness, ignoring the African portion of their heritage. Two other Latino men separately have taken me to task for not seeing people as individuals. Does this mean I can't look at whiteness? A black American wrote that he had been studying white American culture all his life. He found our site a "very thoughtful effort, neither sappy liberalism nor rigid defensiveness." An African woman was "very impressed by this site and what it has to offer." An African-American man was thankful he found our Web site. A high school band director, he observed that "most children of color believe that all white people don't care." It will take responsible white leadership to improve things, he said.

Many writers have a multiracial connection. Some are themselves of multiracial descent. A biracial woman said "you are attempting a great feat" and wished us luck. A biracial man spoke of how contradictory and complex race was and promised to list our site in his organization's newsletter. Others not of multiracial heritage are nonetheless involved in interracial relationships. A white man spoke of his multiracial daughter who claimed she was not white. He accepted her view and acknowledged his own white privilege. A black woman with a biracial son was happy to see a site that would help her discuss the heritage of his father's side. She had been worried about how to do this, especially since her child's father was "not part of his life."

Another African-American woman told how minorities are tired of explaining themselves. She was glad to see we were doing some of that work and our site gave her hope "my 'mixed' daughter will be able to grow up without choosing a side." An African-American man engaged to an European-American woman said it's "time that someone tried to show the white experience in a light that didn't lead down the destructive road of blame and jockeying for superiority." A white woman welcomed our Web page. Married to a black man, she had been feeling a lack of understanding about what it meant to be white.

Some people do not identify their racial heritage, but express opinions. Some are critical. One man called us, inaccurately, an "expression of a racist nonwhite establishment" and cynically thanked us for proving his point to "the children of my elementary school classes." He hoped there would be a backlash against organizations like us in the next generation. Apparently he was doing what he could to see that backlash develops. Another person simply wrote that all white people are evil. It's tempting to think a person of color did that but experience has taught me it might not be so (some white folk are pretty negative on the race/culture).

Among supportive writers, one found us listed in *"Essence* or *Emerge,"* both black-oriented magazines, and sent one of our files to her mom. A woman of color? Perhaps, but again who can tell. I read both *Essence* and *Emerge* myself. Another writer said he liked our ideas. In contrast to our approach, he felt whites often took the backseat and refused responsibility for racial dialogue. One writer appreciated our "invaluable information" and "non-confrontational manner" and thanked us for our effort.

Some white people felt we were being divisive. There was no such thing as white culture they told us. But many white people like what we are doing. One white man congratulated us for creating "such a badly needed Web site." Another white man spoke of the cultural isolation he felt from people of color. Speaking of the child within, he recalled how his ideas of race were shaped when he was six years old. As an adult, he asks "Wouldn't it depress you [too] if you belonged to the group responsible for the majority of hate in the United States?" Another wished us "Godspeed in bringing our races together."

Considering the controversial nature of the Center, it is a welcome experience that the majority of letter writers of all racial/cultural groups are positive. We hear from many academicians as well. They tell us of publications and often I am drawn to a book or article I had not known of before. They also offer us expressions of personal support. Many organizations write to announce their own missions and usually we post their letters. These are simply a sample of the many opinions that exist on the topic of whiteness. Across the United States, for many people, it is becoming a pressing topic. Not simply something contained within our universities, the public discussion of whiteness and white culture promises to continue and grow.

10

Moving Toward a Multiracial Future

Why Think About Whiteness?

The main point of this book is that we who are white Americans should be a little more aware of our race and our culture, that is to say, our whiteness. We need to understand how we presently fit within the racial structure of the United States. When Robert Terry, in 1981, said, *"To be white in America is not to have to think about it,"* he was describing the situation as it was, not as he thought it should be.[1] We do have to think about it. True, even today many white people can blissfully ignore their racial and cultural background and identity. But as the country becomes increasingly multiracial in composition, the space in which we can wear racial blinders is diminishing. There are many good reasons to think about what it means to be white. Here are twelve of them:

1. Awareness of our culture is needed to change it. We cannot change simply by defining ourselves as changed. Whiteness and white privilege operate at subconscious levels. They influence even those who consciously assume ethnic and regional identities, and deny their connection to white culture.

2. Self-awareness is necessary to understanding. In order to understand how cultures shape and influence people, it is necessary to understand how you are shaped and influenced by your own culture. If you are ignorant of your own cultural influences, you are likely to misunderstand and misinterpret the cultural experiences of other people.

3. Being white affects your life chances. This is readily understood by people from other racial groups in the United States. Understanding it yourself depends first on understanding your position as a white person in the racial structure of our country. Not understanding this makes you less credible in a multiracial setting.

4. People of color must contend with white culture. This task becomes more difficult and stressful for people of color when whites are unable to acknowledge our culture. Not understanding your whiteness will make you less able to engage in relationships with people of color in a genuine and supportive manner.

5. White people have common problems. Through our cultural connection, white Americans share many common attitudes, concerns and feelings. These feelings may involve (a) our relationships with people of color; (b) our relationships with other white people; and (c) our feelings about our own whiteness. Acknowledging one's whiteness is a first step to discussing and understanding how these fears shape, and often hinder, our actions in multiracial settings.

6. White culture has both bad and good points. Denying the bad aspects of white culture makes us unable to work for positive change. Denying the good aspects of white culture leaves many of us disconnected from our shared experiences with family, friends, and community.

7. White culture is not American culture. We are all Americans. But for white Americans to insist that we all "just be Americans" without acknowledging the different cultural experiences of people of color is a thinly disguised way of saying everyone should act like white Americans. This makes no more sense than insisting everyone act like black Americans, or Asian-Americans, etc.

8. Lack of awareness preserves the status quo. Lack of awareness by whites of our culture is sometimes seen by people of color as intentional, preserving our privileged position in society. If we do not acknowledge our own culture, we do not hold ourselves accountable for changing it and creating a society that can accommodate other cultures.

9. We fail to meet our ideals. White Americans have proudly opposed foreign tyranny and political oppression in the name of freedom and equality (as have other racial groups in the United States). But we have been oppressors within our own country. This contradictory aspect of our culture has been called the "American dilemma." We fail to meet some of our most cherished ideals through lack of courage to confront, examine, and hold ourselves accountable for changing our own culture.

10. We are not exempt. For the United States to develop a more equitable and less conflicted society, all cultures must change. No culture can define itself as exempt, or opt out of this process if we are to succeed as a nation. In particular, white culture cannot reasonably expect to set itself up as the endpoint of an historic process of assimilation. If the melting pot model is a valid one, we all have a little more melting to do, white Americans included.

11. Why let racists define the culture? In the past, persons claiming to speak specifically for white Americans did so from a white supremacist point of view. This is still largely true today, but it need not be so. As a white American, you have as much of a right to say what white American culture can and should stand for in the future as does any racist demagogue. Being an advocate for developing a positive role for white Americans in multiracial America is an immensely important task.

12. Some of our issues are unique. While cultures of color have struggled to attain power, white Americans must struggle to share the power we have. While cultures of color have struggled to retain their autonomy, white Americans must struggle to make our culture exist without dominating other cultures. We need to develop a public discussion of issues that apply uniquely to us as white Americans in multiracial America.

The Problem of the 21st Century

Nearly 100 years ago African-American sociologist W. E. B. DuBois wrote that the problem of the 20th century would be that of the color line. Events proved him right. Though I'm no W. E. B. DuBois, I predict the problem of the 21st century will be creating a multiracial society. As a nation we already are multiracial *in composition,* and becoming increasingly more so as we move into this century. But this a multiracial *society* does not make. In Chapter 2 I defined a multiracial society as one in which (1) color doesn't matter, especially in determining access to resources and power, and (2) multiracial settings are the norm. If we are to consider what it means to be white people living in a multiracial society, one which we aspire to share in creating, then it's helpful to look at this notion of a "multiracial society" more closely.

Access to Power and Resources

Since the 1960s most antiracism activists have come to define racism as race prejudice plus power. We all have prejudices—some more, some less—and no one is free of bias. Yet these prejudices don't amount to much if we lack the power to enforce them. Racism is a system in which white people have power to make our racial prejudices impact people of color. You can quibble about this definition, as I sometimes have myself. Who has the power? Is it always white people? Are white people inherently racist by this definition? These are hairs this definition invites us to split. But the definition is substantially right. Power is the issue. If you are not talking about how power is managed in race relations, then you simply are not being antiracist. Joseph Barndt goes so far as to divide multiculturalism into racist and antiracist modes. Racist multiculturalism emphasizes the positive aspects of cultural difference, but fails to look at the underlying power differentials that keep white people and white culture in charge.

Who Has the Power?

Let me offer a thought experiment for white people. Suppose you believed a person has unjustly deprived you of your land, labor, or wealth. You get so hopping mad in this nation of law and due process that you decide to fight it all the way to the top. Now depending on your strategy, that top might be the President of the United States, the United States Supreme Court, the United States Congress, or the board of directors of a major corporation. If you were truly starting from the bottom and struggling up through the various levels of the social structure, you would find, on average, the people hearing your appeal at each level are proportionately more white (and male) in number as you move upward. That's how our society is structured. Eventually you would reach the final level and a decision would be rendered.

Leaving aside the actual verdict, let me now pose my experimental question. Suppose that instead of each level becoming whiter, it became blacker. As you move up the steps on your personal mission for justice, the decision makers and holders of power contain a proportionately greater number of black people until the final decision makers are virtually all black (and perhaps female, too). Not only that, the setting, the cultural norms and the accoutrements show a strong African influence. In fact, you might be the only non-black person in the room. Do you think the ultimate outcome will be as favorable to your case? Suppose the person who did you harm was also black. Do you think it would make a difference on how fairly your case was decided? Do you have an opinion about what color you might like your attorney to be?

Along with power is access to resources. Obtaining and controlling resources are the main reasons to hold power, and thus represent the material battleground on which racism plays out. In our past, land, labor, and wealth have all been seized from people of color under a system of white supremacy in the United States. That system has been attacked and weakened in recent years, but it has left us with an historical structure that continues in our society.

If racism is prejudice plus power, the racial structure of our society has concentrated that power in the hands of white people at the expense of people of color. Antiracism, defined as "the process of actively and consistently confronting racism and anti-Semitism wherever they occur," has been the major force aimed at undoing that racial structure.[2] Antiracism is practiced by a number of people of all racial backgrounds and there are many specific theories and approaches to its practice. For the most part these various approaches attempt to create a society in which people of color can live and not suffer from racism. Many practitioners note that white people, too, suffer from racism, though not necessarily in the same way as disenfranchised and disempowered groups of color.

Antiracism often focuses on helping people of color achieve the power and resources they need to pursue the goals their group has defined as important. Depending on the group in question, its historic relationship to white society, and its current aspirations, this may involve becoming part of the dominant culture or, alternatively, preventing the dominant culture from interfering with the internal process of that group and taking resources and power from that group's control. Antiracism also helps white people understand how racism operates. This is not something white culture prepares us to do. Education and training are needed and antiracism fills this role. Once recognized, white people need to confront racism, and antiracism also offers strategies and support for such acts.

What Are We For?

Antiracism, however, is not a positive goal. Its very name and definition are to be against something—racism. This is hardly a new observation and some antiracists, having heard it, reply that antiracism does many positive things. It is part of creating a better world in which racial justice, racial equality, and racial harmony prevail. Truly these are worthy of support. So, too, is ending a war. The analogy is appropriate. Many consider race relations to be in a state of perpetual conflict. But when the war ends, what will the peace look like? Recalling the words of Robert Terry,

> being anti-racist is not enough. Defining what we are against moves into clarifying what we are for. An increasing number of whites is being challenged to articulate alternatives to racism that go beyond simply its elimination. The urgent question that whites must answer is: What alternative models can replace the present American white-male-dominated society?[3]

Antiracist activists have offered visions of alternative models. Joseph Barndt, for instance, calls for institutions to become antiracist, pluralistic and multicultural. Using a model originally developed by Bailey Jackson and Rita Hardiman,

205

he poses a developmental process that organizations need to follow from mono-cultural and segregated beginnings to a final inclusive state of being. Paul Kivel says we need to develop democratic anti-racist multiculturalism. For others, inclusion in the mainstream is not the issue. American Indian activist Russel Means wants only that Indians be free to decide their own fate without impositions by federal, state, and local (non-Indian) government and private interests.[4] Nationalist movements among African-Americans and Latinos also reject a society that does not center on their own cultural and political needs. This is not to say they would necessarily be antagonistic to an inclusive, pluralistic, and multi-cultural model that included other groups. But that same model must recognize the need for some racial/cultural groups to preserve their autonomy and become immersed in their own experience.

Harlon L. Dalton, professor of law at Yale, explored the question of how a society no longer structured by race might look. In his book, *Racial Healing*, Dalton considered that we might not want race itself to be eliminated. "We human beings tend to become quite attached to the familiar, with all its warts and blemishes. At least we know how to negotiate it. We know what to expect. We have already figured out how to adapt to the bad and take advantage of the good" (p. 214).[5] Race, in other words, has cultural elements, as already discussed here. Dalton points out that eliminating race also has implications for ethnicity since black culture is based in resistance and white ethnic assimilation has been based on the scapegoating of blacks. Asians and Latinos may today be experiencing the same process and lack of a societal scapegoat may aggravate ethnic rivalries.

Imagining a situation in which people magically all had the same skin color, Dalton believes race would still have an effect since the memories and experiences of people would be affected by previous racial standing. Furthermore, differences in appearance also signal differences in culture, and cultural differences provide a richness important to many people. He then proposed distributing everyone every place in proportion to their racial numbers, like a massive quota system applying to every facet of life. But he points out this "picture-perfect integration" denies freedom of choice and does not allow group characteristics and preferences to form. Some people may prefer the cultural experience of their own group over that of others. Still other people may like stepping outside their group into the cultural experiences of other groups. Neither would be possible under the perfect proportional distribution idea.

Dalton concludes race needs to be "detached from issues of privilege and power" (p. 222). It's not race that needs to be eliminated, but rather the racial hierarchy to which race is tied:

> In the absence of racial hierarchy, I would not be bothered by the existence of predominantly White, partially Asian-American symphony orchestras. I'd be perfectly happy to have the NBA remain

predominantly Black… On the other hand, the composition of the Senate would have to change dramatically. If it did not do so through the normal electoral process, I would question seriously whether we had succeeded in uncoupling race and power (p. 222).

Uncoupling race and power and creating multiracial spaces is not something that comes easily to white folk. Dalton, an African-American man, speaks of something more than a polite integration where people of different races rub shoulders in workplaces, churches, and other settings where white cultural norms still prevail. We must open our hearts more fully to change, for:

> even in environments that look inviting on the surface, it is important to look past appearances and determine whether an invisible hierarchy is in place. The most promising settings for genuinely egalitarian interaction are ones where White folk are out of their element, where the pecking order is reversed, or where the natives get to bring religion to the missionaries instead of the other way around. Unfortunately, such settings are altogether too rare. Not surprisingly, Whites who find themselves in such settings often have difficulty adjusting to not being on top. But that, of course, is part of the lesson to be learned, for in a world in which race and power are unhinged, power will have to be shared (p. 225).

White people can learn this lesson. Dalton speaks of his experience with the Salt and Pepper Gospel Singers, a group joined in celebration of African-American musical tradition, comprising members of both African and European heritage. White people go through an adjustment phase entering the group, finding their way in a setting where white norms do not prevail. But they persist, for love of the music and, importantly, for "the opportunity to interact with Black people on a genuinely human level" (p. 227). I believe that desire to reach across racial lines and interact on a genuinely human level is a powerful one for many white people. I have felt that power in my personal life, and I personally know many other white people who feel the same way. Indeed, I direct my work to those white friends and acquaintances, and the millions of white people I've yet to meet, all who believe a multiracial community based in genuine humanness transcends any experience white culture may itself offer. We are the future of our people.

Another Model

In 1997 Charley Flint and I proposed another model.[6] Stated briefly, we contend that our present society is based on white values and white culture controls power and access to resources. Whiteness needs to be taken out of the center of our society, and the center replaced with multiracial values. In some respects our model is not very different from suggestions made by many people, including those whose ideas are discussed above. We are not proposing something radically new. Antiracists, multiculturalists, diversity practitioners, and a host of others have been working toward such a vision for many long years. However, we have developed our model in somewhat greater detail than those already presented. We may not be right. Only time will tell that. But as Terry pointed out, we must begin to think about what we are working for, and not simply what we are against.

If we are to undo the racial structure of our society, what will take its place? Our model supposes that there will be a center. To pose a society without a center is to suggest something historically uncommon among large societies. Large societies, and perhaps all societies, need central points of comparison, of social and economic exchange, and of assimilation. These are the means by which a culture realizes and defines itself. The center of a society is the point in which power is held and resources are allocated.

To pose a society without a racial center, when race has been central for more than 300 years, is to suggest a revolutionary change, not an evolutionary one. One problem with revolutionary change is that in the ensuing chaos, disruption, and violence, the new society may be no more just than the former one. There is no magic in encouraging violence and disruption, and there is always the chance that revolutionary change might not take place. A misdirected "revolution" might simply restructure racial relationships in a different way without removing race as a structural feature of society.

The central area of a society can vary remarkably in characteristics from one society to another. In some societies, the center may be diffuse, in others, concentrated. Some societies may support a vertical center with extreme class differences and a powerful, entrenched elite. Other societies may have a horizontal center, with few boundaries among members in terms of access to resources and power. Societies also vary in the type and number of barriers imposed upon outsiders who would like to enter the society. The center can also be oppressive or supportive. In the history of the United States, whiteness as the center has always, on the whole, denied people of color access to power and resources. This has been the net effect, despite many acts of resistance by people who have been racialized as white. The central culture has constructed numerous and real cultural barriers to entry to people of color.

If whiteness, or white culture, is at the center of American society, then color and cultures of color are at the margins. Cultures of color have created and continue to maintain their own historical sets of values which include cultural self-definitions of being different from the center. Consequently, cultures of color have their own centers in which power and resources available to each are controlled and allocated, and values specific to each culture of color are expressed and upheld. However, cultures of color are unable to effectively defend themselves from the overriding presence of white culture, which may impose its values and assert its power against cultures of color, and co-opt the resources that cultures of color still retain.

An important advantage of being white is that only one cultural practice must be acquired by the individual, and it is acquired from birth. At the margins, those wanting access to resources of the center of our society do not have power to simply acquire the access they desire. One might readily think of access to our national institutions, such as the U.S. presidency, the U.S. Senate, our major corporations, universities, etc. People from nonwhite racial/cultural groups must pursue access to resources on terms set by the center, i.e. according to the cultural practices of white people. This necessitates being bicultural. A requirement of biculturality creates considerable overhead for the individual, making his or her efforts inefficient because of the need to think through things that for cultural insiders are unconscious.

Relations Between White Culture and Cultures of Color

In the multiracial/cultural society of the United States, interracial/cultural relations can be viewed from two levels. On the individual level, we can look at how any one person or persons can move within and between various racial/cultural groups. At some more aggregated level, we can look at how various racial/cultural groups have stood in relation to one another. In this latter sense we can make statements such as, "White people have exploited people of color," and understand it describes relations on a grand scale, or in the preponderance through history, but allowing as well that not all individuals' experiences could be condensed to so simple a statement.

On the individual level, people may move among racial cultures, not without cost, but with some greater degree of acceptance, on average, than in the past. Individual movement is still constricted by racial identity and ascribed racial status. Aggregate truths remain. White culture still presents barriers to people of color. Cultures of color erect defensive barriers to protect themselves from white culture, and to a lesser extent, other cultures of color.

Individual variation also exists in the extent that people may gravitate toward or away from the center of their own racial/cultural group. Some people identify closely with their racial/cultural group, and in some cases choose to live as much as their choice will allow within the monoracial/cultural experience of their group. Other individuals may feel constrained by their own racial/cultural group when other racial/cultural groups are readily at hand as counter-examples. Some people prefer a multiracial/cultural lifestyle. People may gravitate toward or away from the center of racial/cultural groups other than their own. Examples of gravitating away from racial/cultural groups are well-known. White people have held cultures of color in disdain. Various cultures of color have, defensively, held white culture in disdain and created boundaries from other cultures of color from time to time. In other cases, people from various cultures of color have formed alliances and mutual living arrangements, as among Native Americans and African-Americans. Some white people have been attracted, individually, to various cultures of color. Whether any people of color have been attracted to white culture is not clear, but many have taken pride in their ability to understand and work its rules to their advantage.

People, within limits, can come and go in multiracial and monoracial settings, seeking their place amidst the larger monoracial/cultural structures. But it is unlikely the structures themselves will dissolve. For a period of time of historical dimension, from several years to many generations, African-American culture, Native American culture, and European-American culture will not effectively blend into one center. Despite the differences and conflicts within each of these racial/cultural groups concerning the location of their own centers, each likely will act to maintain its center independent of the other two. When Asian-Americans and Hispanic-Americans are included in the mix, the possible melding of these racial/cultural groups into a common center seems unlikely. Each group has very distinct circumstances.

The center of each racial/cultural group may undergo radical transformation, and some may converge as others remain static or grow more distant. But to have the centers of all racial groups merge of their own accord and become a single center remains doubtful. Cultures of color have in the past aligned jointly against white culture, and this possibility remains open and to some extent is in practice even today. But this political alignment on a common goal is not the same as these cultural groups merging or assimilating their centers. In all these scenarios, whiteness still remains central.

Figure 10.1 summarizes the current racial/cultural structure of United States society on the aggregate level. White culture occupies the center, and cultures of color are arrayed on the margin. The various monoracial/cultural groups are drawn to a scale that approximates their proportion of the total United States population. The continued position of white culture at the center of American society is problematic because white culture has, on balance, been based on principles of conquest and exploitation. This is not the only relationship that a center might have to the margins, but it has been the one that white culture has maintained from its seminal appearance in Jamestown to this very moment. Time has changed many things, including the nature of power relations between white culture and cultures of color. Elements of exchange and justice are

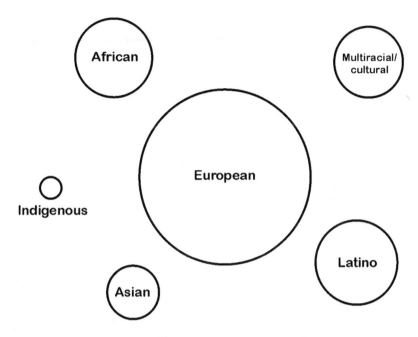

Figure 10.1 The existing racial/cultural structure of United States society on the aggregate level.

beginning to make headway.

But white culture as the center has not offered protection to cultures of color. Its coercive ability alone has been sufficient to hold onto these cultures at the margins by force. The center might conceivably hold onto its margins by offering exchange and justice rather than conquest and exploitation. But white culture has no aggregate experience offering protection such as this, and it is doubtful that it can learn. Cultures act in their own interests. Individuals are not themselves cultures and may step out of the role their own culture might wish to assign them. But cultures themselves as aggregate beings pursue a path of self-interest centered on their own values and past practice. Some white people believe that white culture, after centuries in which it exterminated 98% of the Indian population, enslaved and murdered millions of Africans, and relentlessly exploited Latinos and Asians can now become the benign arbitrator of multiracial justice. Their belief is pollyanish nonsense.

White culture has become more benign. Our world is much smaller now, and cultures of color have learned our ways and fought back. White culture is finally coming to be held in check, and I believe it is to our betterment. But white culture will continue to work for its own interests. White culture will seek white justice and advantage, not multiracial justice and advantage. White culture will seek white community, not multiracial community. That simply is as cultures do. We should not expect anything else of it. Cultures of color seek their own ends as well.

We believe it is unfair that any single racial/cultural group controls the center of our society. Hence whiteness needs to be taken out of the center to join other racial/cultural groups on the margins. Given the power relationships between racial/cultural groups, it is unlikely that the center can remain vacant. Power, like nature, abhors a vacuum. We do not feel any single race should have the advantage of being defined as the center. Thus even if there must be some center to society, no single race should occupy that space to the exclusion of the others. But if each racial/cultural group has its own center, and if it seems likely these centers will not merge, then for any one race to claim the center of our society becomes, effectively, an act of excluding others. With whiteness no longer central, however it might be accomplished, the various racial/cultural groups in the United States will be in a face-off over whose standards prevail. In other words, they each will have to contend for the center. There is no problem with the different racial/cultural groups doing this, provided the contest is fair and it continues to allow access to the center by all groups. However, contests sometimes become lopsided, someone wins and someone loses, and destructive conflict arises as a way of solving disputes. Continual unresolved competition among major cultural groups, without some other structure encouraging cooperation, is a recipe for disaster.

Figure 10.2 shows what we are working toward. The center is now occupied by a multiracial culture and the monoracial/cultural groups, including white culture, are on the margins. Rather than a single monoracial/cultural group forming the center, the center is multiracial. While there is no self-identified multiracial culture in America, there are pockets of multiracial community development. These multiracial pockets, always local, fragile, and subject to the turbulence of relations between the monoracial/cultural groups, might nonetheless exist at the center of several racial/cultural groups that stand in check and balance with one another.

Viewed another way, it is unlikely white culture will displace itself from the center. Cultures simply do not act that way of their own volition. Cultures of color, however, are not likely to unilaterally displace whiteness for many years at the soonest. In effect, with people of color acting unilaterally, the model is more one of surrounding whiteness. This may diminish the scope of white culture, but it still leaves it at the center. It will take a multiracial effort to displace whiteness, one that includes people from all racial/cultural groups.

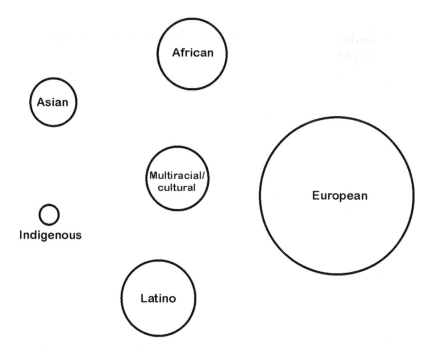

Figure 10.2 Aggregate racial/cultural structure of United States society centered on multiracial/cultural values, with white culture in a decentered position along with other racial/cultural groups.

A multiracial center has the advantage that it can develop a cultural practice of protecting the margins, i.e. monoracial/cultural groups from whence the multiracial culture originates. The monoracial/cultural groups have the means for representation in the multiracial center from within their own groups. Thus no monoracial/cultural group needs to give up its own center in order to attain some measure of participation in the center of American society.

It is critical to understand that our model calls for two conditions. One condition is that white culture be taken out of the center and placed on the margin. The other condition is that the center be a multiracial/cultural group. These two conditions are interdependent. One cannot happen without the other. White culture cannot be moved to the margin unless something takes its place at the center. The center cannot become multiracial unless white culture is moved to the margin. It is not enough to make the center multiracial if white culture is not made marginal. And it is not enough simply to try to make white culture marginal without making the center multiracial. Both conditions must be met. Both are goals to be achieved. We contend that it is not good planning to approach these conditions as if they can be independently accomplished. Whiteness cannot be removed without some thought of what will happen to the power vacuum its removal creates. A multiracial center will not be achieved unless whiteness is decentered.

Comparison to Other Models

Our model does not call for the perfectly proportional distribution of people from different racial groups as posed, and rejected, by Harlon L. Dalton. Nor does it require that race-as-culture be done away with and replaced by a single assimilated cultural group. We allow that the existing monoracial/cultural groups will continue to exist, each with their own cultural centers and we recognize that some people will prefer living experiences that center within those cultures. However, our model does require that racial hierarchy be undone, again fitting Dalton's requirements.

Within the last decade there has been talk in progressive circles of "centering the margins." While the intent of this idea is worthy, its statement as a strategy raises questions. First, it hides the fact that cultures of color have their own centers, which include not only individual people, leaders, or philosophies, but also shared heritage and values. A person on the margin may not want to occupy the center as it is currently defined, i.e., as dominated by the values of white culture. Drawing people from the centers of their respective cultures into an otherwise unmodified and largely white center still leaves whiteness as central. Movement toward the center, after all, means adopting the values that are already in place there. These values may change as the center changes, but then that should be the object, i.e., that the center should be changed, not that the margins should be centered.

Some have suggested that people of color attack and destroy white culture, but assaults on whiteness, depending on their nature, may have the effect of confirming and solidifying the central position of whiteness in American society. Like a prize fighter who by defeating all contenders expands his reputation and retinue, whiteness may find its position reinforced while those who attack it are relegated further to the margins. Thought must be given to how whiteness itself can be made more marginal.

Finally, people have suggested that racial/cultural pluralism is the answer, and we would agree, provided the center of the society is a multiracial culture. Models that call for a monoracial pluralism without calling for a multiracial center, set up conditions that invite competition, conflict, and instability.

Let's Be Clear on Some Things

White people are not bad. I can imagine some people will read our model and believe we are saying white people are inherently evil and should feel guilty. Furthermore, that because of this, all white people should be forced to the margins of society in some gigantic "reverse racism" ploy. This is not the case. White people certainly have a lot to deal with concerning the way our culture has conducted itself in relation to other racial/cultural groups, but we are not calling for the total condemnation and marginalization of white culture. Rather, we are simply calling for equal treatment, culturally speaking. To white people who have been in the center all our lives, this may look and sound like a fall from grace, and it is. There is no getting around that fact.

However, we are not suggesting that white people fall below people of color, but rather to a spot where our own values would place us, i.e., to a point where we all have equal access to the power and resources of our society. Furthermore, those white people who are able to function within a multiracial society should be part of the multiracial culture at the center. Indeed, developing the skills needed to operate in a multiracial setting should be a prime determinant of merit. In fact, simply based on the numerical presence of white people, it would be expected that the multiracial culture comprising the center will have a considerable white, or European-American, influence to it.

So we are not calling for all white people to be marginalized. Realistically, though, many white people who hold positions of power today are culturally incompetent and we expect that they would not function well in a society centered on multiracial values. Furthermore, we would recommend parents of white children see that their children's education includes at least some measure of skills training and experience in multiracial settings.

Do we want a multiracial society? Are white people going to give up our central position? If not, then what do we want? Realistically, what are the alternatives? My crystal ball is cloudy and I cannot answer these questions with certainty. Nor is there any single answer, given the diversity of opinion among white people on these matters. People of color have something to say as well, and the something is just as diverse, if not more so.

Certainly the transition from a white-centered society to a multiracial one will be marked with moments of confusion, frustration and conflict. When the rules change, these things happen. Some of the mighty will fall, and when they do it will not be without a fight. Some of the disempowered will rise, and some of those will forget their oppression and milk their privilege. But on balance I believe the struggle is worth it. And I believe many other people like me feel the same way.

Multiracial Settings Are the Norm

Having looked earlier at the matter of access to power and resources, let us return to the second condition of a multiracial society, the one that says multiracial settings are the norm. Rather than the word "setting," the word "community" might actually be more descriptive. A setting might consist simply of incidental interaction, like in a train station, for instance. Communities imply people working together, relying on one another, sharing resources and common values.

A multiracial community, in the sense that we use it, is a community group in which people from two or more racial/cultural groups work and/or live together. Furthermore, enough people of each racial/cultural group must be present so that they are able to sustain their own cultural experience within the community without having to subsume that experience under a monoracial/cultural orientation. Many white neighborhoods, schools, and workplaces claim to be "integrated" because they have a proportionally small nonwhite population of perhaps three to five percent. With so few people of color, white culture will continue to be in the center, perhaps seeking to accommodate the people of color who are present. But multiracial community-building will not take place.

A second characteristic of multiracial communities, besides living and working in common, is a lack of racial boundaries. Access to the community may require some shared beliefs, but those beliefs never impose skin color and racial origin as boundaries. This is the expression of an ideal, indeed one that white culture and other monoracial/cultural groups also espouse to some degree. Whether a true lack of racial boundaries has ever been realized by any multiracial community at any time in the United States is debatable. But as an ideal, it is more likely to have been lived in practice as well as theory within those communities that have had a multiracial character.

Historically, monoracial/cultural groups, and particularly white culture, have been antagonistic to the formation of multiracial communities. There are few real multiracial communities today, and those that exist are to be found on the margins of the margin, far from the center of our society. To speak the virtues of true multiracial involvement is held by many to be speaking of something odd at best, if not misguided, bizarre, or even disloyal. While many people are willing to espouse colorblindness, brother- and sisterhood, and a common humanity, the actual practitioner of multiracial community-building still feels as if he or she has to apologize to someone for something, or find a spot so secluded that the greater and more powerful racial forces in America do not tear her or his efforts asunder.

People in multiracial communities have an interesting standing vis-à-vis one another and toward their cultures of origin. By definition, they have not located themselves at the center of their own cultures of origin, and also by definition they all share this trait in common, regardless of the cultures from which they originated. Monoracial communities criticize members of their group who participate in multiracial community-building, questioning their "loyalty" and calling them names such as "Uncle Toms," "oreos," "bananas," "apples," "coconuts," "Indian lovers," and "nigger lovers." People who are themselves of multiracial heritage face pressures to "choose sides" and they encounter a set of pejorative names all their own.

Each monoracial community discourages its members from shifting their alliance from a monoracial center to a multiracial one. Each person in a multiracial community is thus subject to pressure from their racial group to recognize the prominence of their monoracial ties, and disavow or place as secondary the task of building a multiracial community. In the face of this, a multiracial community is a mutual act of creation and trust in which the participants place their loyalty to the multiracial process above and beyond their loyalty to their monoracial groups of origin. If any group abandons the process, the multiracial character is lost.

Fortunately multiracial community-building can be done in degrees, else it might never be done at all. People interested in multiracial community-building need to find centers of activity (communities, organizations, employers, etc.) where people from several racial backgrounds are working and living together. A person living in a monoracial family can locate within a multiracial neighborhood, work for a multiracial organization, attend a multiracial church, and generally place a premium on those settings where multiracial norms are explicitly spoken and observed. By a "premium," we mean to say a person is willing to pay more, travel farther, or work harder for access to these settings than they are for access to a monoracial setting, especially the monoracial setting of her or his own racial group. Though few and far between, these multiracial settings exist. When not present, people need to take the initiative to create them.

We are not suggesting that everyone abandon their monoracial communities. Some people prefer their own culture and are not ready for the tumult and uncertainty that a multiracial setting might entail. Furthermore, multiracial community-building need not require its participants to abandon their monoracial heritage. Even persons of multiracial heritage have ties to monoracial communities. Rather it might be expected that people in multiracial communities will still be supportive of efforts among monoracial communities to achieve racial equality and harmony. It must also be expected that people who are attracted to multiracial community-building will take some interest in being involved with other racial/cultural groups.

But multiracial community-building must see itself as something more than a marginal enterprise. We assert that multiracial community-building must become the central force in the United States. Rather than anonymity, it should be highlighted. Rather than socially insignificant, it should claim the significance of being central. It should not be content to be a placid side tributary; it should claim the mainstream, the styles, the trends, the attention of the country. Not odd, but normal, the multiracial community should not have to explain itself. It should ask why monoracial communities choose to be isolated, and it should demand that they reach out. It should demand economic, social, and moral support for its expansion and growth. Multiracial community-building, if it is to become significant, requires people to commit themselves to the interest of this community above and beyond their monoracial interests.

Decentering Whiteness

Difficult as it may be to build multiracial community, it's not enough. White culture must also be moved from the center of our society to the margin, side by side with other monoracial/cultural groups. We have termed this process "decentering whiteness." Decentering whiteness is a collective process that can take place in organizations, sectors of society, personal lives, etc., over periods of days, months, years, and generations. Anyone so willing can take the goal of decentering whiteness and attempt to develop transition plans that affect their local sphere of influence. Larger alliances can be sustained to exert influence on a broader scale.

Many of these efforts and alliances are already underway, though not necessarily under the name of decentering whiteness. While we feel there is a need to make the process of decentering whiteness a broadly accepted goal, these ongoing efforts, such as those stemming from multiracial/cultural education and activism, are important. We do not believe there is anything incompatible with our approach and these existing efforts. As much as anything, we are suggesting a reason for their continued and renewed use.

It is possible to imagine some of the circumstances that must take place as whiteness is decentered. Those of us who wish to decenter whiteness need to question its unspoken role as the standard and ask what other standards exist, from what other racial/cultural groups. Rather than letting white culture form the background, we need to assume whiteness, and race, always structures our experience, and thus needs to be consciously considered as part of any social process. We need to make it clear that "normal" is defined by one's culture. Different racial/cultural groups have different definitions of normal. A central definition of normal should be a multiracial one and a desire for multiracial contact should be assumed to be normal. When whiteness passes as the "common" understanding, we need to ask, "Understood by whom?" and listen to see if both white people and people of color

answer. When only white people answer, the "commonness" of the understanding among all Americans becomes questionable.

Not all white people are equally immersed or involved in white culture or
cultures of color. Some whites prefer monoracially white settings. Others
prefer and are more knowledgeable about multiracial settings or nonwhite
monoracial settings. Some white people are of full European parentage.
Other white people are of partial European parentage. We should not let
white culture appear undifferentiated. Degrees of immersion in white culture should be articulated. Whiteness still observes the "one drop" that says
to be considered white, a person cannot have any black ancestors. This
should be modified to allow any person with a cultural and/or genetic tie to
European-American culture to identify as white. Identification should not
be posed as an either/or situation. People of mixed ancestry, and people
who gravitate to a mixture of cultural influences, should be able to acknowledge all these influences, including whiteness.

We need to dispute that white culture can determine who is "American"
and who is not. White culture should be characterized simply as one of
many racial/cultural groups, all of whom have a more or less equal standing
and claim on the American experience and American society. It should not
be treated as the "glue" that holds things together, particularly since there
are severe problems with the "glue" experienced by nonwhite people. The
glue (shared heritage and privilege) that holds white people together is not
the same as the glue (power and coercion) that holds cultures of color to an
American society that is white at the center. This glue needs to be changed
to a multiracial one.

It's presently difficult for white people to be comfortable with our culture
with any sense of integrity. But white people do not have to surrender our
racial/cultural style or identity, just our centrality. We need to create a circumstance in which each group's culture, including our own, is protected
from harm by a mutual agreement among racial/cultural groups to work
cooperatively and not to exploit one another. Rather than relying on the
absolute power of white culture to dominate, security should be provided
by the multiracial center and agreement among racial/cultural groups.
Avenues for economic support and professional advancement should
extend from a multiracial center, and not from assimilation to white culture.
Acquisition of the customs and habits needed to function in a multiracial
center should be a prerequisite for personal and professional growth.
Limited growth opportunities should remain available to white people
unable or unwilling to master the skills needed to function outside of white
culture, but these should be modest in comparison to opportunities available
in the multiracial center.

Rather than being understood as the bland and familiar, whiteness should
be seen as a cultural expression with European roots that stands alongside

other cultural groups. This cultural expression has a unique character that differs from other racial/cultural groups, and may be appreciated by people from both white culture and cultures of color. Rather than the obvious way of doing things, it should be viewed as one alternative among many. We need to distinguish between making universal statements (e.g., "The way every person does it...") and statements which really are more culturally specific (e.g., "The way every white person does it...").

Rather than setting itself up as not open to contradiction, white culture must contend for the center and for understanding as one of many racial/cultural groups. In the process, it can be contradicted, like any other group. White values may be morally correct within their local cultural context, but not above those of the multiracial center, and not according to any absolute biological or cultural principle. White culture should be understood as not naturally dominant. In the past it has had many advantages and acted upon them. But in a society centered on multiracial values, white culture will be somewhat marginal, influencing the center but not central itself. Those who believe the dominance of whiteness was ordained by God will have to reconsider their theology.

White culture is somewhat self-centered and this need not change if the culture itself no longer forms the center of our society. Those who prefer a white cultural experience are welcome to pursue it. White culture will still control some measure of power and resources, but the greater measure of power and resources should be controlled by the multicultural center. People will no longer be coerced into accepting white values, or forced to assimilate to white culture in order to participate in the center of our society. Rather, white people will need to adopt multiracial values in order to participate in the center. A value of self-centeredness in white culture will have limited impact on people from other racial/cultural groups. Nonetheless, a value of self-centeredness will hinder functioning in the multiracial center, and thus will keep those who hold this value from gaining access to resources the center controls.

Where to Begin?

Last night I happened to see David Duke on a TV talk show. Though a former KKK leader, he now says he is not a white supremacist. Instead, he has started a civil rights organization for white people. A white male caller said he had been denied a job because his industry had to hire lesser qualified minorities. He was going to join Mr. Duke's organization. For many white people the notion of a white civil rights organization is appealing.

As I have voiced in this book, the idea of a multiracial society also appeals to many white Americans. It need not be one or the other. I believe it possible for a person to be concerned for both the welfare of white people and for the creation of a society centered on multiracial values. But in the big bad political world we live in, we are often forced to choose. White demogogues throughout our history have forced this choice, sometimes as part of mainstream white culture, and other times over a less organized majority favoring multiracial cooperation.

I don't claim to be objective. I've made my choice. If something pits the self-interest of white culture against the interest found in creating a multiracial society, then I choose the latter. Looking at it another way, it's a matter of how self-interest is defined. For me, it lies not in grabbing everything we can for white people, again.

My self-interest does not lie in convincing white people we are the newest victims in the dynamics of racism in the United States. Cries of white victimhood are an old, old game that go back more than 170 years when free white immigrants decried their economic exploitation and pointed to the slave who had shelter, food, and clothing provided. Yet there is absolutely no record of any white person ever volunteering to become a slave for even the most benevolent of masters. And the masters themselves imagined their own victimhood. They constantly complained of ingratitude and unjust lack of effort from those whose labor they stole. White whining, it seems, has a long history.

My choice is made. I don't believe it forces me to work against the interest of white people. Rather I believe our interests are best served by learning how to live in a multiracial society. But at some point a decision on values is required. Where are you going to put your effort?

I can't answer this for you. And I won't try. But if you have invested the time to read this book, then I imagine you probably believe creating a multiracial society is a worthy goal. I'm not claiming to convince people on the point. I simply believe that those who are into their white victimhood will not have made it to the end of this book. Yet you are here.

There is much work to do. I struggle to say something profound, to guide you on your way. It doesn't come to me. The only advice I can offer is to educate yourself, and to stay with it. There is much to learn about the racial structure of our society, and ample means to learn it. Read, listen, dialogue, join, witness, protest, and participate. Keep with the journey. Ever since whiteness arose as the dominant force in the racial structure of our society it has been opposed as such by people it called white. We've been beaten down, beaten up, and beaten back, but still we continue to move forward. Today we continue a struggle that has taken generations, and will take generations to come. Friend, please stay with it. We need you. It's about our future. You've got to keep going.

Appendix

Works cited in tour of white studies
in Chapter 8, pages 167–172

Alba, Richard D. *Ethnic Identity: The Transformation of White America*. New Haven, Connecticut: Yale University Press, 1990.

Allen, Theodore W. *The Invention of the White Race. Volume One: Racial Oppression and Social Control*. New York: Verso, 1994.

———— *The Invention of the White Race. Volume Two: The Origin of Racial Oppression in Anglo-America*. New York: Verso, 1997.

Almarza, Dario J. "The Construction of Whiteness in History Classrooms: A Case Study of Seventh- and Eighth Grade Mexican American Students." *Dissertation Abstracts International* 58, no. 12, Section A: 4609.

Ani, Marimba. *Yurugu: An African-Centered Critique of European Cultural Thought and Behavior*. Trenton, New Jersey: Africa World Press, 1994.

Athey, Stephanie. "Contested Bodies: The Writing of Whiteness and Gender in American Literature." *Dissertation Abstracts International* 54, no. 8, Section A: 3026.

Bay, Mia Elisabeth. "The White Image in the Black Mind: African American Ideas about White People." *Dissertation Abstracts International* 54, no. 12, Section A: 4554.

Bergstrom, Maria Joy. "'Old Gold and Old Races': Whiteness and Gender in Narratives of the American West." *Dissertation Abstracts International* 57, no. 6, Section A: 2472.

Bernardi, Daniel Leonard. "The Wrath of Whiteness: The Meaning of Race in the Generation of 'Star Trek'." *Dissertation Abstracts International* 56, no. 10, Section A: 3776.

Davy, Kate. "Outing Whiteness: A Feminist/lesbian Project." *Theatre Journal* 47, no. 2 (May 1995).

Day, David V. and Christina A. Douglas. "De-centering Whiteness: Toward an Inclusive Model of Race in Organizations." Paper presented at the 14th Annual Conference of the Society for Industrial and Organizational Psychology, Inc. (May 1, 1999).

Deguzman, Maria. "'American' in Dependence: Figures of Spain in Anglo-American Culture." *Dissertation Abstracts International* 58, no. 5, Section A: 1781.

Dickar, Maryann. "Teaching in Our Underwear: The Liabilities of Whiteness in the Multi-Racial Classroom." *The Researcher* 11, no. 2.

Doane, Ashley W., Jr. "Dominant Group Ethnic Identity in the United States: The Role of 'Hidden' Ethnicity in Intergroup Relations." *The Sociological Quarterly* 38, no. 3 (summer 1997): 375–397.

duCille, Ann. "The Shirley Temple of My Familiar." *Transition* 73: 10–32.

Feagin, Joe R. and Hernán Vera. *White Racism: The Basics.* New York: Routledge, 1995.

Fernandez, John P. "The Impact of Racism on Whites in Corporate America." In *Impacts of Racism on White Americans,* Second Edition, eds. Benjamin P. Bowser and Raymond G. Hunt. Thousand Oaks, California: Sage, 1996.

Fishkin, Shelley Fisher. "Interrogating 'Whiteness,' Complicating Blackness: Remapping American Culture." *American Quarterly* 47, no. 3 (September 1995): 428–466.

Flagg, Barbara J. *Was Blind But Now I See: White Race Consciousness and the Law.* New York: New York University Press, 1998.

Frankenberg, Ruth. *White Women, Race Matters: The Social Construction of Whiteness.* Minneapolis: University of Minnesota Press, 1993.

Gaertner, Samuel L., John F. Dovidio, Brenda S. Banker, Mary C. Rust, Jason A. Nier, Gary R. Mottola, and Christine M. Ward. "Does White Racism Necessarily Mean Antiblackness? Aversive Racism and Prowhiteness." In *Off White: Readings on Race, Power and Society,* eds. Michelle Fine, Lois Weis, Linda C. Powell, and L. Mun Wong. New York: Routledge, 1997.

Gallagher, Charles A. "White Reconstruction in the University." *Socialist Review* 94, nos. 1-2 (1995): 165–187.

Giroux, Henry A. "Rewriting the Discourse of Racial Identity: Towards a Pedagogy and Politics of Whiteness." *Harvard Educational Review* 67, no. 2 (summer 1997): 285–320.

Hale, Grace Elizabeth. *Making Whiteness: The Culture of Segregation in the South, 1890–1940.* New York: Pantheon Books, 1998.

Harris, Cheryl I. "Whiteness as Property." *Harvard Law Review* 106, no. 8 (June 1993): 1710–1791.

Hartigan, John, Jr. "Locating White Detroit." In *Displacing Whiteness*, ed. Ruth Frankenburg. Durham, North Carolina: Duke University Press, 1997.

Helms, Janet E. *Black and White Racial Identity: Theory, Research and Practice.* Westport, Connecticut: Preager Publishers, 1993.

hooks, bell. "Representing Whiteness: Seeing Wings of Desire." In *Yearning: Race, Gender and Cultural Politics.* Boston: South End Press, 1990.

———. "Representing Whiteness in the Black Imagination." In *Cultural Studies*, eds. Lawrence Grossberg, Cary Nelson, and Paula Treichler. New York: Routledge, 1992.

Howard, Gary R. "Whites in Multicultural Education." *Phi Delta Kappan* 75, no. 1 (September 1993).

Howell, Sharon L. "The Learning Organization: Reproduction of Whiteness." In *White Reign: Deploying Whiteness in America,* eds. Joe L. Kincheloe, Shirley R. Steinberg, Nelson M. Rodriguez, and Ronald E. Chennault. New York: St. Martin's Press, 1998.

Ignatiev, Noel. *How the Irish Became White.* New York: Routledge, 1995.

Klotz, Marcia. "White Women and the Dark Continent: Gender and Sexuality in German Colonial Discourse from Sentimental Novel to Fascist Film." *Dissertation Abstracts International* 56, no. 1, Section A: 208.

Lipsitz, George. "The Possessive Investment in Whiteness: Racialized Social Democracy and the 'White' Problem in American Studies." *American Quarterly* 47, no. 3 (September 1995): 369–387.

López, Ian F. Haney. *White by Law: The Legal Construction of Race.* New York: New York University Press, 1996.

Lott, Eric. "The Whiteness of Film Noir." In *Whiteness: A Critical Reader,* ed. Mike Hill. New York: New York University Press, 1997.

Marty, Deborah Lynn. "Accounting for Racial Privilege in White Antiracist Rhetorics." *Dissertation Abstracts International* 57, no. 10, Section A: 4188.

McIntyre, Alice. *Making Meaning of Whiteness: Exploring Racial Identity with White Teachers.* Albany: State University of New York Press, 1997.

McLaren, Peter. "Whiteness Is...: The Struggle for Postcolonial Hybridity." In *White Reign: Deploying Whiteness in America,* eds. Joe L. Kincheloe, Shirley R. Steinberg, Nelson M. Rodriguez, and Ronald E. Chennault. New York: St. Martin's Press, 1998.

McMichael, Robert Kenneth. "Consuming Jazz: Black Music and Whiteness." *Dissertation Abstracts International* 57, no. 9, Section A: 3999.

Melnick, Jeffrey. "'Story Untold': The Black Men and White Sounds of Doo-Wop." In *Whiteness: A Critical Reader,* ed. Mike Hill. New York: New York University Press, 1997.

Morrison, Toni. *Playing in the Dark: Whiteness and the Literary Imagination.* New York: Vintage Books, 1993 (First published by Harvard University Press, 1992).

Munfaro, Giavanna Jo. "The Properties of Whiteness: Contemporary American Women Novelists and the Figuring of White Womanhood." *Dissertation Abstracts International* 57, no. 8, Section A: 3497.

Perkinson, James Willard. "Signified Upon and Sounded Out: A White Theology of Black Salvation." *Dissertation Abstracts International* 58, no. 7, Section A: 2706.

Perry, Martha Groves. "Reinventing the Nation: Anglo-Saxon Romantic Racial Nationalism from Dixon to James." *Dissertation Abstracts International* 56, no. 8, Section A: 3129.

Pfeil, Fred. *White Guys: Studies in Postmodern Domination and Difference.* New York: Verso, 1995.

Phoenix, Ann. "'I'm White! So What?' The Construction of Whiteness for Young Londoners." In *Off White: Readings on Race, Power and Society,* eds. Michelle Fine, Lois Weis, Linda C. Powell, and L. Mun Wong. New York: Routledge, 1997.

Roediger, David R. *The Wages of Whiteness: Race and the Making of the American Working Class.* London: Verso, 1991.

Roman, Leslie G. "Denying (White) Racial Privilege: Redemption Discourses and the Use of Fantasy." In *Off White: Readings on Race, Power and Society,* eds. Michelle Fine, Lois Weis, Linda C. Powell, and L. Mun Wong. New York: Routledge, 1997.

Rosenberg, Pearl M. "Underground Discourses: Exploring Whiteness in Teacher Education." In *Off White: Readings on Race, Power and Society,* eds. Michelle Fine, Lois Weis, Linda C. Powell, and L. Mun Wong. New York: Routledge, 1997.

Sacks, Karen Brodkin. "How Did Jews Become White Folks?" In *Race,* eds. Steven Gregory and Roger Sanjek. New Brunswick, New Jersey: Rutgers University Press, 1994.

Sleeter, Christine E. "Reflections on My Use of Multicultural and Critical Pedagogy When Students Are White." In *Multicultural Education, Critical Pedagogy, and the Politics of Difference,* eds. Christine E. Sleeter and Peter L. McLaren. Albany: State University of New York Press, 1995.

Squire, Corrine. "Who's White? Television Talk Shows and Representations of Whiteness." In *Off White: Readings on Race, Power and Society,* eds. Michelle Fine, Lois Weis, Linda C. Powell, and L. Mun Wong. New York: Routledge, 1997.

Thompson, Becky. "Time Traveling and Border Crossing: Notes on White Identity Development." Research Paper 17, Center for Research on Women, The University of Memphis (Tennessee), March 1994.

Twine, France Winddance. "Brown-Skinned White Girls: Class, Culture and the Construction of White Identity in Suburban Communities." In *Displacing Whiteness,* ed. Ruth Frankenburg. Durham, North Carolina: Duke University Press, 1997.

Valli, Linda. "The Dilemma of Race: Learning to be Color Blind and Color Conscious." *Journal of Teacher Education* 46 (March 1995).

Wald, Gayle. "One of the Boys? Whiteness, Gender, and Popular Music Studies." In *Whiteness: A Critical Reader,* ed. Mike Hill. New York: New York University Press, 1997.

Watkins, James Hull. "Locating the Self: Southern Identity, White Masculinity, and the Autobiographical 'I'." *Dissertation Abstracts International* 56, no. 11, Section A: 4401.

Winant, Howard. "Behind Blue Eyes: Whiteness and Contemporary U.S. Racial Politics." In *Off White: Readings on Race, Power and Society,* eds. Michelle Fine, Lois Weis, Linda C. Powell, and L. Mun Wong. New York: Routledge, 1997.

Wray, Matt. "White Trash Religion." In *White Trash: Race and Class in America,* eds. Matt Wray and Annalee Newitz. New York: Routledge, 1997.

Notes

CHAPTER 1: White People—What Do We Want?

1. Although it has not been my personal experience, it is not uncommon for interracial couples and mixed-race individuals to experience overt acts of hostility, rejection, and even violence because of their interracial status.

2. Michel Guillaume Jean de Crèvecoeur, *Letters from an American Farmer*, (1782) reprint (New York: Albert and Charles Boni, 1925), 55–55. Quoted in Vincent N. Parrillo, *Diversity in America* (Thousand Oaks, California: Pine Forge Press, 1996), 9.

3. Parrillo, *Diversity in America*, 9.

4. This and subsequent quotations of DeMott in Chapter 1 are from Benjamin DeMott, "Put on a Happy Face: Masking the Differences between Blacks and Whites" (*Harper's Magazine*, September 1995) 31–38.

CHAPTER 2: What Will It Take to Create a Multiracial Society?

1. Based on data from the U.S. 2000 Census. The census collects racial identification of Hispanics, and often includes both Hispanics and non-Hispanics together in presenting racial tallies. The figures here break out Hispanic-Americans as a separate "racial/cultural" group. The multiracial group is most impacted by this procedure. With Hispanics included, multiracial Americans comprise 2.43% of the U.S. population, due to the comparatively large number of Hispanic-Americans who identify as multiracial. The census also tallied a catchall group of "other." This group amounted to much less than 1% to the total population (0.17%). To simplify the presentation, figures for the "other" group were not included in the calculation of the percentages given here.

2. "Overestimating minority numbers," *Boston Sunday Globe*, 21 December 1997, sec. A, p. 40.

3. Cooper Thompson, *White Men and the Denial of Racism*, The WHITENESS PAPERS, no. 2 (Roselle, New Jersey: Center for the Study of White American Culture, Inc., 1997), 7.

4. "Observations Concerning the Increase in Mankind," (1751), *Papers of Benjamin Franklin*, ed. Leonard W. Labaree (New Haven, 1959). Quoted in Straughton Lynd, "Slavery and the Founding Fathers," in *Black History: A Reappraisal*, ed. Melvin Drimmer (Garden City, New York: Anchor Books, 1969), 117–131.

5. Parrillo, *Diversity in America*, 68. This figure is for the area of the United States prior to its expansion beyond the Mississippi River. If the complete area of today's 50 states were included, the percentage of white people would be reduced even further since west of the Mississippi the population at that time was mostly Native American and Hispanic.

6. Ibid., 142–7.

7. Ibid., 180.

8. Several studies confirm that the quality of healthcare in the U.S. follows racial lines, even when other factors, such as socio-economic class, are equal. The February 24, 1999, edition of *Nightline*, with Ted Koppel, documented many such disparities and reviewed the findings of a study to be published in the *New England Journal of Medicine* the following day that demonstrated subconscious, but

substantial, racial bias on the part of medical doctors. A recent article in the March 21, 2002, issue of *The* (Newark, New Jersey) *Star-Ledger*, by Maggie Fox, titled "Report finds U.S. health care short-changes minorities," provided additional details of this problem. Black and Hispanic patients are significantly less likely than white patients to receive diagnostic and/or surgical procedures for illnesses such as cancer, heart disease, diabetes, and kidney disease. These differences in treatment are mirrored in greater rates of mortality among people of color for any given illness. To the extent this occurs among the elderly, the ratio of white people to people of color will be magnified. Differential healthcare along racial lines also exists in regard to infant care, and is reflected in greater rates of infant mortality among people of color. This circumstance would tend to counter the trend portrayed in Figure 2.1. In other words, if rates of infant mortality were equal between white people and people of color, then the ratio of white people to people of color would be lower than that shown in Figure 2.1.

9. *Gabe Grosz, "Just the Facts," Interrace Magazine*, fall 1997, 6. The 2000 U.S. Census showed only a minuscule change from this figure, with 96.87% of married white Americans having a white partner.

10. R. Roosevelt Thomas Jr., *Beyond Race and Gender: Unleashing the Power of Your Total Work Force by Managing Diversity* (New York: AMACOM, 1992).

11. Thomas made another point the major focus of his book. Organizations have been set up with organizational cultures that benefit white men but do not allow other employees to reach their full potential. Programs designed to integrate other employees into such organizations will fail. What is needed is a comprehensive effort to remake the cultural "roots" of the entire organization. I am telling the story here from my own personal perspective, highlighting a point I found significant to my own circumstance.

12. Marimba Ani, *Yurugu: An African-Centered Critique of European Cultural Thought and Behavior* (Trenton, New Jersey: African World Press, Inc., 1994).

CHAPTER 3: Remedial Education for White Folk

1. Here I am talking about information from social scientists, historians, and other scholars, along with information produced by people working for social change and racial justice. There is also a large body of literature produced by white supremacists and other groups who dress their ideas in the semblance of rational and objective discussion, but who shape their work to support their beliefs that white ways are superior, and therefore white people deserve all the power we have, and more. Some readers may feel my insistence on creating a multiracial society clouds my objectivity. However, I question that any stance can be neutral and objective in a society that is already racially structured. We each have a bias, whether we see ourselves as promoting white supremacy, promoting a multiracial society, or standing in the middle trying not to choose one over the other.

2. Sharon S. Brehm and Saul M. Kassin, *Social Psychology* (Boston: Houghton Mifflin Company, 1990). A description of this classic 1936 experiment by Muzafer Sherif may be found in virtually any introductory social psychology textbook.

3. These are four common examples. Of course a culture of poverty implies also a culture of the middle class and a culture of wealth, and a gay culture implies a straight culture. Regarding the notion of male culture and female culture, see Deborah Tannen, *You Just Don't Understand: Women and Men in Conversation* (New York: Ballantine Books, 1990).

4. American Indians, for instance, have over 700 ethnic groups (nations, or tribes), making them the most ethnically diverse of the racial/cultural groups in the United States. See Roger Herring, "Native American Indian Identity: A People of Many Peoples," in *Race, Ethnicity and Self: Identity in Multicultural Perspective*, ed. Elizabeth Pathy Salett and Diane R. Koslow (Washington, DC: NMCI Publications, 1994).

5. Frank Gonzales. *Mexican American Culture in the Bilingual Education Classroom*. Unpublished doctoral dissertation, The University of Texas at Austin, 1978.

6. The first two quotes in this sidebar are from "Press Release/OMB15," dated September 8, 1997; the middle three quotes are from "American Anthropological Association Statement on 'Race,'" adopted May 17, 1998; and the final two quotes are from "American Anthropological Association Response

to OMB Directive 15: Race and Ethnic Standards for Federal Statistics and Administrative Reporting" ca. 1997. These references may be viewed at http://www.ameranthassn.org, the Web site of the American Anthropological Association.

7. Ironically, the early environmental theorists may have been right, at least in regard to skin color. Contemporary scientific thought suggests that dark skin protects against the harmful effects of intense solar radiation, while light skin allows a person to receive more sunlight, which is needed by the body to manufacture vitamin D. However, these variations change on an evolutionary time scale, which may require thousands of years and not simply a few generations to appear.

8. For a detailed discussion of this point, see Stephen Jay Gould, *The Mismeasure of Man*, revised and expanded (New York: W.W. Norton & Company, Inc., 1996).

9. Michael Omi and Howard Winant, *Racial Formation in the United States: From the 1960s to the 1990s*, Second Edition (New York: Routledge, 1994).

10. Quoted in Jeff Hitchcock, "Undoing the 'White Problem'," *Quarterly Newsletter* [of the Center for the Study of White American Culture] (summer 1997): 9–10.

CHAPTER 4: Colorblindness, Personified

1. Name changed. Although this quote is published here for the first time, a detailed description of other findings may be found in Jeff Hitchcock, "When We Talk among Ourselves: White-on-White Focus Groups Discuss Race Relations" (Alfonso Associates, Inc., Jersey City, New Jersey, bound report), available also online at http://www.euroamerican.org/library/report/repindex.htm.

2. "Playboy Interview: John Wayne, a Candid Conversation with the Straight-Shooting Superstar/Superpatriot," *Playboy Magazine*, May 1971, 75.

3. R. C. Rist, "Race, Policy and Schooling," *Society*, v. 12, no. 1, 59–63. Cited in Janet Ward Schofield, "Causes and Consequences of the Colorblind Perspective," in *Prejudice, Discrimination, and Racism*, ed. John F. Dovidio and Samuel L. Gaertner (Orlando, Florida: Academic Press, Inc., 1986), 232.

4. Lerone Bennett Jr., *Before the Mayflower: A History of Black America*, Sixth Revised Edition (New York: Penguin Books, 1988), 260.

5. Lois Mark Stalvey, *The Education of a WASP* (Madison, Wisconsin: The University of Wisconsin Press, 1989) 326.

6. A first-hand description of an incident like this may be found in Malcolm X, *The Autobiography of Malcolm X* (New York, Ballantine Books, 1973), 36.

7. This defeat was heralded most eloquently at the outset by James Baldwin, who wrote nearly fifty years ago, "This world is white no longer, and it will never be white again." From "Stranger in the Village," *Harper's Magazine*, October 1953. Reprinted in James Baldwin, *The Price of the Ticket: Collected Nonfiction 1948–1985* (New York: St. Martin's, 1985), 79–90.

8. Frequently the "culture wars" between the colorblind and multiracial positions do just that— hold one level of experience above another. Colorblindness denies that social groups have any meaning and multiracialists deny that individuals have any power.

9. Renae Scott Gray, Donna Bivens, Marian (Meck) Groot, and Nancy Richardson, *Why Can't We Just Get Along?*, The Brown Papers: A Monthly Essay of Reflection and Analysis from the Women's Theological Center [of Boston], v. 3, no. 9, June/July 1997, 4.

10. Names changed. This exchange was reported originally, in greater detail, in Jeff Hitchcock, "White Habits: Questioning Colorblindness," *Quarterly Newsletter* [of the Center for the Study of White American Culture] (spring 1996): 4–6. Also see note 1 above.

11. "What Keeps Us from Talking about Race?," *The (Raleigh, North Carolina) News & Observer*, 22 June 1997.

12. Beverly Daniel Tatum, *"Why Are All the Black Kids Sitting Together in the Cafeteria?" and Other Conversations about Race* (New York: Basic Books, 1999) 43.

13. Martin Luther King Jr., *Where Do We Go from Here: Chaos of Community?* (New York: Harper & Row, 1967), 9.

14. "Integration the Army Way." Online Newshour (www.pbs.org/newshour/gergen /may97/race_5-

20.html) 20 May 1997. The Online Newshour interview and the discussion in the next seven paragraphs in the text draw upon Charles C. Moskos and John Sibley Butler, *All that We Can Be: Black Leadership and Racial Integration the Army Way* (New York: BasicBooks, 1996).

CHAPTER 5: How Did It All Begin?

Some of the historical quotes given in this chapter are cited in several articles and books. In each case, for the sake of brevity, I have given a single secondary reference in order that the reader might locate additional material and a reference to the primary source documents.

1. The United States did not exist as a political entity until the Revolutionary War and its aftermath. Here I am using the term to denote a geographic area that came under the dominion of a common European people, the English.

2. I first encountered the idea that English settlers in Jamestown and the Virginia colony went through an early period of common identity formation in Richard Williams, "Reward and Punishment as Dimensions of Lower Rung White Identity," Department of Sociology, Rutgers University, April 1997.

3. Quotes and material in this sidebar are from James Axtell, "The White Indians of Colonial America," *William and Mary Quarterly*, 3rd ser., 32 (1975): 55–88.

4. David E. Stannard, *American Holocaust: The Conquest of the New World* (New York: Oxford University Press, 1992), 106. This quote, and others, are taken from reports made by witnesses recording events in the same period as they took place. Spelling was not consistent in the 1600s and 1700s, hence many words still familiar to us today may be spelled in unfamiliar ways. The reader is encouraged to make a commonsense interpretation of these quotations. For instance, in the quote cited here the observer reports (using modern spelling and language) that the colonists threw the kids in the water and shot their brains out.

5. Edmund S. Morgan, *American Slavery, American Freedom: The Ordeal of Colonial Virginia* (New York: W.W. Norton & Company, 1975), 103.

6. Although this incident is mentioned in several books, a most detailed account can be found in George F. Willison, *Saints and Sinners: Being the Lives of the Pilgrim Fathers & Their Families, with Their Friends & Foes; & an Account of Their Posthumous Wanderings in Limbo, Their Final Resurrection & Rise to Glory, & the Strange Pilgrimages of Plymouth Rock* (Cornwall, New York: Cornwall Press, 1945).

7. Theodore W. Allen, *The Invention of the White Race, Volume Two: The Origin of Racial Oppression in Anglo-America* (New York: Verso, 1997), 75-96.

8. Quote cited in Ronald Takaki, "*The Tempest* in the Wilderness: The Racialization of Savagery," *The Journal of American History*, v.79 (December 1992): 909. Information on this incident may also be found in Karen Ordahl Kupperman, "Thomas Morton, Historian," *The New England Quarterly*, v. 50 (December 1977): 660-664; Michael Zuckerman, "Pilgrims in the Wilderness: Community, Modernity, and the Maypole at Merry Mount," *The New England Quarterly*, v. 50 (June 1977): 255-277; and Willison, *Saints and Sinners*, 1945.

9. Francis Jennings, *The Invasion of America: Indians, Colonialism, and the Cant of Conquest* (New York: W.W. Norton & Company, 1975), 223.

10. Morgan, *American Slavery, American Freedom*, 162. According to Morgan, mortality experience proved women were better able than men to withstand the hardship and disease rampant within the colony.

11. Quotes and material in this sidebar are from Mechal Sobel, *The World They Made Together: Black and White Values in Eighteenth-Century Virginia* (Princeton, New Jersey: Princeton University Press, 1987).

12. Allen, *Invention of the White Race*, 159.

13. Lerone Bennett Jr., *Before the Mayflower*, 37–38.

14. Morgan, *American Slavery, American Freedom*, 156–157.

15. Allen, *Invention of the White Race*, 162.

16. Morgan, *American Slavery, American Freedom*, 153.

17. Ibid., 209.

18. Ronald Takaki, *A Different Mirror: A History of Multicultural America* (New York: Little, Brown and Company, 1993), 59.

19. Terrence W. Epperson, "Whiteness in Early Virginia," *Race Traitor*, no. 7 (spring 1997): 14.

20. Quakers were often outspoken against slavery prior to the Revolutionary War, but some members of the sect held people in slavery until the late 18th century.

21. George Fox, *Gospel Family Order, Being a Short Discourse Concerning the Ordering of Families, Both of Whites, Blacks and Indians* (1676), 13–15. Italics are Fox's; bold emphasis has been added. See also Epperson, "Whiteness in Early Virginia."

22. Epperson, "Whiteness in Early Virginia," 11.

23. Winthrop D. Jordan, *White Over Black: American Attitudes Toward the Negro, 1550–1812* (Chapel Hill, North Carolina: The University of North Carolina Press, 1968), 79.

24. Material in this sidebar is from James W. Loewen, *Lies My Teacher Told Me: Everything Your American History Textbook Got Wrong* (New York: Simon & Shuster, 1995) and Judith Nies, *Native American History: A Chronology of a Culture's Vast Achievements and Their Links to World Events* (New York: Ballantine Books, 1996).

25. Takaki, *A Different Mirror*, 62.

26. Ibid., 62.

27. Epperson, "Whiteness in Early Virginia," 11.

28. Takaki, *A Different Mirror*, 67.

29. Epperson, "Whiteness in Early Virginia," 11–12.

30. Allen, *Invention of the White Race*, 172.

31. Epperson, "Whiteness in Early Virginia," 12.

32. Allen, *Invention of the White Race*, 143.

33. Quotes and material in this sidebar are from Noel Ignatiev, *How the Irish Became White* (New York: Routledge, 1995) and Ronald Takaki, *A Different Mirror*.

34. Jordan, *White over Black*, 137.

35. Bennett Jr., *Before the Mayflower*, 299.

36. Jordan, *White over Black*, 338.

37. Gary B. Nash, *Red, White, and Black: The Peoples of Early America* (Englewood Cliffs, New Jersey: Prentice-Hall, 1974), 214.

38. Morgan, *American Slavery, American Freedom*, 378–379.

39. Nash, *Red, White, and Black*, 229, 237–238.

40. Nash, *Red, White, and Black*, 230–234.

41. Jordan, *White over Black*, 295.

42. Ibid., 280.

43. Ibid., 278–279.

44. Material in this sidebar is from Lawrence R. Tenzer, *The Forgotten Cause of the Civil War: A New Look at the Slavery Issue* (Manahawkin, New Jersey: Scholars' Publishing House, 1997).

45. Earl Conrad, *The Invention of the Negro* (New York: Paul S. Eriksson, 1966), 48.

46. Figure 5-1 portrays the structure of white American culture. It does not purport to represent the structure of all of American culture, nor does it represent the structure of any of the other racial/cultural groups in the United States. The inclusion of cultures of color at the bottom of the diagram is an integral part of the definition of white American culture as our culture has structured itself. A diagram for African-American culture or a diagram for Native American culture would look quite different. So, too, would a diagram of the entirety of American culture.

47. I thank my colleague, Lowell Thompson, who first drew my attention to the seminal role of Jefferson in the formation of post-Revolutionary War racial attitudes in his book, *"WHITEFOLKS": Seeing America Through Black Eyes,* (Chicago, 1996).

48. Jordan, *White over Black*, 524.

49. Loewen, *Lies My Teacher Told Me*, 125.

50. Bennett Jr., *Before the Mayflower*, 178.

CHAPTER 6: Looking at White American Culture

1. Material and quotes in this sidebar are from Marian Meck Groot, *The Heart Cannot Express Its Goodness*, The Brown Papers: A Monthly Essay of Reflection and Analysis from the Women's Theological Center [of Boston], v. 3 (February 1997).

2. Ian F. Haney López, *White By Law: The Legal Construction of Race* (New York: New York University Press, 1996), 38.

3. Loewen, *Lies My Teacher Told Me*, 138.

4. Judith H. Katz, "The Sociopolitical Nature of Counseling," *The Counseling Psychologist*, v. 13 (October 1985): 617.

5. Thomas Kochman, *Black and White Styles in Conflict* (The University of Chicago Press, 1981), 122.

6. Material in this sidebar is from Kochman, *Black and White Styles*.

7. Ralph Wiley, *Why Black People Tend to Shout* (New York: Birch Lane Press, 1991), 1.

8. Ruth Frankenberg, *White Women, Race Matters: The Social Construction of Whiteness* (Minneapolis: University of Minnesota Press, 1993). The discussion in the foregoing paragraph and the following six paragraphs in the text draws upon this work.

9. Ibid., 197.

CHAPTER 7: Inside the White Experience

1. Janet E. Helms, ed., *Black and White Racial Identity: Theory, Research, and Practice* (Westport, Connecticut: Praeger, 1993) 4.

2. Rita Hardiman, "White Racial Identity Development in the United States," in *Race, Ethnicity and Self: Identity in Multicultural Perspective*, ed. Elizabeth Pathy Salett and Diane R. Koslow (Washington, DC: NMCI Publications, 1994).

3. Material for this sidebar, aside from comments identified as my own, is from Janet E. Helms, "An Overview of Black Racial Identity Theory," in Helms, *Black and White Racial Identity*, 1993.

4. Helm's model emphasizes black and white relations as the context within which white racial identity develops. Nevertheless, it is possible to extend the model to account for relations between whites and other nonwhite groups. Other models, like Hardiman's, explicitly state that white racial identity development can take place in relation to any of several nonwhite groups, and furthermore, that a white person may be in one stage of development in relation to one nonwhite group (e.g., American Indians) and a different state of development in relation to another nonwhite group (e.g. black people).

5. Janet E. Helms, *A Race Is a Nice Thing to Have: A Guide to Being a White Person or Understanding the White Persons in Your Life* (Topeka, Kansas: Content Communications, 1992), 31.

6. Material for this sidebar is from Larke Nahme Huang, "An Integrative View of Identity Formation: A Model for Asian Americans," in *Race, Ethnicity and Self: Identity in Multicultural Perspective*, ed. Elizabeth Pathy Salett and Diane R. Koslow (Washington, DC: NMCI Publications, 1994).

7. Helms, *A Race Is a Nice Thing*, 33. Helms credits Hardiman's work for Helms's later inclusion of the Immersion/Emersion stage in her own model.

8. James Baldwin, "White Man's Guilt," in *The Price of the Ticket* (New York: St. Martin's, 1985); Shelby Steele, "White Guilt," in *The Content of Our Character: A New Vision of Race in America* (New York: HarperPerennial, 1991); Andrew Hacker, "White Responses: Right and Left, Guilt and Sex," in *Two Nations: Black and White, Separate, Hostile, and Unequal* (New York: Ballantine Books, 1993).

9. James Oakes, *The Ruling Race: A History of American Slaveholders* (New York: Alfred A. Knopf, 1982), 114. One enslaved woman, Martha Harrison, "remembered her master as a man so frightened by his imminent death that he offered thousands of dollars to secure his salvation." (p. 116).

10. Baldwin, "White Man's Guilt," 410.

11. Haresh B. Sabnani, Joseph G. Ponterotto, and Lisa G. Borodovsky, "White Racial Identity

Development and Cross-Cultural Counselor Training: A Stage Model," *The Counseling Psychologist*, v. 19, (January 1991): 76–102.

12. Thandeka, *Learning to Be White: Money, Race and God in America* (New York: Continuum, 1999).

13. Ibid., 10.

14. Ibid., 13.

15. Ibid., 86.

16. Ibid., 3–19.

17. Lillian Roybal Rose, "White Identity and Counseling White Allies About Racism," in *Impacts of Racism on White Americans*, Second Edition, ed. Benjamin P. Bowser and Raymond G. Hunt (Thousand Oaks, California: Sage, 1996), 42–43.

18. Ibid., 44.

19. Elaine Pinderhughes, *Understanding Race, Ethnicity, and Power: The Key to Efficacy in Clinical Practice* (New York: The Free Press, 1989), 91–92.

20. Rose, "Counseling White Allies," 45.

21. Personal communication. The nearly identical term of "internalized domination" appears in Gail Pheterson, "Alliances between Women: Overcoming Internalized Oppression and Internalized Domination," *Signs: Journal of Women in Culture and Society*, v. 12, no. 1. (1986): 146–160. As often happens, the concept of internalized dominance, as a companion concept to internalized oppression, was independently conceived by Walker and Pheterson. My first exposure to the term came from Dr. Walker. The ideas I discuss here are informed by both Walker and Pheterson, but contain my own formulation and extension of their work as well.

22. William Larkin and Maureen Walker, "Internalized Dominance and Workplace Dynamics," Workshop handout, National Multicultural Institute, May 1994.

23. Ibid.

24. Various authors have discussed the effects of racism on white people. This list has drawn extensively on the following: Bowser and Hunt, "Introduction" and "Conclusion" to *Impacts of Racism on White Americans*, 2ⁿᵈ ed.; John P. Fernandez, "The Impact of Racism on Whites in Corporate America," in ed. Bowser and Hunt, *Impacts of Racism on White Americans*, 2nd ed., 157–178; Judith H. Katz and Alan E. Ivey, "White Awareness: The Frontier of Racism Awareness Training," *Personnel and Guidance Journal*, v. 55 (April 1977): 485–488; Peggy McIntosh, *White Privilege and Male Privilege: A Personal Account of Coming to See Correspondences through Work in Women's Studies*, Working Paper Series, No. 189 (Wellesley, Massachusetts: Center for Research on Women, Wellesley College, 1988); Pheterson, "Alliances between Women"; Pinderhughes, *Understanding Race, Ethnicity, and Power*; Walker and Larkin, "Internalized Dominance."

25. Often we are unaware of being seen as having the characteristics on this sublist. In other words, these are our common blind spots.

CHAPTER 8: The Academy Awakens

1. Gunnar Myrdal, *An American Dilemma: The Negro Problem and Modern Democracy* (New York, Harper & Row, 1969), 1:lxxv. Myrdal used the phrase "a white man's problem" as a section heading in his Introduction and offered three pages explaining his formulation. It's noteworthy, however, that the "problem" remained "the Negro" in the subtitle of the complete work.

2. David R. Roediger, ed., *Black on White: Black Writers on What It Means to Be White* (New York: Schocken Books, 1998).

3. Ray Stannard Baker, *Following the Color Line: An Account of Negro Citizenship in the American Democracy* (Garden City, New York: Doubleday, Page and Company, 1908), 65. Quoted in Myrdal, *An American Dilemma*, 1:43.

4. Two white American authors, for instance, each published books taking a critical look at white Americans and our dominant role in race relations shortly after World War II. Margaret Halsey, a best-selling humorist, heralded a new age of activism in her *Color Blind: A White Woman Looks at the Negro* (New York: Simon and Schuster, 1946). Halsey's critique of segregation and racism was witty,

cutting, and common-sensical. A deeper, partly self-analytical, and painful examination of Southern white consciousness emerged from Lillian Smith. Smith, having sold 4 million copies of her first novel, *Forbidden Fruit*, exposed the heart of white racism in her book, *Killers of the Dream* (New York: W.W. Norton & Company, 1994; orig. pub. 1949). The book suffered from poor sales and a public unwilling to hear its message. Despite the lack of commercial success, Smith's book came to be recognized by many during the 1960s as a forceful and accurate analysis of white schizophrenia and the damaging effects of racism on the humanity of all. Today it stands as a classic and heroic work.

5. Sig Synnestvedt, "White Faces and White Studies," *Commonweal*, v. 92 (1970): 182–183.

6. The terms "whiteness studies" and "white studies" are both in use and refer generally to the same thing. Though "whiteness studies" suggests looking at political hegemony and social dominance, and "white studies" suggests a more rounded view of cultural and social aspects of whites (akin to "black studies"), few seem to have made much of what seems an important distinction.

7. From the conference description appearing at the conference Web site at http://violet.berkeley.edu/~ethnicst/conference/description.html, 11April 1997.

8. Liz McMillen, "Lifting the Veil from Whiteness: Growing Body of Scholarship Challenges a Racial 'Norm'," *The Chronicle of Higher Education*, 8 September 1995.

9. David W. Stowe, "Uncolored People: The Rise of Whiteness Studies," *Lingua Franca* (Sept./Oct. 1996): 68–72, 74–77.

10. Quentin Hardy, "School of Thought: The Unbearable Whiteness of Being," *The Wall Street Journal*, 24 April 1997, pp. A1, A12.

11. Margaret Talbot, "Getting Credit for Being White," *The New York Times Magazine*, 30 November 1997, pp. 116–119.

12. Noel Ignatiev, "The Point Is Not to Interpret Whiteness but to Abolish It." (paper read at the conference, "The Making and Unmaking of Whiteness," Berkeley, California, 11–13 April 1997). Although his paper was read at the conference, Noel Ignatiev did not attend the event.

13. From the conference description appearing at the conference Web site at http://violet.berkeley.edu/~ethnicst/conference/description.html, 11 April 1997.

14. See "A Symposium on Whiteness," *the minnesota review*, n.s. 47 (fall 1996) 115.

15. Race does not determine intellectual views by any means, but it does impact our experiences, and these experiences do bear upon our intellectual development. Of the many people who have written about whiteness, including several I cite in this chapter, I do not always know their ascribed racial identity. White studies in the 1990s has been described by others as predominantly white in the corpus of its practitioners (see David W. Stowe, "Uncolored People," 68). Personal accounts I received of the Berkeley conference also pointed out that most of the scholars present were white. Activists were critical of this fact, expressing their concern from the audience that the conference on whiteness was itself very white in nature. In this chapter, when and where it seems relevant and where the racial identity of the scholar/writer is known to me, I will identify it.

16. Joel Kovel, *White Racism: A Psychohistory* (New York: Pantheon, 1970).

17. Robert W. Terry. *For Whites Only*, rev. ed., reprinted 1994 (Grand Rapids, Michigan: William B. Eerdmans Publishing Co., 1975).

18. Katz and Ivey, "White Awareness," 485–489.

19. Judith H. Katz has continued to write about white awareness. See also her *White Awareness: Handbook for Antiracism Training* (Norman, Oklahoma: University of Oklahoma Press, 1978); "The Socio-Political Nature of Counseling," *The Counseling Psychologist*, v. 13 (October 1985): 615–624; and *White Culture and Racism: Working for Organizational Change in the United States*, The WHITENESS PAPERS, no. 3, (Roselle, New Jersey: Center for the Study of White American Culture, 1999).

20. David T. Wellman, *Portraits of White Racism* (New York: Cambridge University Press, 1977).

21. Benjamin P. Bowser and Raymond G. Hunt, eds., *Impacts of Racism on White Americans*, (Beverly Hills, California: Sage Publications, Inc., 1981). See also the second edition under the same title and publisher, released in 1996 and cited in Chapter 7, notes 17 and 24. The latter edition contains nearly all new material.

22. bell hooks, *Ain't I a Woman: Black Women and Feminism* (Boston: South End Press, 1981). In particular, see Chapter Four—"Racism and Feminism: The Issue of Accountability." Many women of

color shared hooks's critique and several wrote of their concerns and experiences with an otherwise unnamed white middle and upper class feminism. See also, Cherríe Moraga and Gloria Anzaldúa, eds., *This Bridge Called My Back: Writings by Radical Women of Color* (Watertown, Massachusetts: Persephone Press, 1981).

23. Marilyn Frye, "On Being White: Toward a Feminist Understanding of Race and Race Supremacy," in *The Politics of Reality: Essays in Feminist Theory* (Freedom, California: The Crossing Press, 1983), 110–127.

24. This line of thought is remarkably similar to that incorporated more recently by the New Abolitionists as one of their organizing precepts. See Chapter 9.

25. McIntosh, *White Privilege.*

26. Richard Dyer, "White," *Screen,* v. 29 (1988): 44-64. An article by Jane Gaines titled "White Privilege and Looking Relations: Race and Gender in Feminist Film Theory" appeared in the same issue and in fact had been published in earlier form two years prior in *Cultural Critique.* However, it failed to command the same attention as Dyer's article, perhaps because it looked at "white privilege," an increasingly familiar concept to cultural and feminist studies, and limited its discussion to the intersection of those fields. Dyer posed a broader question about the nature of whiteness itself and explicitly called for a study of its implications.

27. Toni Morrison, "Unspeakable Things Unspoken: The Afro-American Presence in American Literature," *Michigan Quarterly Review,* v. 28 (Winter 1989): 1–34.

28. Ibid., 14–18.

29. Ibid., 17.

30. See Janet E. Helms, "Toward a Theoretical Explanation of the Effects of Race on Counseling: A Black and White Model," *The Counseling Psychologist,* v. 12, no. 4 (1984): 153–165; and John F. Dovidio and Samuel L. Gaertner, eds., *Prejudice, Discrimination, and Racism* (Orlando, Florida: Academic Press, 1986).

31. Morgan, *American Slavery, American Freedom.* See Stowe, "Uncolored People," 70–71.

32. Kochman, *Black and White Styles in Conflict,* and Elaine Pinderhughes, *Understanding Race, Ethnicity, & Power.*

33. This question begs another. If whiteness is not a "universal" American perspective or culture, what, if anything, is? There seems no sense of urgency at present to either ask or answer this, though at least some scholars have suggested the universal American culture is mulatto or mestize, in other words mixed and multiracial. Whiteness studies is still preoccupied with taking whiteness out of the center. This seems a necessary task before the center can be seen for what it is.

34. An example of one course offered during this period may be found in Marlene Applebaum, Arlene Avakian, Christina Cincotti, Kelly Facto, Brenda Fitzpatrick, Sarah Gold, David Hanbury, Keisha Kenny, Kathryn McGarvey, Nicole Lisa, Nicole Morse, Judith Schneider, Andrew Susen, and Katie Thoennes, "'Unmasking the Beast': Learning and Teaching about Whiteness," and "Syllabus: The Social Construction of Whiteness and Women," *Transformations: The New Jersey Project Journal,* v. 9 (Fall 1998): 212–239.

35. See, for instance, "A Symposium on Whiteness,"116, in which Mike Hill, introducing the topic of a 1995 symposium, spoke of "the extra-intentional effects of a new whiteness studies…"

36. Henry A. Giroux. "Rewriting the Discourse of Racial Identity: Towards a Pedagogy and Politics of Whiteness," *Harvard Educational Review,* v. 67 (Summer 1997): 289. The present listing of works is intended to show the variety and specificity of topics examined by whiteness studies, but it is partial at best, containing many, though by no means all, well-known works along with a selection of lesser known works. As of 1999, over 1,000 and perhaps as many as 3,000 articles and books have been published in white studies. If you count papers and presentations at conferences, that number might easily double. This listing represents something less than 5%, and maybe as little as 1%, of the available material. Assignment of works to specific fields is also somewhat problematic. White studies has been interdisciplinary, and a single article might, for example, embody American studies, history, literary criticism, women's studies, and/or gender studies. I have assigned articles to fields not to make an authoritative statement on where they belong, but rather to organize the listing for the reader in a way that illustrates the many disciplines contributing to white studies. In doing so, I recognize that scholars, including the various authors themselves, may disagree in some instances with the assignments I have made.

37. In 2000 an annual conference series on white privilege was inaugurated at Cornell College in Mount Vernon, Iowa. In April 2002 the conference held its third annual sessions at Central College in Pella, Iowa where the series founder, Eddie Moore Jr. is presently Director of Intercultural Life.

CHAPTER 9: Grass Roots—Old, Deep, and Spreading

1. That is, the first conference during the contemporary period of heightened white consciousness that arose in the early 1990s. As mentioned in Chapter 8, an earlier wave of activity took place in the early 1970s. During this first wave of antiracist white consciousness, the Oakland Conference on the White Minority took place in Oakland, California on August 17, 1970, where a statement titled "The World Future of the White Minority—A White Point of View," was drafted. It read, in part:

> Oppression by the white minority has produced among Third World peoples a res-
> olute spirit of revolt. White western nations will no longer be permitted to continue
> arrogant disrespect for the rights and humanity of others. The days of white domina-
> tion are over; the tide is turning. Suppressed peoples are rising to meet their oppres-
> sors.

See Joseph Barndt, *Liberating Our White Ghetto* (Minneapolis, Minnesota: Augsburg Publishing House, 1972), 109–110. A description of the 1996 conference may be found in Jeff Hitchcock, "WHITE-NESS: The Conference at Burlington, NJ, November 1996," *Quarterly Newsletter* [of the Center for the Study of White American Culture] (winter 1997): 4–9.

2. Charles A. Gallagher, "White Reconstruction in the University," *Socialist Review*, v. 94, no. 1–2 (1995): 165–187; and "White Racial Formation: Into the Twenty-First Century," in Robert Delgado and Jean Stefancic, eds., *Critical White Studies: Looking behind the Mirror* (Philadelphia: Temple University Press, 1997), 6–11.

3. Ben Stocking, "'European American' Month Put on Calendar. California Lawmakers Approved Resolution," *San Jose Mercury News*, 19 September 1998.

4. *Report of the National Advisory Commission on Civil Disorders: Special Introduction by Tom Wicker of* The New York Times (New York: Bantam Books, 1968), 2.

5. Ibid., v.

6. Stephen Thernstrom and Abigail Thernstrom, *America in Black and White: One Nation, Indivisible* (New York: Touchstone, 1997).

7. Advisory Board to the President's Initiative on Race, *One America in the 21st Century: Forging a New Future* (Washington, DC: U.S. Government Printing Office, 1998).

8. Frederick R. Lynch, "Managing Diversity: Republicans Have Embraced 'Diversity' Doctrines for a Variety of Reasons—None of Them Good," *National Review*, v. 49, 13 October 1997.

9. Geoffrey Colvin and Eileen P. Gunn. "Special Report: The 50 Best Companies for Asians, Blacks, & Hispanics," *Fortune*, 19 July 1999. *Fortune* has continued to compile an annual list of the 50 best companies for minorities. During the economic downturn of 2001, *Fortune* found many firms, in a departure from past trends, retained a concern for maintaining the diversity of their workforce even in the face of cutbacks and layoffs (see Jeremy Kahn, "Diversity Trumps the Downturn," *Fortune*, 9 July, 2001). Nor does a racist past always guide present action. Kahn reports, "That a company can bounce back from a troubled history is evident from our No. 1 company [on *Fortune's* fourth annual list of the best companies for minority employees], Advantica. The owner of Denny's Restaurants was hit with a series of legal claims in the early 1990s but responded with aggressive minority hiring and a supplier-diversity effort. It has led our ranking for two years in a row."

10. Lou Schoen. "Racism Is Prejudice Plus Power, but There Are Ways to Combat It," *Minneapolis Star Tribune*, 15 August 1998, 19A. On the matter of diversity displacing race as a focus, see Cora Daniels, "Too Diverse for Our Own Good?" *Fortune*, 9 July 2001.

11. One widely reported 1999 study by Korn/Ferry International found that 6% of corporate directors are minorities. Women of color hold less than 1% of corporate board seats (see http://www.ewow-facts.com/wowfacts/pdfs/diversity/4corporateamerica.pdf). In contrast, *Fortune* reported that minorities

hold 11% of the board seats in firms that made the *Fortune* list of the 50 best companies for minority employees (see Jeremy Kahn, "Diversity Trumps the Downturn." *Fortune*, 9 July 2001).

12. For more information: Lowell Thompson, 1507 E. 53rd St., #132, Chicago, IL 60615.

13. Gregory Freeman, "Big Corporations Aren't Seeing the Benefits of Diversity," *St. Louis Post-Dispatch*, 28 July 1998, B1.

14. David A. Thomas and Suzy Wetlaufer. "A Question of Color: A Debate on Race in the U.S. Workplace," *Harvard Business Review*, (September 1997).

15. Judith H. Katz, *White Culture and Racism*, 1.

16. David V. Day and Christina A. Douglas, "De-centering Whiteness: Toward an Inclusive Model of Race in Organizations" (paper presented at the 14th Annual Conference of the Society for Industrial and Organizational Psychology, Inc., May 1, 1999).

17. Marian Meck Groot, *The Heart Cannot Express Its Goodness*, 3.

18. Mark Twain, "Slavery in Hannibal," in *Voices in Black and White: Writings on Race in America from Harper's Magazine* (New York: Franklin Square Press, 1993), 1–2.

19. The House of Bishops of the Episcopal Church, "The Sin of Racism: A Pastoral Letter," 1994.

20. First quote in sidebar from Joseph Barndt, *Dismantling Racism: The Continuing Challenge to White America* (Minneapolis, Minnesota: Augsburg Fortress, 1991), 41. Second and third quotes from Charles E. Fager, *White Reflections on Black Power* (Grand Rapids, Michigan: William B. Eerdmans Publishing Co., 1967), 90–91.

21. Joseph Barndt and Charles Ruehle. "Rediscovering a Heritage Lost: A European-American Anti-Racist Identity," in *America's Original Sin: A Study Guide on White Racism* (Washington, DC: Sojourners, 1995) 73–77.

22. Barndt, *Dismantling Racism*, 5.

23. Jody Miller Shearer, *Enter the River: Healing Steps from White Privilege toward Racial Reconciliation* (Scottdale, Pennsylvania: Herald Press, 1994). The *Free Indeed* videotape, with study guide, is available from the Mennonite Central Committee, 21 S. 12th St., P.O. Box 500, Akron, PA 17501-1151.

24. From http://www.soujourners.com/magazine.html.

25. Myke Johnson, *Wanting to Be Indian: When Spiritual Searching Turns into Cultural Theft*, The Brown Papers, v. 1, (April 1995). The Women's Theological Center (WTC) may be contacted at P.O. Box 1200, Boston, MA 02117-1200. Quotes taken from "looking back," a 4-page description of the first 15 years of WTC.

26. Barbara Ehrenreich, "The Unbearable Being of Whiteness," *Mother Jones*, June 1988, 12.

27. Martin Mull and Allen Rucker, *The History of White People in America* (New York: Perigee, 1985) and *A Paler Shade of White: The History of White People in America—Volume II* (New York: Perigee, 1986). Donald A. Clement, "A White-Male Lament," *Newsweek*, 2 July 1990.

28. David Gates, "White Male Paranoia: Are They the Newest Victims—or Just Bad Sports?," *Newsweek*, 29 March 1993, 48–53; John Leo, "The Demonizing of White Men," *U.S. News & World Report*, 26 April 1993, 24; Michele Galen with Ann Therese Palmer, "White, Male & Worried," BusinessWeek, 31 January 1994, 50–55.

29. Chris Adams, "Both Elusive and Exclusive, Whiteness Sets Itself Apart, *New Orleans Times-Picayune*, 17 October 1993, 22A; "White Like Who?," The Village Voice, 18 May 1993; Richard Leiby, "White Like Me," *The Washington Post*, 1 August 1993, F1, F5.

30. See http://www.eaif.org/enter.htm (13 September 2000) regarding EAIF's self-description. Quote of city Supervisor Mabel Teng may be found in Joyce Nishioka, "Seeking Equal Time: European American Issues Forum Disputes Stats," *AsianWeek*, v. 20, 22 July 1999.

31. Description of *Race Traitor* as "intellectual center" quoted from "Editorial: Abolish the White Race—by Any Means Necessary," *Race Traitor*, no. 1 (winter 1993), 2. Tag line appears on cover of same issue. For more about *Race Traitor*, see www.postfun.com/racetraitor, or write Race Traitor, P.O. Box 499, Dorchester, MA 02122.

32. Shawn Setaro, "Political Entanglements #8 (column), *Instant Magazine*, 1999. See http://www.instantmag.com/columns/polit_08.htm or write P.O. Box 2224, Woburn, MA 01888. For a description of the conference, see Jeff Hitchcock, "Race Traitor: the Conference," *Quarterly Newsletter* [of the Center for the Study of White American Culture, Inc.] (summer 1997): 6–7.

33. Copwatch program described in *Race Traitor*, no. 6 (summer 1996), 18–23. For quote, "we know...," see Hitchcock, "Race Traitor, the Conference," 6.

34. Recovering Racists Network Web site, http://www.jmckenzie.com/rrn/ .

35. Horace Seldon, *Convictions about Racism in the United States of America*, Third Edition. (Boston: Community Change, Inc., 1995).

36. Quote from "Mission Statement of European Dissent, New Orleans," *The Journey of European Dissent* (May 1997), 8. For more information: European Dissent, c/o The People's Institute for Survival and Beyond, 7166 Crowder Blvd., Suite 100, New Orleans, LA 70127; Crossroads Ministry, 425 S. Central Park, Chicago, IL 60624.

37. For more information: Community Change, Inc., 14 Beacon St., #605, Boston, MA 02108.

38. For more information: CWS Workshop, 2440 16th St. PMB #275, San Francisco, California 94103; Training for Change, 4719 Springfield Ave., Philadelphia, PA 19143; for "What White People Can Do" workshop by Judith Katz, contact Caryn Cook, The Kaleel Jamison Consulting Group, Inc., 279 River St., Suite 401, Troy, NY 12180.

39. Becky Thompson and White Women Challenging Racism, "Home/Work: Antiracism Activism and the Meaning of Whiteness" in Michelle Fine, Lois Weis, Linda C. Powell, and L. Mun Wong, eds., *Off White: Readings on Race, Power, and Society* (New York: Routledge, 1997), 354–366.

40. Center for the Study of White American Culture, 245 W. 4th Avenue, Roselle, NJ 07203, (908) 241-5439, contact@euroamerican.org. See our Web site at http://www.euroamerican.org.

41. Anthony J. Ipsaro, *White Men, Women & Minorities in the Changing Workforce* (Denver, Colorado: Meridan Associates, 1997), 17.

CHAPTER TEN: Moving Toward a Multiracial Future

1. Robert W. Terry, "The Negative Impact on White Values," in Benjamin P. Bowser and Raymond G. Hunt, *Impacts of Racism on White Americans* (Beverly Hills, California: Sage, Publications, 1981), 120.

2. Paul Kivel, *Uprooting Racism: How White People Can Work for Racial Justice* (Philadelphia: New Society Publishers, 1996), 211.

3. Robert Terry, *For Whites Only*, 1.

4. Russell Means with Marvin J. Wolf, *Where White Men Fear to Tread: The Autobiography of Russell Means* (New York: St. Martin's Press, 1995).

5. Harlon L. Dalton, *Racial Healing: Confronting the Fear between Blacks and Whites* (New York: Doubleday, 1995).

6. Jeff Hitchcock and Charley Flint, *Decentering Whiteness*, The WHITENESS PAPERS, no. 1 (Roselle, New Jersey: Center for the Study of White American Culture, Inc., 1997).

Index

antiracism, 156, 172, 193, 208
  critique of, 192
  defined, 205
  examines power relations, 203, 204
  and first conference on whiteness, 177
  must create positive models, 205
  role of white people in, 189
  training programs, 10, 156, 188,
    194–195
AntiRacist Action, 192
antiracists, 60
Asian ethnics, 48
Asian-American identity development, 48,
  130
Asian-Americans, 1, 17, 32, 52, 109, 182,
  198, 210
  assimilating as Asian, 49
  assimilating as white, 19, 20, 50, 206
  clubs for, 178
  victimized by whites, 48, 211
assimilation to racial groups, 47–49, 50,
  62–63
Athey, Stephanie, 170
autokinetic effect, 36
aversive racism, 155
Axtell, James, 75

B

Bacon, Nathaniel, 85, 86
Bacon's Rebellion, 84–87, 89
Baker, Ray Stannard, 151
Baker, Russell, 183
Baldwin, James, 133, 135, 228n
Baptists, 80
Barbados, 83, 84
Barndt, Joseph, 10, 188, 194, 205
Bay, Mia Elisabeth, 167
Bennett Jr., Lerone, 81, 90
Bergstrom, Maria Joy, 170
Berkeley conference, 152, 153, 154, 166,
  169, 176, 190, 233n
Berkeley, Gov. William, 85, 86
Bernardi, Daniel Leonard, 170
Beyond Race and Gender (Thomas), 26
Beyond the Pale (Ware), 166

black American culture, 48, 80
  rules about expression, 116, 117
black Americans, 1, 17, 22, 52, 68, 182,
  198–199
  appearing white, 106
  assimilating as black, 48
  clubs for, 178
  in colonial Virginia, 81–82
    as Christians, 83
    faced heightened oppression, 87, 88,
      89
    and start of slavery, 83
  in Continental Army, 96
  and doo wop, 171
  excluded from whiteness, 21, 107–108
  freemen in North, 90
  IQ and, 45
  long roots in U.S., 28
  rejected by whites after Revolution, 99,
    106
  resisting white supremacy, 57
  seeking autonomy, 206
  seen by whites as human, 94
  seen by whites as subhuman, 56, 94, 96,
    98–99, 100
  in the U.S. Army, 69–70
  victimized by whites, 18, 48, 100, 211
Black and White Racial Identity (Helms), 166
Black and White Styles in Conflict
  (Kochman), 115, 165
black culture, 210
black ethnics, 49, 66
black men, 58, 81, 88, 90, 91, 100, 160,
  181
Black on White (Roediger), 151
black racial identity, 125
black women, 3, 22, 81, 88, 90, 159, 161,
  170, 171, 199
Boas, Franz, 56
Boston Globe poll, 17
Bowser, Benjamin P., 158
Brown Papers, The, 189
Brown, John, 100, 164, 192
Burlington, New Jersey, 176
Business Week, 190
Butler, John Sibley, 69, 70

C

D

Dachau, 58
Dalton, Harlon L., 206, 207, 214
Dangerous Minds (film), 168
Davy, Kate, 172
Day, David V., 167
de Crèvecoeur, Michel Guillaume Jean, 3
de Tocqueville, Alexis, 191
decentering whiteness. *See* whiteness: decentering of
Declaration of Independence, 55
Deguzman, Maria, 167
Democrats, 90, 180, 181
demographic information
  by age (chart), 20
  black people in early Virginia, 81, 87
  black personnel in Armed Forces, 69
  estimate for year 2050, 19
  geographic distribution, 17
  historical, 17–19
  immigration, 18
  interracial marriages, 25
  lay bias in estimating, 17
  marriages, if race preference were random, 22–23
  monoracial white marriages, 23
  2000 Census, 16
  U.S. by race, 16, 18
DeMott, Benjamin, 5–6, 25
  and friendship model, 5–6, 7–8
Dickar, Maryann, 168
Dismantling Racism (Barndt), 188
Doane Jr., Ashley W., 172
dominative racism, 155
Douglas, Christina A., 167
Douglass, Frederick, 90
Dovidio, John F., 165, 171
dual consciousness, 179
DuBois, W. E. B., 179, 203
duCille, Ann, 169
Duke, David, 220
Dunn, Diana, 50

E

El-Shabazz, El-Hajj Malik, 45. *See also* X, Malcolm
Elsie Y. Cross Associates, 185
Emerge, 199
English colonies in America
  egalitarianism in, 92–93
  lacked class of nobility, 92
  lacked idea of limited good, 92
  opportunity in, 92
  preference for English culture, 91, 96
  prejudice arising in, 94
English commoners, 74, 78, 93
  degraded by elite, 74
English elite, 74, 93
enslaved people, 80, 83, 85, 87, 95
enslavers, 80, 83, 84, 90, 102, 108, 186
  controlled by own debts, 95
Enter the River (Shearer), 189
Episcopal House of Bishops, 187
Episcopalians, 187
Epperson, Terrence W., 84, 88
Essence, 199
Ethnic Identity (Alba), 166
Eurocentric history, 73, 89, 106, 169, 178
European American culture. *See* white American culture
European American Heritage Month, 178
European American Issues Forum (E/AIF), 191, 193
European Americans. *See* white Americans
European aristocrats, 92
European Dissent, 193–194
Evangelical Lutheran Church, 188

F

Feagin, Joe R., 171
Federal period, 96
  nation seeking new identity, 96
  rejecting English identity, 98
feminists, 158–162
Fernandez, John P., 167
Fishkin, Shelley Fisher, 167
Flagg, Barbara J., 170, 172

X

Y

Give the Gift of
LIFTING THE WHITE VEIL
to Your Friends and Colleagues

CHECK YOUR LEADING BOOKSTORE OR ORDER HERE

❑ **YES**, I want _____ copies of Lifting the White Veil at $22.95 each, plus $4.95 each for shipping and handling. (New Jersey residents add $1.38 sales tax per book.) Canadian orders must be accompanied by a postal money order in U.S. funds. Allow 15 days for delivery.

❑ **YES**, I am interested in having Jeff Hitchcock speak or give a seminar to my company, association, school, or organization. Please send information.

My check or money order for $_____ is enclosed.

Please charge my ❑ Visa ❑ MasterCard

Name _____

Organization _____

Address _____

City/State/Zip _____

Phone_____ E-mail _____

Card # _____

Exp. Date_____ Signature _____

Please make your check payable and return to:
Crandall, Dostie & Douglass Books, Inc.
245 West 4th Avenue • Roselle, NJ 07203

Call your credit card order toll-free to: 877-679-6119
or Fax: 908-245-4972